1960

JEAN

Laurent LeSage

GIRAUDOUX

HIS LIFE AND WORKS

The Pennsylvania State University Press 1959

LIBRARY OF CONGRESS CATALOG CARD NO. 59-12342

PRINTED IN THE UNITED STATES OF AMERICA BY

THE HIMES PRINTING COMPANY, STATE COLLEGE, PENNSYLVANIA

DESIGNED BY MARILYN SHOBAKEN

I wish to express my gratitude to the Administrative Committee on Research of The Pennsylvania State University for several grants during the preparation of this book.

Laurent LeSage

CONTENTS

PART ONE: Life and Career

PART TWO:
The Testimony of Giraudoux's Creative Work

PART ONE

Life and Career

Chapter 1

YEARS OF FORMATION AND PREPARATION

In an age when writers, mindful of posterity and the curiosity of their readers, leave abundant records of their problems and preoccupations, the case of Jean Giraudoux is unusual. No journal, no correspondence, no confession. Sartre's thought that "cet écrivain si discret et qui s'efface devant ses fictions"[1] might one day speak to us directly of himself was never realized. Perhaps he might have if he had lived longer. But nothing in the miscellaneous papers he left indicates a serious intention to do so, and one might say that, in regard to his personal life, Jean Giraudoux wished to leave the earth without having trod so heavily as to leave a mark.[2]

To trace his life and career we have recourse only to his works, which confuse the pedestrian researcher by their polite ambiguity and jovial blending of fact and fancy; to scanty records; and to the reminiscences of friends and colleagues, whose testimony cannot always be taken at face value. These sources, for want of autobiographical papers, have to suffice at present. It may be expected that as time passes new documents will be brought to light, and more persons close to Giraudoux will be willing to share with the public their intimate knowledge of the man. As such material gradually becomes available, biographers will correct and amplify the presentation they find here.

Notes to Chapter 1 begin on page 211.

Boyhood and School Days

Bellac and environs.

Hippolyte-Jean Giraudoux was born October 29, 1882, in Bellac, Haute Vienne. No poet has lavished more lyricism and eloquence upon the place of his birth than Giraudoux, who, with tongue in cheek, ascribed to Bellac every idyllic virtue and made of it a fitting place for genius to be born. For this exceedingly banal provincial town of 4,800 souls, he created a legendary past with saints and heroes and a symbolic present, whereby it appears to all the world as an archetype, the model of the French community, which (of course) is the goal of civilization in general:

> Bellac, bâti sur le bord des roches les plus anciennes de France, point précis où l'herbe jaunâtre du Poitou et du Berry devient le gazon anglais dru et vert sur lequel tomba le grand corps de Richard Cœur de Lion, tué à quelques lieues, Bellac que je croyais une oasis soustraite aux vicissitudes de l'histoire, n'en a pas évité une seule. Son nom, son nom pacifique qu'on m'avait dit venir de *bella aqua,* belles eaux, veut dire, en fait, *Belli vicus,* c'est-à-dire le bourg de la guerre. Son fondateur, mauvaise affaire et mauvais présage, fut empoisonné par sa femme. En l'an mille, un dragon y parut dans un nuage et le mal des ardents ravagea la ville.[3]

Towards his native soil and childhood surroundings, Giraudoux is a Barrès who knows that he is joking. He invites us into the house where he was born, to eyes untouched by magic a very ordinary dwelling on the Poitiers road, consisting of six rooms on two floors, the ground floor of which is now a mechanic's shop:

> A Bellac, entrez, je vous prie, dans la maison où je suis né, et, du second étage, vous devrez reconnaître, bon gré mal gré, que c'est bien la plus belle ville du monde à cause du mail à colonnades où jouent les filles d'officiers et du château Marmontel, d'où Mme. de Begorce, dans une hotte, se faisait porter chez le procureur son amant par des domestiques fidèles.[4]

Since March 1, 1944, a plaque by the front door proclaims the proud distinction of this house.

Giraudoux's devotion to the little town of Bellac is all the more surprising since he spent there only the first seven years of his life. Actually young Giraudoux had no real home, for his father was obliged to lead the quasi-nomadic life of a civil servant. From Bellac, where Léger Giraudoux had been employed as *conducteur des Ponts et Chaussées,* he moved his wife and two sons to Pellevoisin, where he assumed the duties of *percepteur,* then to Cérilly and to other little towns on a provincial circuit of government employees that Giraudoux would later point out bears no relation to a Cook's tour of celebrated places.[5] Jean first went to school at Mlle. Degude's in Bellac, then attended the communal school of Pellevoisin and the *collèges* of Cérilly and of Saint-Amand, where his aunt lived. He was from the first a star pupil. M. Corneille, his teacher at Saint-Amand, judged him "très bon élève, sous tous les rapports."[6] In the classroom and outside as well, Giraudoux was already a leader. His ascendancy over his companions is succinctly demonstrated by the report that it was he who led the others marching to the village square to sing "Sur le front de nos bataillons, le drapeau s'avance."[7]

We assume that, in spite of his personal distinction, Giraudoux's childhood was little different from that of all small town children — home, school, and the countryside explored alone or roamed together with his playmates. Fleeting pictures of it pass before our eyes as we read Giraudoux's first writing. He seems to have had the usual portion of pleasures and sorrows — the joys all boys know of games and comradeship balancing the misery of cold, solitary bedrooms and the loss of beloved pets. Every time he lost one — he would later remember with the amusement we feel at the recollection of distant woes — his father refused to let it be replaced by another of the same species. As a result, with each successive tragedy — dog run over, cat stolen, goat sold — little Jean was forced to seek lower and lower on the scale of intelligence and affection — a squirrel, then a turtle. By the time he started school he had arrived at the level of silkworms! A salmon has the honor of being his first memory. Not as a pet, however. The story Giraudoux tells is that once when his father was going fishing with a colleague, he was taken along. To his misfortune, his father happened to mention to his friend that Jean was exactly eighty centimeters tall. So, every time they caught a fish in the net stretched across the river, the fishermen laid the child on the ground, in spite of his shrieks, and measured their catch. "Il y en avait un énorme (as enormous as this story, we may suspect), dont la tête était à la hauteur de la mienne. Frère siamois d'un saumon voilà comment je me vois dans ma première mémoire . . ."[8]

Can we take Giraudoux's confidences as really autobiographical? Some of the things he tells us in *Simon le Pathétique* are not literally true. Critics have noticed the passage where Simon declares that his mother lived only five hours after he was born and have pointed out that Anne Lacoste Giraudoux was to die only two months before her son. They should have noticed, however, that Simon, as well as Giraudoux, is making believe in this passage, for he is deliberately inventing for himself a tragic childhood to satisfy a mood of the moment. Although Giraudoux never attempted to portray his mother in his writing, his enduring fondness for her is attested by the inscribed special editions he habitually had made for her whenever he published a new book. Doubtless she was as good a woman as the old nurse Jeanne remembered her to be. Speaking of Jean and his mother, she told a reporter, "Ah! il était mignon, toujours bien habillé. Un beau petit. Et vif. Il ressemblait à sa mère. C'était une femme remarquable, d'une intelligence! Quand quelqu'un voulait faire quelque chose d'extraordinaire à Bellac, il venait lui demander conseil. Ah! son petit Jean."[9] Mme. Giraudoux saw to it that her children were warmly and neatly clad as they went off to school, and to enliven his lonely hours at the *lycée* in Châteauroux, she sent Jean stories that she had cut out of the newspapers and carefully stitched together.

The random remarks that Giraudoux makes concerning his father suggest less fondness for his other parent. The reproach that he let his children's eyes and teeth go neglected strikes a more authentic tone than some of the sentimental griefs that Simon invented.[10] Whether Léger Giraudoux actually sent Jean off to boarding school with a Polonius speech such as the one recorded in *Simon le Pathétique* is more doubtful. In form, it follows too closely a typical pattern of Giraudoux's irony and rhetorical whimsy to be a verbatim copy:

> — Tu entres dans la lutte avec une chance incroyable. Je t'envie! Pas de charge: je suis toute ta famille. Pas de tare: ton grand-père était paysan; il n'y a eu entre lui et toi ni comptables, ni perruquiers, ni maquignons. Ton nom, tu peux en faire ce que bon te semble; il est neuf; il n'a jamais figuré sur une enseigne, ni sur le papier où sont enveloppées les côtelettes. Félicite-toi de tous ces privilèges et pose cette pomme.[11]

Moreover, we know that Giraudoux's father was not his whole family. Yet the scene is probably not entirely imaginary, and it is quite likely that on the eve of Jean's departure for Châteauroux his father made some sort of gruff farewell address. If we allow for stylization and simplification prompted by artistic reasons — and for the occasional caprice of a lively imagination — we can take what we read as essentially accurate. Giraudoux's deviations from literal facts do not seem like deliberate attempts to misrepresent himself or to cover his tracks. Besides, the childhood he depicts is so classic that it would indeed be strange if most of the experiences described in his books were not inspired by personal recollection. At any rate, we need not try to draw a harder and faster line between fact and fancy than Giraudoux himself has done, for just as the Bellac he invested with legendary and symbolic virtues is more real for us than the one in the *Guide Bleu,* so the childhood he evokes has more pulsating life than any strictly factual account.

Thus we may imagine young Giraudoux himself when he describes Simon preparing to go off to school — packing his belongings and putting his room in order. The bed, which he had kept pushed out into the room to make it seem more like a raft or a desert island (depending on which course his flight of fancy took), goes back against the wall. All traces of his childish games must be suppressed, all toys put away: "Pour le cas où jamais je ne reviendrais, je ne voulus laisser, par orgueil, que les empreintes d'une grande personne, — une carafe, un encrier, un buvard avec ses marques, et j'enfermai tous les jouets dans un placard . . ."[12] Jean Giraudoux is now ready — to use one of his favorite metaphors — to pass through his first *écluse,* and move up to a new level in life.

The lycée *at Châteauroux.*

In 1893 Jean Giraudoux, along with his older brother Alexandre, arrived at the *lycée* of Châteauroux. We are told that the account of his journey as given in *Simon le Pathétique* is not quite accurate. It does, in effect, seem unlikely that such a bold and proud lad would be crying — if only out of anxiety over his luggage — in a railway station and have to be comforted by a stranger. It is regrettable that there is not a good photograph of Giraudoux from this time. The only one we know is an enlargement from a group picture, so retouched as to make him look distressingly like the mummy of a boy.[13] Friends remember him as looking quite alive — reddish blond hair with a lock over his forehead, blue-gray eyes, freckles, and a dimple in his chin. The regulation dark blue jacket (two issued annually to scholarship pupils) became Giraudoux, and on Sundays and special occasions when he donned the jacket with gold buttons and carried white gloves, his appearance was even elegant. The distinction with which Giraudoux wore his uniform reflects a basic quality of character. This showed up too in his language and deportment, free from all vulgarity or the rowdiness one associates with schoolboys. His classmates soon perceived that somebody special was in their midst:

> Il n'était pas de ceux qui cassaient ou déformaient trop savamment la visière de leur casquette. Même ses gros godillots donnaient des illusions de bottines. Le pantalon avait allongé et tombait, dans la mesure de ses faibles moyens, mais Giraudoux savait lui faire prendre tout naturellement un petit air repassé, sinon tuyau de poêle, du meilleur effet. Tout ceci instinctif, et innocent, et seulement remarquable après coup, mais tout de même significatif d'une évolution imperceptible, qui l'élevait peu à peu au-dessus du commun des élèves, autrement que par la régularité dans le travail, la sagesse et le succès.[14]

At Châteauroux, Giraudoux continued the fine scholastic record he had established at his other schools. He was a docile pupil, conscientious, alert, intelligent, striving to do to perfection whatever he undertook. He read works as well as critics, and supplemented his assignments with corollary readings. Not a prodigy pupil à la Musset, but rather a model pupil whose gifts, although very real, obtained their luster by assiduous labor at the study table. Needless to say, he was the joy of his teachers. As one of them exclaims in *Simon le Pathétique,* "Vous êtes un peu notre bien, Simon."[15] On only one occasion did he bring down a teacher's wrath, and then upon another pupil's head, literally. This was in Latin class with M. Dorey, the irascible *Sixième* teacher, who, exasperated by the new pupil's slowness in taking his books from his desk, rushed over, clutched Giraudoux's pen box and flung it across the room. The missile struck young Marc Aucuy on the head. From this episode Aucuy dates the beginning of his friendship with Giraudoux, a friendship which remained close all the seven years they were together in the *lycée.* Two other events make the year of *Sixième* memorable. Giraudoux was taken with his classmates to the theater, "dans la formation par files qui nous menait à la chapelle ou au bain," where he saw Silvain play the role of the father in *Horace.*

"Tout le Berry adolescent l'attendait passionnément au 'qu'il mourût!' "[16] The other event of *Sixième* is Giraudoux's First Communion, which took place on June 11, 1894.

It is to Marc Aucuy's reminiscences that we owe much of our knowledge of Giraudoux's progress through the classes at Châteauroux. After his year with M. Dorey, who interrupted the lessons frequently to read *Tartarin* and other novels, Giraudoux began Greek under teachers who were as severe and careful as Dorey had been lax. In later life Giraudoux would express gratitude to those who pitilessly drove him on in French grammar, Latin, and Greek during *Cinquième.* In *Quatrième* the class forged ahead particularly in Greek, even beginning to translate some Thucydides. Giraudoux's zeal won for him a privileged place in his teachers' hearts. The anecdote is told that one of his teachers was so angry when he noticed a prankster had pinned the classic placard "donkey" on his model pupil's back that he cried, "Je n'admets pas qu'on se permette de pareilles facéties vis-à-vis d'un de mes meilleurs élèves. Ce ne sont même pas des grossièretés de paysans, mais la marque d'une bassesse stupide."[17]

It was a Spartan life at Châteauroux, laborious and regimented. Days in the classroom and study hall, nights in the unheated dormitory. The diversions possible to the *lycéens* were not lavish, and Giraudoux, by his discrimination and standoffishness, denied himself a good many that the other boys enjoyed. He shared their enthusiasm for amateur theatricals, however, and in *Quatrième* scored what seems like a facile triumph in a Labiche play by wrinkling up his nose when he recited the line, "Ça sent le Romain, ici." Fond, too, of singing, he performed on at least two occasions while at the *lycée* — in 1894 he was heard in a comic song entitled "Le Bal à l'Hôtel de Ville," and in 1896 in another *chansonette,* "La Journée d'un Flâneur."[18] Sundays young Giraudoux served as acolyte, presenting the water and the wine while replying correctly "*Et cum spiritu tuo.*" The good Abbé Jouve was fond of his young server, so blond, gentle, and discreet. He himself was a great favorite with all the students. Often when the period of religious instruction was over he entertained them by readings from profane works, such as the *Inondation* of Zola. Perhaps this priest, who was also an author and an ornithologist, made a particularly deep impression on Giraudoux. His collection of corals and bright-plumaged birds may have stimulated the exotic fancy that produced *Suzanne et le Pacifique.*

Athletics were, however, Giraudoux's chief escape from his books. During *Quatrième* he joined the sports club and organized the track meet. On the running track he would drive himself close to exhaustion, frequently to the amusement of his comrades. What did their derision matter, since he won? "Tu peux toujours rire," he would say, "moi, j'ai gagné."[19] There are persons who cannot be satisfied with anything but first place, and Giraudoux was of this breed. The testimony of friends is interesting on this point, even though jealousy may have dictated the emphasis: "Je n'ai jamais connu d'homme plus orgueilleux; au jeu, Giraudoux détestait perdre, non par avidité, mais à cause d'une sensation d'infériorité qu'il supportait mal, même passagère; il voulait exceller en tout, souffrait d'occuper la seconde place."[20]

Pride, the sin that Giraudoux would mention so frequently in his writing, always kept this schoolboy from knowing the pleasure of unself-conscious participation, the warm comradeship in which the mediocre bask. He recognized himself as a superior person, and applied himself diligently to maintain himself as such. Friendly towards his classmates, he nevertheless betrayed a sort of condescension that they were quick to recognize. The young man who liked to sign his name Gerald Houe du Bel Lac, and who finished his meticulous toilet with eau de cologne, could scarcely regard as kindred spirits the oafish young Berrichons who bathed once a week and cut their toenails only when they began to hurt. One gathers from Marc Aucuy's account of their seven years together that he was as close a friend as Giraudoux ever had in school. Yet it is apparent that they were not real chums. Giraudoux's swan-like attitude towards the ducks at Châteauroux precluded any possibility of comradeship on the basis of equality. What suited him better was the sort of prince-and-page friendship that he began with little Louis Bailly.[21] Giraudoux was very fond of this little cherub — as Aucuy calls him — who always waited for Giraudoux by the second pillar to the left of the yard. The older boy took him in hand and directed his studies. Notes began to pass between them several times a day. This unfortunate practice proved the undoing of their fervent friendship when the censor one day intercepted a message. He would have separated Orestes and Pylades, Giraudoux reflected bitterly!

So Giraudoux walked rather much alone at Châteauroux. He would sometimes take his books with him into the dining commons and, lost in *Le Capitaine Fracasse* or a volume of Lamartine, forget the noise of dishes and companions. The beans would pass time after time under his nose without his deigning to partake, while on all sides plates were voraciously being cleaned. Only when the chef prepared something special like chicken or orange flan did it seem unwise to set the dish down first before Giraudoux. Sometimes on his way back to the study he would linger for a moment listening to some noisy singing, but if he were tempted to join, he never showed more than an aloof interest. The model for "Jacques l'égoiste" is surely Giraudoux himself. "Mes maîtres s'inquiétaient de me voir si souvent isolé et silencieux."[22] When one of them asked him one day what he intended to do with his life, Jacques had no reply. Feeling no compelling urges, no need of a formula for life, he preferred to be an indifferent spectator.

As a rule, Giraudoux was treated with deference and left alone to take his walks and study his books. Only when a professor accused him one day of false modesty did his fellows feel bolder about considering him a snob. The one recorded encounter with overt hostility and ridicule is connected with his enthusiasm for the writer Charles-Louis Philippe.

One year when Giraudoux went home for the summer holidays, he discovered that the house in Cérilly, to which his family had moved during the year, was next door to Philippe's. Delighted to be able to observe a real writer at close range, Giraudoux posted himself at an attic window from which he could watch his comings and goings. Acquaintance was eventually struck up, and Giraudoux accompanied his literary neighbor on long rambles through the countryside, listening to his conversation and advice. Through Philippe, Giraudoux discovered Michelet, whose *Histoire de France* he began to read passionately. When he returned to school that fall, he took with him a precious *plaquette,* the first version of Philippe's *La Mère et l'Enfant,* which he showed to his schoolmates. Baffled at their indifference, Giraudoux tried to harangue them into an admiration and appreciation for the peasant author, but failed utterly. The more insistent he became, the firmer the opposition, until the subject turned into a playground issue. Made fun of by the older students, Giraudoux raged and fumed, then retreated into somber disdain. But having championed this poet, he was never to forsake him. The essay he would write years later on Charles-Louis Philippe is a labor of love and a belated rebuke to the boys of Châteauroux, who would not be convinced that a genius could live so near them. If they had fallen in with Giraudoux's enthusiasm, perhaps he himself would have quickly got over it. Happily, it persisted, and his own style bears the trace of this writer in its earthy and homely touches.

The Philippe episode widened and deepened the moat that Giraudoux, by his distinction and superiority, had dug between himself and his fellows. Naturally proud and distant, he became more so, and lived virtually a recluse. One does not know whether his family was as neglectful of him as Simon's is painted, but it is certain that Giraudoux spent many short holidays almost alone in the deserted *lycée*. He rarely ventured outside the school and into the town. The streets of Châteauroux, "ville la plus laide de France,"[23] held no charm for him, and only an occasional invitation to dinner at a professor's house could draw him forth. Books were his life and his refuge. With books spread out before him on the study table, he could soar high above his drab prison on the wings of his imagination. The old table was his best friend and confidant:

> Enfant, me disait-elle, tu me plais car tu ne fais pas de profondes entailles avec ton canif, car tu ne prends pas plaisir à me faire grincer sous ton talon. Aussi je t'apprendrai les secrets du bois; je te dirai quelle joie prennent les vieilles tables à sentir sur elles un enfant travailleur et aimant; je t'enseignerai bien des choses que je sais seule en ce bas monde.[24]

Before it he would sit, with one leg tucked under him, tapping with his pencil as he balanced, harmonized, elaborated the sentences of a composition. "Travail, cher travail, toi qui terrasses la honteuse paresse! Travail d'enfant, généreux comme un amour d'enfant."[25] Although as a mature writer Giraudoux doubtless wrote as spontaneously as he always claimed, as a student he worked hard over his style. Even then, however, he preferred to give the illusion of facility and did not like to have it noticed how painstakingly he orchestrated his compositions. Six of them were entered in the school's *Cahier d'honneur.*[26] Possibly an even greater honor, bits of Giraudoux's prose or verse found their way into other students' notebooks. The idea of a literary career must have already been in his mind, for he wrote to writers, requesting advice. We have two of the answers he received in November, 1898, one from his idol Charles-Louis Philippe, and the other from a celebrated poet, thought to be Edmond Rostand.[27] Philippe's modest suggestions make an interesting contrast with the pompous counsel offered by the celebrated writer — a contrast which even an eighteen-year-old was fully aware of.

The *Palmarès* of Châteauroux records, after the grammar years, an increasing number of scholarly triumphs for Giraudoux: the *premier prix de français,* the *prix de latin,* the *prix de grec,* the *prix d'histoire,* and nominations in other subjects. But although Giraudoux was a distinguished pupil, his record — as Christian Marker points out[28] — reveals him to have been less phenomenally so than is sometimes assumed. M. Marker cautions likewise against rating Giraudoux's themes too highly. Close scrutiny reveals in them facility, but not great originality. Better augury for the great writer Giraudoux would become, Marker suggests, may be found in a little comedy in verse which dates from the year *Première. La Rosière de Chamignoux* is Giraudoux's first theatrical venture on record. The text was handwritten and illustrated by the author. It was performed during the summer at Saint-Amand, where Jean and his cousins put on plays in his aunt's workshop.[29]

In *Première,* Giraudoux had the good fortune to study under an exceptionally fine teacher, Léonce Gain. It was he who had organized the circulating library of new books, which were eagerly read and discussed by the students. He also instituted the free recitation period each Monday, which became a weekly contest to see who could memorize the longest passage. Giraudoux made the *Contes du lundi* his monopoly, preferring Daudet to Hugo and not caring for Zola or Maupassant at all. In April (the year is 1899) Giraudoux was selected to give a speech at the alumni banquet. For this annual affair, the student speeches were semiofficial in character, submitted beforehand to the professors, who would add a few embellishments and see that due homage was paid to the guests. With his habitual independence of spirit, Giraudoux kept his composition to himself, and the simple dialogue between a student and his study table (from which we have already quoted[30]) met with faint applause.

The *bachot* was taken without incident in June. Giraudoux was sure to pass — in spite of writing to his aunt, "Si je ne suis pas admissible, je vais me jeter dans l'Indre"[31] — and after the formality he went home for the summer holidays. He returned to school in the fall for the year of philosophy, to find as usual the fat concierge with his fat cat, the red beans, and the drum roll that would fix his daily schedule for another year. This was the time of the Dreyfus Affair. Giraudoux seemed unconcerned over the issue, although it had become a hot one even within the walls of provincial *lycées*. At the end of the year he made another trip to Poitiers to take the second part of the *baccalauréat*. In October, 1900, he was ready to enter a new phase of his schooling. His life in Châteauroux was over: "Il était temps, et, après tout, je n'avais plus rien à faire dans cette ville. J'y étais venu souder à moi le passé des grands hommes, des petits hommes, de l'univers. C'était fait, solidement fait."[32] A *bachelier* and a *lauréat de concours général,* he was off to Paris, where a scholarship would permit him to prepare for the Ecole Normale at Lakanal.

What had seven years spent within the dreary *lycée* walls done for this young man, still proud and independent in spite of his discipline? Giraudoux tells us in the tribute Simon pays his teachers, which begins:

> Je leur devais, en voyant un bossu, de penser à Thersite, une vieille ridée, à Hécube; je connaissais trop de héros pour qu'il y eût pour moi autre chose que des beautés ou des laideurs héroïques. Je leur devais de croire à l'inspiration; — à des chocs, à des chaleurs subites qui me contraignaient, en cour ou en classe, un oiseau divin me coiffant, à graver sans délai sur l'arbre ou le pupitre mon nom en immenses lettres. Je leur devais de croire à ces sentiments qu'on éprouve au centre d'un bois sacré, d'une nuit en Ecosse, d'une assemblée de rois, — à l'effusion, à l'horreur, à l'enthousiasme . . .[33]

Lakanal, Ecole Normale, and Budding Friendship

The loss of the archives at Lakanal during the last war hinders our investigations of Giraudoux's career at this famous *lycée,* situated near Paris in the woods and fields that once belonged to the vast domain of the Duchesse du Maine. With some reservation, we can believe Simon's word, however, that he continued to be an assiduous pupil.[34] As at Châteauroux, it took him a little time to get started. But he finished brilliantly. The *Palmarès* for 1901-02, Giraudoux's second year, registers awards in Latin and French composition, the first prize in the *Concours général* for Greek translation. Honors went to him, too, in athletics.[35] His name was inscribed upon the *tableau d'honneur*, and he was accepted for the Ecole Normale.[36] The transfer to the rue d'Ulm is recorded on a plaque in the hall of the main building at Lakanal. There is his name, along with those of other distinguished alumni we recognize — Ernest Tonnelat, Paul Hazard, Alexandre Guinle — also admitted to the Ecole Normale Supérieure from Lakanal. Giraudoux's class was a brilliant one, but he was its star, long to be remembered by his classmates, who recounted his exploits to the classes that followed:

> Au lycée Lakanal, qu'il avait quitté deux ans avant mon arrivée et dont il était avec Péguy la première gloire, son passage avait été marqué d'un si vif éclat que nos anciens ne parlaient guère que de lui. . . . Il avait été l'étoile de la fameuse promotion, restée unique, qui vit entrer, la même année, dans la vénérable maison de la rue d'Ulm, sept élèves de Lakanal.[37]

Before going on with his scholastic career, Giraudoux found himself obliged to return to Châteauroux for his year of military service. The only personal testimony we have of this year is a schoolmate's recollection of a letter Giraudoux wrote from his post. In remarking upon how grateful he is when an accident or an illness relieves the monotony of his garrison life, he puns, "Varus, Varus, rends-moi mes lésions!"[38] After basic training, he was stationed at Clermont-Ferrand and at Lyon with the 298th Infantry Regiment. He was released with the rating of Reserve Sergeant.

"Il est doux, pour une âme bien née, de gravir pour la première fois les pentes de Sainte-Geneviève, et de découvrir . . . l'Ecole Normale Supérieure."[39] The tall, sparse young man with the wellborn soul can be seen, like Juliette, passing the Panthéon, hesitating before the street to the left that leads to Polytechnique, then suddenly turning into the rue d'Ulm and stopping before Normale. The picture Giraudoux paints in *Juliette au Pays des Hommes* is of the way the building used to look, just as it did when he himself stood before it for the first time:

> Première cour carée où le passant était épié par les soixante bustes des grands hommes qui surent le mieux observer, Lavoisier, Cuvier ou Chevreul, puis un jardin bordé par la rue Claude-Bernard et où tout promeneur était épié, plus scientifiquement encore, par soixante concierges.[40]

This is the Ecole Normale, "école de réalisme spirituel," where the flower of French intellectual youth is nurtured and carefully watched over:

> De leurs loggias, les bustes de Racine, de Pascal, de Montaigne et de trente autres écrivains contemplent avec ravissement et attendrissement, vautré en bras de chemise et sans col sur le gazon, le jeune normalien en proie au délire qui lui dicte le deuxième paragraphe de son diplôme d'études sur la césure dans le vers anapestique ou sur la métaphore dans les hymnes d'Alamanni.[41]

Unlike students at Polytechnique or Saint-Cyr, young men attending Normale wear civilian clothes. Yet they are clad forever henceforth in the "esprit normalien," a uniform recognizable to everyone. Giraudoux gives his own subtle and whimsical definition of it in the short essay from which we have quoted. It is easy to see in the nonchalant erudition, the playful pedantry that fills his works. His humor is that of the *canular,* the peculiar invention of the merry and often boisterous monks of learning in the rue d'Ulm.

Testimony by Giraudoux's friends at Normale indicates that he had not lost the quiet reserve and the correctness in language and costume already noticed at Châteauroux and Lakanal. He listened more than he spoke, but was not above leading his condisciples into little traps to show off their ignorance. Apparently they were not so resentful as the boys at Châteauroux had been, for Giraudoux at Normale was summed up as an amiable fantast.[42] It does indeed seem that, although continuing to do brilliant work in school, he was beginning to relax the discipline that had formerly kept him at his study table. Frequently he cut his courses, ostensibly to go to the Bibliothèque Nationale, but rarely getting beyond the Seine. For he loved the book stalls and spent hours leafing through *bouquins* on the quays. The Latin Quarter, too, had its distractions. Giraudoux started going to Vachette's and other cafés, even out as far as the Closerie des Lilas, where Paul Fort presided. Thursday evenings he was regularly to be seen at the Bal Bullier. No longer could it be said that Giraudoux lived exclusively in his books.

The years 1903 to 1905 were marked by a very significant step in Giraudoux's education and literary orientation. We know he had studied German at Châteauroux, for his *Palmarès* indicates it among his studies from *Sixième* through *Première.*[43] But his work in French and

Latin appears to have been considerably more distinguished. It is assumed he went on with his German at Lakanal, although the loss of the school archives prevents our establishing his curriculum there with precision.[44] However, since among all the prizes which are listed for Lakanal's star pupil there is no mention of any award in German, it is doubtful whether Giraudoux was particularly directed towards German studies before entering the Ecole Normale. His decision to work in the German field dates from his encounter with the great German teacher, Charles Andler, whose lectures were opening new vistas to students of literature both at the Ecole Normale and at the Sorbonne.[45] As Professor Andler expounded before them the theories of the German Romantic authors, students like young Giraudoux, trained in the rigorous patterns of French classicism and rationalism, listened with excitement to this new gospel of liberty and fantasy in letters.

Under Andler's guidance, Giraudoux prepared himself to take the *licence* in German. The program for the year 1903-4 included Greek, Latin, and French authors representing many periods.[46] The German portion concentrated on the nineteenth century. At the end of his first year at the Ecole Normale (July, 1904), Giraudoux obtained his degree. His *mémoire de licence* was on the Pindaric odes of Ronsard.[47]

Giraudoux's second year at Normale was devoted to "la culture générale et l'initiation philologique."[48] The library records indicate that, beginning in October, 1904, the books Giraudoux borrowed were almost exclusively German — eighteenth, nineteenth, and twentieth-century authors, with particular concentration upon the Romantics. The Schlegel brothers, Achim von Arnim, Novalis, Tieck, La Motte Fouqué, and Kleist are on the list.

At the same time Giraudoux was reading intensively in German literature, he was doing some writing of his own. "Le Dernier Rêve d'Edmont About" appeared in the December 15, 1904, issue of a student review, *Marseille-Etudiant*.[49] It is a comic dream-fantasy about a soldier in love with a prefect's wife. His discourses to her — arranged as prelude, declaration, objection, declaration, and finale — jumble mock lyric and heroic phrases with old saws. The two dainty lovers gaze at each other, weep hopelessly, and travel about in a phaeton driven by the prefect himself. After a visit to the Pope, they continue their extravagant journey through forests and gardens of gladioli, stopping to munch macaroons behind a hedge of rose-laurel. The editor's fulsome introduction to Giraudoux's piece is of interest:

> Nous sommes heureux de publier dans notre numéro du 15 décembre une nouvelle d'un jeune littérateur qui ne tardera pas à se faire un nom dans les lettres et qui, pour le moment, se contente d'être un des plus brillants élèves de l'Ecole Normale. M. Jean Giraudoux, l'auteur en question, n'est pas ennemi de la fantaisie la plus truculente et de la plaisanterie la meilleure; il se complaît dans le domaine du fantasque et de l'irréel, mais un fantasque savoureux à l'excès et un irréel particulièrement attachant. Sa nouvelle, qui est un petit chef-d'œuvre de malice, une merveille d'ironie, de verve caustique et mordante, pourra paraître bizarre; n'oublions pas qu'il s'agit d'un rêve, c'est-à-dire d'événements qui sont d'une invraisemblance voulue, mais dont la succession, purement imaginaire, présente un intérêt. Et ce que l'on appréciera surtout dans l'œuvre de M. J. Giraudoux, c'est l'art charmant qu'il a su y introduire, un style remarquablement exact, nerveux et sûr, et enfin des qualités de forme, de pensées et de sentiments qui dénotent un véritable tempérament littéraire.

It is unusual that a first critical estimate, based exclusively upon one brief sketch, should prove such an adequate description of an author's talent. The implication is obvious and easily confirmed by a perusal of the text: the fundamental pattern of Giraudoux's art was fixed from the outset of his career. The years of maturity disciplined and refined his manner but brought about no radical change in it. Here in this first work we may observe his characteristics in all their youthful excessiveness. He indulged himself unrestrainedly in verbal antics, piling up jokes, puns, *coq-à-l'âne*. Rhapsodical tirades and lyric effusions break off abruptly to give place to sheer buffoonery:

> Je ne vous aime pas avec des pommes, des branches d'aubépine, des baisers sur le cou.
>
> La nature est lâche et désolée, mon amour l'habite et ne lui ressemble pas: Ce n'est pas l'hiver que les oies sont le plus blanches . . .
>
> Beaucoup d'hommes t'aimeront: que la qualité de leur amour ne te dupe pas, parût-il aussi fou que le mien. Rien ne ressemble plus à la queue du lion que la queue du bœuf . . .

Giraudoux achieves his effects by his characteristic method: an improvisation sustained and directed only by the loose association of words and images which flash through his mind:

> Nous ne cessions de pleurer très haut, nos sanglots couraient sur la surface de l'eau, revenaient en écho, se buttaient, se choquaient, avec des rebonds et des glissades, comme des billes folles sur un billard.

One word merely leads to another in the intricate meanderings which cut across all rational categories. Metaphors crystallize and dissolve before others in kaleidoscopic succession. The basic compositional technique of all Giraudoux's later works will not be different.

Not only does "Le Dernier Rêve" reveal that Giraudoux's manner was fixed from the beginning, it offers also striking evidence of the models by which he was guided to his characteristic expression. This student essay reads like a German fantasy. One would say that its author had borrowed all the stock in trade of an E. T. A. Hoffmann — illusion, enchantment, shifting and imprecise identities, farcical incongruity. Thus Giraudoux's debut piece appears to us as a key work, at one and the same time prefiguring his work to come, and harking back to those German writers whom the student author was reading at the time.

Sojourn in Germany

In the spring of 1905, Giraudoux won a traveling scholarship to the country whose literature he had been studying. Franz Toussaint and Maurice Martin du Gard tell us that he had been teaching three days at the Lycée Janson-de-Sailly when he heard the good news.[50] If this is true, he quit his job immediately and left for Munich. For one who took as dim a view of teaching as Giraudoux professed, this must have been a great relief. By his docile behavior and good marks in school, Giraudoux had always seemed cut out for the professorship; but it was a joyless prospect for him, and kindly fate intervened in the nick of time:

> Professeur, tant qu'ils voudraient, dès que j'aurais atteint soixante, cinquante-cinq ans, mais je voulais aller d'abord là où me seraient utiles leur latin, leur histoire, — voyager. . . . Mes professeurs obtinrent pour moi une mission à l'étranger et arrangèrent, d'eux-mêmes, le voyage que l'on offre au fiancé dont le mariage est rompu . . .[51]

The account of a young man's *voyage d'études* that Giraudoux composes in "L'Ecole du Sublime" is essentially his own story. In the countries he passed through, he wanted to see all the things he had read and heard about from his professors: "Ce fut longtemps un voyage silencieux, consacré à m'acquitter des mille commissions dont mes professeurs m'avaient chargé, sans le savoir, pour ce monde qu'ils ne connaîtraient jamais."[52] With so many commissions to accomplish — to visit the museums, the belfries, and the towers of Belgium and Holland — he arrived in Germany only by easy stages, and lingered for a time in Charlottenburg[53] before going south to Bavaria.

The exhilaration of this young French intellectual, foot-loose in the magic city of Munich, is still vividly recalled fifteen or so years later in the various versions of *Siegfried.*[54] With adolescent fervor heightened by poetic reminiscences, Giraudoux was ready to delight in everything he encountered. Baedeker in hand, he explored Munich's monuments, carefully noting details of dimension and items of historical interest. From his student window, he surveyed a panorama of statues and steeples. And he sauntered through streets haunted by the shades of Hoffmann and other authors he had studied. Out in the country, the heather and pines at dawn might seem common property to others, but for Giraudoux:

> L'aube . . . était luisante et correcte comme une aube d'Albert Dürer . . . Pas un lapin, pas un lièvre, pas un genièvre, et un noyer avec une grive dans l'angle comme une signature, pas une croix, que je ne connusse déjà par le Petit ou le Grand Testament. J'étais dans ce temps épique du Saint Empire qui continue à vivre en Allemagne le matin, alors que l'époque romantique n'y reparaît que vers midi, et, au crépuscule et dans les environs des villes celle du Sturm und Drang. Je prenais dans l'air le plus frais ce bain de moyen âge que donne la Bavière à son réveil, quand ne sortent encore que les êtres et les animaux qui n'ont pas changé depuis Wallenstein, les belettes, les vairs, les courriers à cheval dont les cors éveillent . . . les chambrières qui entr'ouvrent un volet doucement, et de l'épaule, car il faut empêcher l'autre sein de paraître et le pot de verveine de tomber . . . Un paysage vu tant de centaines de fois, . . . dans Altdorfer ou dans Wohlgemüth, qu'on s'attend à apercevoir soudain dans l'air, comme dans leurs dessins et leurs gravures, un gros petit enfant tout nu, ou des mains seules priant, ou des gibets célestes . . . Une aube de conjuration, de pillage, et qui s'obstinait à ne rien révéler de l'Allemagne moderne.[55]

It may be noticed from the last line that modern Germany falls outside the enchantment. What Giraudoux loved and was disposed to see was the old Germany of *Gemütlichkeit* and the *Märchen.* To it he gave himself up wholeheartedly and, thanks to literature and fancy, lived happy months beyond the Rhine.

It was in Munich that Giraudoux first met Paul Morand. Morand's father, the curator of the Dépôt des Marbres in the Beaux-Arts administration, had gone there to represent France in the International Painting Exhibition. Paul, who was with him, needed a tutor to prepare him for the philosophy oral, which he had just failed but wished to take again in October. The Bavarian minister recommended Giraudoux. We have Morand's first impressions of Giraudoux that day in July when he came to present himself:

> Personne n'avait une plus glissante démarche, et toute sa vie il la conserva; une foulée longue et pliée, très souple des reins, avec une avancée de l'épaule qui était la grâce même (plus tard, après l'Amérique, à cause des talons de caoutchouc qu'il en rapporta, son pas fut, de plus, silencieux, ce qui lui donna quelque chose de félin).
>
> Giraudoux était encore assez mal assemblé, habillé étroit, la moustache rousse coupée dru, les cheveux en brosse, le regard mal assuré derrière le lorgnon (il n'adopta les lunettes que dix ans plus tard).
>
> Ce n'est qu'après plusieurs années de Paris qu'il devint élégant, mais d'une élégance qui ne fut jamais "empruntée"; Paris révéla simplement une distinction native qui apparaissait dans tout, dans la voix, dans les paroles naturellement, dans les gestes, dans le rire, dans le sérieux. Jamais je ne l'entendis prononcer un gros mot, pas même un mot d'argot. Mes parents avaient la même retenue; ce n'était pas du rigorisme; c'était le genre naturel et universel d'une époque où personne ne parlait avec cette grossièrté que nous affectâmes plus tard, par drôlerie ou par veulerie, à partir de 1914.
>
> Le Giraudoux qui entrait dans ma chambre d'Amalienstrasse n'avait pas l'air jeune. Je ne lui trouvai, comme on dit, "pas d'âge." Ce n'est que vingt ans plus tard qu'il devint jeune, comme, vers la cinquantaine, il cessa d'être myope.[56]

They talked seriously and impersonally about Morand's studies. Giraudoux spoke well, and Morand listened in admiration:

> Je me souviens des douces inflexions de sa voix, traduisant avec une aisance parfaite une pensée nuancée, classique, inspirée de l'étude directe des maîtres, une pensée extrêmement subtile mais qui déjà tendait à se simplifier, à s'humaniser, comme elle le fit complètement dans son théâtre.[57]

But both were too lazy to pursue the lessons very assiduously, and soon the times they spent together were chiefly good times.

The summer days passed quickly and pleasantly. Giraudoux would meet Morand at the Café Luitpold, a convenient spot since Giraudoux's *pension* was in the same building, and he liked to drop in there the first thing every morning to read *Le Figaro*. Together they might go to Lake Starnberg, where they would swim in a pool equipped with artificial waves. The Bavarians were proud of the machinery that produced them, and Giraudoux found highly amusing the sign inviting foreign tourists to inspect it: "Les machines seront en examination les jours pas propres de prendre bains *[sic]*."[58] Sometimes they went to the Ungererbad out in Schwabing to take sun baths, a daring practice unknown in France at the time. They would come back to town by the streetcar that took them through the artist quarter, the colorful Bohemia that Giraudoux loved and where he would be living during the winter.[59] Rainy days they went to the Volksbad, a covered pool, where Giraudoux dived for perforated pennies. Afterwards, they would stop at Tieck's, across from the station, to lunch on smoked salmon and go on to have a taste of roast goose in the old Hofbräuhaus, or drink wine in the cellars of the Rathaus. By then it was time to separate for dinner. Giraudoux would go back to his *pension*. In the evening the friends would meet again in the Spatenbräuhaus to drink beer and listen to the orchestra playing gypsy music.

Their conversation never turned into those feverish discussions to which young men are often inclined, wherein all the problems of the soul and of destiny are threshed out. Their talks were not very intellectual either, for Giraudoux was discreet about displaying his learning. Politics did not interest them, nor business. They preferred stories and songs. We have noticed before Giraudoux's fondness for singing. At Lakanal, so André Beucler reports,[60] he had once been expelled for a week because of singing in class! What his baritone lacked in precision it made up in volume, and his rendition of airs from *Manon, Siegfried, Griselidis* was memorable.

Often Giraudoux took leave of the tavern company in time to go to concerts and the opera. Reminiscing in *Siegfried,* he speaks of hearing Wagner from the *Stehplätze,* standing in tennis shorts; and, leaning on his racket, of watching Mottl, Strauss, and Weingartner each direct one act of his beloved Mozart.[61] His press card from *Le Figaro* let him in theaters free. It is said that he owed it to the kindness of Wanda de Boncza, of the Comédie Française, who had been moved by his demonstration of enthusiasm after one of her performances at a classical matinée.[62] He held another card from the *Revue d'Art Dramatique,* for which, thirty years later, he thanked its director, Gaston de Bellefonds, in a preface to Bellefonds' book on bridge.[63] According to his statement in this preface, he saw two hundred plays and two hundred operas in Germany, a figure we need not take literally, for in the previous sentence he exaggerates the time spent abroad.[64]

Sometimes, though, they did talk of literature at the red and white checked table in the Spatenbräuhaus while the pretty *Kellnerin* brought them foamy steins. Giraudoux spoke of his grave and deep friendship for Charles-Louis Philippe, who had taught him to love Michelet, of Paul Claudel, of Laforgue, and of Anna de Noailles, who was the idol of the French youth of the period. He still ignored Flaubert, Zola, and Maupassant, and instinctively disliked Realism. Among the young German writers, Wedekind inspired his greatest admiration.

Once he took his pupil Morand to see two spinsters whose prestige in Giraudoux's eyes lay in their being relatives of this playwright. On their front lawn, Giraudoux proposed his favorite pastime, the 100-meter dash. Long after his days at Châteauroux, he delighted in running races and in beating his opponents. While at Lakanal he ran in the Bois de Boulogne, and in Munich anywhere where the spirit moved him — on front lawns or out the Ludwigstrasse, where startled sentries watched this tall young man running, glasses in hand, with great, easy strides. We gather that Giraudoux had made many acquaintances in Munich. Morand speaks of his having given "plusieurs semaines de suite des leçons de français dans les milieux de la Cour de Bavière."[65] The tutorship to the Prince of Saxe-Meiningen, reported by early biographers, must fit in here. This German prince, whose residence was just outside Munich, is doubtless the inspiration for the Prince de Saxe-Altdorf in "Visite chez le Prince."[66]

Giraudoux made contacts also in art circles. Morand's father took him several times to Dachau where there was a thriving young school grouped around Ferber.

When September came, the lessons were over. Paul returned to Paris to his *philo* exam, and Jean Giraudoux went off southward on a sight-seeing trip. It is impossible to trace his movements during the next months with exactitude. What he himself tells us in his later works — *Simon le Pathétique, Nuit à Châteauroux, Siegfried et le Limousin* — is always open to question. Reports by others are conflicting and equally untrustworthy. Giraudoux enjoyed spoofing, and his biographers repeat each other's errors or make new ones. He is said to have made extensive tours, much of the time on foot — Berlin, the Scandinavian countries, the Balkans, and Italy. Paul Morand says Bosnia, Herzegovina, Agram, Austria, and Venice. The itinerary described in *Simon* probably combines the meanderings Giraudoux took out of Munich with other travels he would make later. Simon went to Denmark and Sweden, Russia, and England, always "servi par le hasard." "Il me suffisait d'entrer dans un pays pour que le monarque en mourût, ou se mariât, ou entrât en conflit avec son Parlement."[67] Simon caught Ibsen and Gladstone on the edge of their graves, and was the last Frenchman to see Bismarck![68] If Giraudoux visited all these north countries, it was probably only after he joined the diplomatic service. During the month of September, 1905, his travels were most likely confined to the Balkans and north Italy. A hotel bill found among his papers testifies that he spent the night of September 10 in Trieste, and a postal card establishes his presence in Venice later in the month.[69] Before October, presumably, he was back in Munich where he advertised in the newspaper for a German companion to increase his proficiency in the German language.[70]

The following was among the letters he received in reply:

Mons. Jean M. H. Giraudoux, Hier, Amalienst 14, I, Eberlein.
(postmarked Munich, 28 September 1905)

P. P.

Ich las zufällig Ihr Inserat und wäre gern bereit, demselben näher zu treten. Von Geburt Nordd. 27 Jahr alt, bin ich fein gebildet und weitgereist. Ich wünsche Anschluss an j. Herrn, der möglich etwas Interesse für Literatur, Theater, Kunst u. Natur haben sollte. Noch bemerke ich, dass ich mich in angesehener Stellung befinde und Beziehungen zu den besten Kreisen habe . . .

Haben Sie die Güte, auch wenn Sie meine Zeilen nicht berücksichtigen, mir kurze Mitteilung zu machen.

Hochachtend
D. Graz
D. G. Akademiepost[71]

In *Siegfried et le Limousin,* Giraudoux speaks of having solicited "pour jeune étudiant français hôtes de marque et de culture," phrasing recommended by the newspaper. Doubtless this letter, which Giraudoux never threw away, is the one referred to in the novel as from a "jeune israélite de Charlottenburg, nommé Walden."[72]

Siegfried confirms much that Paul Morand tells us about the summer in Munich together. We gather from it (and from Morand's personal testimony) that the winter Giraudoux spent in the artist district of Schwabing was just as diverting. The district in those days surpassed the Latin Quarter in opportunities for disguise, escapades, and merry student life. A life of perpetual carnival, it would seem, with Giraudoux in Bavarian costume: "une culotte noire passepoilée de grenat et coupée aux cuisses . . . une chemise gaufrée à revers brodés de zinnias, et . . . un chapeau émeraude à blaireau de chamois!"[73]

In spite of carnival, sight-seeing, and outings with friends (every Saturday he took the train to Schleissheim with Martha-Eva, etc.), Giraudoux found time to do some work. In the library, he studied the manuscripts of von Platen-Hallermünde for the thesis he would present on his return to Paris.[74] It seems unlikely that he ever undertook more formal study while in Germany than this library research; the account of matriculation at a German university is probably fictitious and the assertion of memorialists that he attended Heidelberg erroneous.[75] Besides Platen, however, he read other German writers, and, in a notebook which has been preserved,[76] he tried his hand in the German language. Among the fragments we find there, one little sketch concerns life at a spa. Other entries record his observations on Karl Immermann, on the novel *Niels Lyhne,* on Impressionist painters. Between pages of his own composition we find verses in violet ink, a portion of *Der Tor und der Tod* by Hofmannsthal. Giraudoux's German was quite nonchalant, and these jottings bristle with errors in gender and syntax and with questionable diction.

Aside from these exercises in German, Giraudoux was probably doing other writing during his sojourn abroad. In January, 1906, the *Athena, revue de lettres et d'art,* published some curious bits of poetic whimsy by one Jean-Emmanuel Manière, the pseudonym Giraudoux would use more than once. One of the pieces is recognizable as the spring allegory in *Provinciales.*[77]

The *D. E. S.* and the *Agrégation*

Sometime in the spring Giraudoux returned to Paris and on June 23, 1906, received the *Diplôme des Etudes Supérieures* in German. The subject of his *mémoire* was the *Festgesänge* of Platen. We have noted the proof of his researches in Platen manuscripts while in Munich.[78] Whether he accomplished more than that towards his *mémoire* while abroad — in view of his many distractions — is highly doubtful. We are not surprised to learn from Professor Maurice Boucher that only by the collaboration of obliging comrades who ransacked the library of the Ecole Normale on his behalf was Giraudoux able to bring the paper to its required length.[79]

It is obvious that somewhere between Lakanal and Munich a change had overcome the model *lycéen.* The hard-working solitary student had become a happy-go-lucky, gregarious young man, for whom life seemed too brimming full to permit the assiduousness in his studies that had characterized him previously. Native wit would henceforth serve him, with less and less support from application. To be sure, we remember the schoolboy who would not have it thought that he slaved over his themes, and the *lycéen* at Lakanal who cut classes to stroll along the bookstalls. But now facility and offhandedness seem to have crystallized into a code of conduct consciously adopted. It would remain a guiding principle in life, and if study or labor were ever required of Giraudoux, nobody saw evidence of it. This *désinvolture* must always be reckoned with in explaining his failures and his successes, for — as a writer and as a diplomat — Jean Giraudoux refused to make work out of anything he undertook.

Fortunately, at least to nonspecialist eyes, Giraudoux's essay on Platen does not betray the haste and nonchalance in which it is reported to have been prepared. The work appears to be honest and carefully thought out. It is a sister study to his *mémoire de licence,* since the poetry Giraudoux is analyzing has again Pindar as its model. In the introduction, he refers immediately to Ronsard. But after stating the obvious kinship between the works of the two poets, he hastens to indicate their dissimilarity.[80] Of greater interest to us here than Giraudoux's discussion of metrics and form is what he notes concerning Platen's thought. He finds in the aristocratic German poet a stoic attitude towards life and a lofty concept of the role of the poet that he will make part of his own philosophy. Giraudoux's academic studies left a strong mark on him.

With the *D.E.S.* out of the way, Giraudoux looked towards the *agrégation.* He resumed the life of the typical student and fledgling author of the Latin Quarter. He lived in hotel rooms — the Descartes, for example, next to Polytechnique — and took his meals in a boarding house. Giraudoux's boarding house was the Pension Laveur. Much has been written about this famous *pension* just off Boul' Mich', where students were fed well and copiously and where their credit was good.[81] In the crowded dining room decorated with a portrait of Gambetta and Millet's *Angelus,* Giraudoux sat down to table with other young writers and students whose names have become famous — Curnonsky, Emile Clermont, André Billy, J.-P. Toulet. They were good comrades, whom Giraudoux would remember all his life long.

Sunday afternoons he often went to see the Morands at the Dépôt des Marbres. Paul and he played tennis with their girl friends Suzanne Lalique, the daughter of the artist, and Denise Rémon, later Mme. Bourdet, whose father was at that time enjoying great success on the Paris stage with his Sudermann translations. Or, if not playing tennis, the two young men engaged in their usual horseplay, such as leapfrog over the busts of fallen sovereigns which had been exiled by successive régimes to this museum. Sometimes they would spend the afternoon in Paul's room in the little house hidden under the chestnut trees and the lilacs behind the bleak façade of the museum. When Giraudoux was with M. and Mme. Morand, he chatted about many things: his mother's health (in spite of her weak heart, she lived into the eighties), his brother's splendid medical career, his own future, and especially about literature. The tradition of Sunday dinner with his friends dates from these Sundays at the Morands'.

One may suspect that during the summer following his *D.E.S.* Giraudoux did not apply himself very seriously to his books. In August we find him traveling again. With his friends Louis Bailly and Max Vidal, he visited Prague and Dresden.[82] In the fall of 1906, however, he registered again at the Ecole Normale and began to study for the *agrégation d'allemand.*[83] It is doubtful that he applied himself seriously though, even now. A good part of his time — we imagine — he idled away in the Pension Laveur, in the cafés, or in jolly excursions. What else he was doing we do not know. He may well have had a job of some sort in order to earn his livelihood. Perhaps he was taken up with his writing. "De ma fenêtre," the opening piece of *Provinciales,* appeared in the magazine *L'Ermitage,* December 15, 1906, under the pseudonym J.-Emmanuel Manière.

Whatever the cause, Giraudoux's *agrégation* examination was a remarkable disaster. The high grade he obtained in French composition (18/20), a grade almost unique in the annals of the *concours,* could not offset the eliminative grade of 2, or 3/20, on his German exam. One wonders what happened. The samples we have of his German composition, although full of errors, would have been worth more.[84]

He was not long to brood over this mishap, however. The opportunity to live abroad again presented itself, and Giraudoux packed his things to spend the academic year 1907-08 at Harvard. He had met the wealthy young American philanthropist James Hazen Hyde, who, while president of the Harvard French Club, had inaugurated an exchange professorship program. Hyde was now interested in fostering student exchanges, and through his efforts Giraudoux was offered a year in the United States. His prompt acceptance did not mean, however, that his interest in German had flagged. It has been asserted even that he went to Harvard for the purpose of studying German.[85] We know for certain that he was enrolled in Kuno Francke's course on Goethe during the year.[86]

Harvard University

Evocations of the year at Harvard are scattered through Giraudoux's early writings. "Don Manuel le Paresseux,"[87] for example, describes the experiences and impressions of a foreign student at that university. He undergoes the hazing that is part of initiation into a fraternity. To become a Phi Gamma, Don Manuel had to get up and offer his seat in an almost empty streetcar to every lady who got on. And under the elm where Washington called his armies together, he had to play the banjo while other initiates, dressed as dancing girls, performed to the music. The haughty *lycéen* of Châteauroux has changed a great deal, one would say. Through the eyes of this visitor from abroad, the Boston of 1908 lives again: little girls on roller skates, Radcliffe women in cars with a teddy bear on the seat or on the hood. It is Saturday on Tremont Street between the park and the stores:

> Les ouvriers de Cambridge et de Chelsea, villes prohibitionnistes, ont passé le Charles River pour boire leur paye à Boston. Les footballeurs verts de Dartmouth, qui viennent de nous battre, défilent avec leur musique et leurs animaux favoris en lançant mille serpentins à leur couleur.[88]

At Wellesley the girls put on *Le Monde où l'on s'ennuie* in knickerbockers.

Many years later, in one of his lectures on *La Française,*[89] Giraudoux would recall that it was during the year at Harvard that he made his debut as a public speaker. He addressed the *Alliance Française* of Portland, Maine, on the subject of the fox and the rabbit in French literature! Because of a severe snow storm, only six of the ladies turned out to hear him, but — according to Giraudoux's account, which may not be exactly factual — President Eliot of Harvard was present.

Like all exchange students, Giraudoux tried to see something of the country during his vacations. A trip to Canada is recorded in a short article entitled "Conversations Canadiennes," which appeared in the review *Idées modernes,* February, 1909.[90] At Ottawa he visited the Parliament; at Montreal, McGill University; at Quebec, the French theater. In recording his impressions, one may note, he soon leaves the United States and Canada to deal with a subject of more passionate interest to him — the comparison of France and Germany:

> On pourrait dire de votre France qu'elle ne se reproduit pas par boutures, comme les autres nations, mais par marcottage. Chaque plante rejoint l'autre de toutes ses fibres. Ce n'est pas ainsi qu'on fait du commerce. Les Allemands émigrés perdent leur nationalité au bout d'une génération à peine, mais ils restent les clients assidus de leur pays. Ils ne font pas venir de la métropole des conférenciers qui, à chaque conférence, leur rappellent que leur place au foyer restera toujours vide, mais de bons voyageurs de commerce, qui précèdent la bière Royale ou le piano Bechstein.

Giraudoux may well have gone as far west as Niagara Falls on his Canadian trip. This supreme tourist attraction figures in *Jérôme Bardini* and provides the setting for the satiric piece on American publicity methods, "La Surenchère," published in *Le Matin* in 1910. However he probably did not go so far as Texas, the setting for another satiric piece, "Une Carrière," in which American upstart universities are lampooned. Both stories are interesting reactions to what Giraudoux saw and heard in this country in 1908.[91]

Although the United States will provide the background for several other later works too, it is noteworthy that the people described against an American background are either French or German visitors or immigrants (Jérôme and Fontranges at Niagara Falls, Edmée in California, Stéphy in the German-American colony of New York City). Giraudoux really knew the Americans very little, and their place in his works is slight and superficial. Canadians figure even less, and the Canadian disguise of the narrator in *Siegfried* is not at all elaborated.

The preoccupation with Germany, alluded to above, is further reflected in a curious document which we come across among the author's papers, a manuscript of a newspaper article that was never published.[92] Written in 1912, just before France and Germany would go to war, it mocks the tactics their diplomats use in advancing the cause of their countries abroad. Particularly the Germans, whose methods of propaganda at Harvard constitute the theme of the piece. The German Club there thrives because it offers beer, he declares, but other German enterprises meet with failure. Hugo von Münsterberg was thwarted in his effort to monitor André Tardieu's lectures. Kuno Francke's ambition to found a Germanic museum led only to a collection housed in a gymnasium (in view of the eventual realization of Francke's highest hopes, this example today seems unfortunate); Francke's insistence that all German instructors be chosen from among students of German nationality was ignored, etc. With cutting words, Giraudoux notifies the Germans that they are sending the wrong kind of persons to represent them abroad:

> Mais si ce peuple, qui manquaint déjà d'éducation, renonçait lui-même à sa culture; si, pour succéder aux émigrés libéraux de 1848 il envoyait maintenant aux Etats-Unis des professeurs juifs — ou étrangement pangermanistes — il fallait l'avertir qu'il faisait fausse route.

One might wonder how much the highly accusing tone of this article was prompted by the general atmosphere that existed at the time it was written, shortly before the outbreak of World War I — whether Giraudoux was not viewing the events at Harvard with a hostility he felt only in retrospect. Nothing substantiates such a supposition, however, and it must be remembered that the anti-German feeling was strong, too, in 1907-08. Giraudoux's tone here is no more violent than that of the editorials he was reading that year in the *Courrier des Etats-Unis*, a French language daily published in New

York City. We conclude then that, in spite of his recent sojourn in Germany and his profound attachment to German culture, Giraudoux was never, even at this early date, an uncritical Germanophile. The testimony of the journal he kept while in Germany[93] and of *Siegfried et le Limousin,* which we will turn to later, further bears us out.

THE LATIN QUARTER AGAIN, JOURNALISM, AND THE END OF STUDENT LIFE

When Giraudoux returned from America in the spring of 1908, he found Paul Morand waiting for him on the docks at Naples, eying with candid admiration the pigskin suitcase and the wardrobe trunk acquired in the States. He showed Morand his trophies — but Paul was less impressed by the Harvard pennant and the blue stocking cap one wears for ice skating than by the mechanical razor and the dental floss. Morand noted his carefully manicured finger nails and his expensive American shoes. Surely the year in America had wrought great changes in Jean Giraudoux. Before long he was going to wear his hair with a part, abandon his glasses for a monocle, and buy his suits at an English tailor near Saint-Philippe-du-Roule. But these subsequent transformations were probably not entirely inspired by his American sojourn. The American style was affected by all the young men of the Ecole. Velvet berets and artist capes persisted only in Montmartre, where the Chat Noir had renewed the tradition of Murger. On the Boul' Mich', the ideal was that represented by the "High Life Tailor"—impeccable grooming, hair plastered down, and the crush hat.

With his new finery Giraudoux proceeded to Paris to pick up the threads of the life he had left the year before. He still had the *agrégation d'allemand* in view and may have thought of doing some work with Professor Andler, or with Ernest Lichtenberger, the adviser for his *D.E.S.* thesis. He did not, however, enroll officially at Normale. His plans were not very certain, we suspect, but the future did not preoccupy Giraudoux unduly. Soon after his return, he ran into Marc Aucuy in the Luxembourg Gardens and took him back to his room in the rue des Fossés-Saint-Jacques, where, the new luggage and fancy shoes properly admired, the conversation turned to Aucuy's legal studies and Giraudoux's own circumstances. Giraudoux probably told Aucuy that the *Mercure de France* and the *Grande Revue* were soon to publish two of his stories. "La Pharmacienne" had already appeared in *La Revue du Temps Présent.*[94] His literary career seemed to be his chief preoccupation, and the failure in the *agrégation* exam and the decision against teaching caused him no anxiety. The two young men were in perfect agreement that persons like themselves could with impunity change the course of their lives many times. After all, as Giraudoux summed up their thought: "lorsqu'on a quelque chose dans le ventre, un jour ou l'autre cela se montre!"[95]

While waiting for that day to arrive, Giraudoux slipped back into the pleasant routine he had known before he left for America. The Pension Laveur, D'Harcourt's, the Cluny, the Balzac (where the beer was exceptionally good) were among his haunts, but above all the Vachette, that Café de Flore of the *Belle Epoque,* where Jean Moréas played bridge and gathered the faithful around him. Giraudoux's lifelong addiction to the game probably began here. The Vachette is the restaurant Giraudoux has in mind when he speaks of "un café disparu, mais jadis célèbre, sur le boulevard Saint-Michel, où je rejoignais quelquefois mes amis aînés ou cadets: Moréas, Toulet, Apollinaire, Albalat, Morand et Guinle."[96] Victor, the waiter in *Cantique des Cantiques,* is doubtless the famous Victor of Vachette's. Giraudoux often took Paul Morand to his favorite haunts and invited him to lunch at the Vachette, to be joined by "le Cricri-Ravageur" or other girls they met there. Paul, who detested Vachette's, invited Jean to Prunier's for oysters and white wine. Sometimes during that summer, they went to Bullier's to see the bear dance, to the Closerie des Lilas, or to the summer Alcazar, where they saw Colette assume "poses plastiques" in a panther skin.

Towards fall, Giraudoux took a job as secretary to Bunau-Varilla, son of the owner of *Le Matin.* Inventor of modern journalism and pioneer in the field of fanatic anti-Communism, this conspicuous and controversial personality was not the sort of association that some of Giraudoux's friends could have wished for him. At a very celebrated trial of the day in which a former Minister of Education was suing *Le Matin* and its editor-in-chief Henry de Jouvenel, Marc Aucuy was painfully surprised to see his friend enter the courtroom with Bunau-Varilla, carrying the latter's brief case. At the recess, Giraudoux defended his employer to Aucuy, but Aucuy doubted his sincerity. He believed that in the portrait of Jacques de Bolny in *Simon le Pathétique* Giraudoux was painting Bunau-Varilla: "Bolny n'avait qu'une ambition: passer pour avoir l'âme noble, et il ne parvint jamais à la réaliser pour la simple raison que cette âme était basse . . ."[97] Aucuy was probably right because Giraudoux later told other friends that the Bunau-Varilla house had been for him a jail which he got out of as soon as he could.[98]

In addition to whatever duties were implied by his title of secretary, Giraudoux was asked to collaborate with Franz Toussaint in providing for the Thursday literary page of the newspaper. The history of their co-editorship is amusingly recounted by Toussaint in his *Souvenirs distingués.*[99] Their career was exciting, but brief. To supply the necessary "Contes des mille et un Matin," they solicited works of their friends, and Giraudoux inserted some of his own under the pseudonyms of E.-M. Manière and Jean Cordelier. Their first misfortune was to request a contribution from Charles-Louis Philippe, Giraudoux's idol. They received an edifying account of a miserly old woman who put false two-franc pieces in the collection basket. One day at Communion, the priest, who wanted to teach her a lesson, placed one of her counterfeit coins upon her tongue. Terrified at not being able to swallow the Host, she kept it in her mouth until Mass was over, then rushed to the priest to have him deliver her of it. He thanked God for having performed such an avenging miracle. When the story was published, over one hundred pious persons wrote canceling their subscriptions to *Le Matin.* Jouvenel sent his literary editors an amiable but firm rebuke. Things had not got along very far before they published an item of Toulet, whom Giraudoux was seeing a great deal of at the time and with whom he was even thinking of doing a play.[100] Toulet's story about a drunkard who behaved shockingly after a number of Pernods brought forth five hundred letters of protest. This time Jouvenel felt obliged to thank Toussaint and Giraudoux for their services.

The newspaper stories that Giraudoux composed for *Le Matin* and later for *Paris-Journal,* with the exception of two items to be incorporated into *Elpénor,* stand outside the main current of his literary career. They were written for the general public and lack the poetry and fine writing that we identify with Giraudoux. It is interesting to observe from them that Giraudoux was capable of fairly conventional prose; that he could, if he wanted, tell a story in a direct and realistic manner. Not without the sustained ironical humor, however, or the characteristic word-play and verbal acrobatics.

I have already alluded to the two stories in which the inspiration of the country where he had just spent a year is evident.[101] Another major inspiration is the Paris street scene. "Le Banc," "Au cinéma," "Guiguitte et Poulet" are amusing little sketches of pre-war Paris that seem very quaint today. The young provincial who had come from the Limousin to accept a scholarship at Lakanal soon fell under the charm of the capital. He never tired of exploring its parks, its streets, all its characteristic aspects. Nowhere more charmingly does he evoke the city than in these juvenile pieces. Standing apart from the other stories is "L'Ombre sur les joues," a grim and bitter tale of leprosy in Iceland. It is a curious pastiche of J. P. Jacobsen, whom Giraudoux had discovered while studying in Germany.[102] One would say that Giraudoux was experimenting with several literary styles before he developed his definitive manner.

While Giraudoux was working for *Le Matin* and writing his realistic *contes,* his first book, *Provinciales,* was offered for sale. The bulk of the stories that comprise this volume had already appeared in the reviews. Giraudoux's memorable encounter with the publisher Grasset is often told. One day while having a drink at a sidewalk café, he struck up a conversation with a stranger who happened to be the young philanthropist whose publishing house was to become one of the most important in France. Bernard Grasset told Giraudoux about the authors he had signed up already — Emile Baumann, Faguet, and others — and invited him to submit some of his stories as a volume. Giraudoux's literary career really dates from this meeting, and through the years to come he repaid his benefactor with a fidelity that contrasts with Proust's early abandonment of Grasset for a firm he found more chic.

For a time Giraudoux's writing continued on two levels. Newspaper stories of the "Mille et un Matin" sort appeared even as late as 1911. But the encouragement offered by the publication of *Provinciales* disposed Giraudoux gradually to abandon journalism and to cultivate his more original style of writing. Besides, in left-bank literary circles Giraudoux was making a name for himself. Gide's favorable notice of *Provinciales* was a great boost:

> Jean Giraudoux sait écrire. Je n'admire pas seulement ici de belles qualités naïves, mais aussi leur mise en valeur, leur culture, leur retenue. Ces qualités acquises sont si remarquables dans ce livre

qu'elles me laissent croire que l'auteur, sur lequel, du reste, je ne sais rien, a déjà passé la première jeunesse.[103]

Giraudoux would have had the Goncourt prize in 1909 if Jules Renard had had his way.[104] His picture appeared now and again in magazines with captions like the following: "Un de nos tout jeunes confrères en journalisme débute dans les lettres par un livre de nouvelles et de croquis: *Provinciales,* qui annonce un original écrivain."[105]

The *nouvelles* that make up Giraudoux's second book, *L'Ecole des Indifférents,* appeared in the *Nouvelle Revue Française,* the *Grande Revue,* and the *Mercure de France.* When the volume came out in 1911, Giraudoux received further acclaim from discerning spirits. His gratification can be measured by the lofty ambition he had for his work. Together with his young companions in the Latin Quarter who discussed literature with revolutionary passion, Giraudoux aimed at nothing less than breaking the mold into which they claimed French prose had hardened, to let it flow melodiously and poetically as once before! In an interview granted Simonne Ratel some years hence, he would recall the spirit that possessed them during those years:

> Vers 1910, 1912, il y avait des jeunes gens qui peut-être préparaient, comme moi, l'Ecole Normale: ils n'avaient pas la mine de révolutionnaires. Ces jeunes gens se sont mis à voyager. Ils ont échappé à l'influence stérilisante de Paris, où l'homme de lettres était à cette époque une sorte de fonctionnaire exécutant sa besogne dans des cadres tracés une fois pour toutes. Ils ont plongé dans de grandes ondes poétiques dont les cercles de dressage littéraire et mondain semblaient ignorer l'existence. Je ne veux pas dire que la France tout entière se tenait à l'écart du mouvement: il s'était déjà manifesté, en poésie, par Verlaine, Rimbaud et le symbolisme. Mais la prose était figée dans le moule stéréotypé du langage que nous avaient légué le dix-huitième et le dix-neuvième siècles, coupables d'avoir desséché et compliqué le beau langage vivant du dix-septième et du seizième. Et la littérature romanesque était une route monotone, creusée d'ornières dans lesquelles on s'engageait docilement à la queue-leu-leu.
>
> Nous avons voulu réagir, briser les moules, donner du champ à l'invention.[106]

On the strength of the praise his handful of stories had received from a few persons — even though they were of the *N.R.F.* — this beginning writer, one should say, was remarkably self-confident. Of course, the future would prove that his self-confidence was perfectly justified and that he, at least, accomplished the ambition that inflamed those of his generation.

But glory and gratification did not, unfortunately, imply financial success for Jean Giraudoux. He received little from *Le Matin* — seven louis a month, according to Paul Morand. Nor could he live on the money Grasset paid him. Only thirty copies of *Provinciales* sold in four years. The magazines to which Giraudoux contributed paid little or nothing. He pondered the problem of income. Mr. Adams, the husband of an American friend, urged him to return to the United States. His thoughts turned towards business. To the youth of the Latin Quarter, the capitalist tycoon had become the new hero, and Giraudoux doubtless shared the general dream of fortunes amassed through business deals and financial manipulations. Jean de Pierrefeu, who describes very wittily his own *crise affairiste* at this time, recalls how Giraudoux once served as contact man between a chum of his who had some mine shares to sell and two businessmen of Giraudoux's acquaintance who represented vast mine holdings in South America. Giraudoux took Pierrefeu and his friend to a room in the Grand Hôtel, where — intimidated and enchanted by the atmosphere of big business — they presented their offer. All bright hopes of profits and commissions faded when the men agreed only to take an option on the stock. Giraudoux remained in Pierrefeu's eyes a financial giant, notwithstanding.[107]

It is amusing to think of young Giraudoux aspiring to be one of the "mecs" he would denounce in *La Folle de Chaillot*. His efforts, whatever they were, could not have been very successful or long-enduring.[108]

Although he was not making money, Giraudoux was nevertheless living as if he were. When he went to work for Bunau-Varilla he had given up student rooms for good to establish himself in a pretty Louis XV apartment on the fourth floor of 16 rue de Condé, the building where Stechert-Hafner now has its Paris office. Aucuy had noticed that Giraudoux always managed to give his surroundings some of his own distinction and elegance. This apartment, with its windows on three sides, seemed delicately suspended in mid-air. Paul Morand had helped Giraudoux shop for furnishings. The first acquisition was a superb Boule chest of drawers, for which Giraudoux paid out 800 francs over a four-year period. Above this piece — magnificent with its polished ebony and brass hardware — they placed a picture of a bewigged nobleman in an oval frame. The bed was installed in the alcove opposite, and a small, rickety table by its side. Since Giraudoux had very few books, the absence of bookcases was not important. The vestibule, the kitchen, another small room, and the bath were probably even more sparsely furnished. Madame Morand supplied some curtains for the windows of the big room, through which the two young men could look up the street to see one side of the Odéon, and at noon watch the young ladies come out from the Lycée Sévigné. Long before Giraudoux had paid for the chest of drawers he had acquired a dainty harpsichord, on which he played Couperin, not well, but with elegance and nonchalance.[109]

In his newly acquired *chez-soi* Giraudoux took great pleasure in receiving his friends. Here he gave his first luncheon parties to which young ladies were invited. About the loves of his youth we have little specific information, but Morand tells that he was enamored of a beautiful foreign girl whom he saw regularly, and Franz Toussaint alludes to his infatuation for "la jeune fille rose" and "la jeune fille bleue." In *Sentiments distingués,* Toussaint sketches provokingly the good times he and Giraudoux had as gay and prankish young blades whom the young ladies could rarely resist. Giraudoux himself gives an account of his sentimental life in the story of *Simon le Pathétique.* Gabrielle, Hélène, and Anne are lovely creations of poetry and whimsy, but we can be sure they had their prototypes among young Giraudoux's feminine acquaintances.

It may be surmised from Giraudoux's literary activity and his casting about to establish himself financially that he was doing little or no reading for the *agrégation.* Paul Morand was busy preparing for the *Concours des affaires étrangères et sciences politiques.* While he was away at Caen to spend "deux mortelles années au 36me d'infanterie,"[110] Giraudoux poked into his manuals one day and decided that he, too, should prepare for the *Grand Concours.*[111] Time was too short to study adequately for international law and the second language, and Giraudoux failed. But several months later when he took the examination for *élèves vice-consuls, petit concours,* he won first place. On June 14, 1910, he received his appointment; on September 15, he was assigned to the political and commercial section. Giraudoux's student days were over, the *agrégation d'allemand* forgotten, and his connection with *Le Matin* severed. The question of his profession and his livelihood was now settled.

Chapter 2

DIPLOMACY AND AUTHORSHIP: GIRAUDOUX'S NOVELS AND PLAYS

First Years in the Consular Service. *Simon le Pathétique*

Giraudoux's first assignment on the Quai d'Orsay was in the foreign press section, the bureau that he himself would direct fourteen years later. The following spring he made contact with Philippe Berthelot, then *sous-directeur* of the European desk, who immediately took a personal interest in the new foreign service officer. If we can believe Giraudoux's own statement, this is how his career began:

> Philippe Berthelot m'a fait appeler. Il est directeur du cabinet du ministre. Il s'enquiert de mon travail et de mes goûts. En le quittant, il m'explique d'où vient son intérêt pour moi: "Dimanche dernier, j'ai vu un de nos ambassadeurs rire en lisant le Mercure de France." Je lui ai demandé pourquoi. "Il lisait une phrase d'une de vos nouvelles: un cheval passa. Les poules suivirent, remplies d'espoir." Voilà à quoi je devrais peut-être ma carrière.[1]

The ambassador in question must have been Paul Claudel, for Claudel speaks of having noticed Giraudoux's writing for the first time in the pages of the *Mercure,* and of having pointed out the pages to Berthelot. Berthelot "partagea mon appréciation et il voulait connaître le jeune écrivain qui nous consolait de la disparition de Jules Renard."[2] Soon Giraudoux was on very friendly social terms with Berthelot. We know of their tennis games on the courts at *Affaires Etrangères,* and we read that in a duel Giraudoux expected to fight

Notes to Chapter 2 begin on page 217.

early in 1913, it was Berthelot — along with Paul Morand — whom he asked to serve him as second.[3] In Berthelot, Giraudoux had found a protector and friend.

During the first years of Giraudoux's service, he remained in Paris. There seems to have been no question of an assignment abroad. He may have carried the diplomatic pouch, however, which would account for the allusions to travels to Russia and Central Europe that we note in *Simon le Pathétique.* Morand declares Giraudoux once went to England with the mail-pouch. He had volunteered to go so as to visit Morand there, but the rough Channel crossing discouraged him from making the trip a second time.

Giraudoux preferred to refresh himself in the French provinces, and we know of several outings and vacations which he enjoyed in the years before the war. The summer of 1911, he was a frequent visitor at the little château of Feugerolles which the Morands had rented to be near Paul, who was doing his military service at Caen.[4] During the day Giraudoux worked on his book *Simon le Pathétique.* The next year, when Morand too was in the diplomatic service, attached to "Protocole," Giraudoux persuaded his friend to lend him his diplomatic uniform to wear during a holiday in the Limousin. Obligingly, Morand lifted from the wardrobe of foreign decorations enough stars, medals, and ribbons to bespangle Giraudoux like a Christmas tree.

In July, the excursion to Commercy that Franz Toussaint relates in "Pégase"[5] took place. Franz's father was commanding two infantry regiments stationed there. Giraudoux was invited to go riding and, being an inexperienced horseman, disgraced himself most entertainingly in his handling of "Pegasus." Commercy, incidentally, was the home of "la jeune fille rose" (Laure de Messey) and "la jeune fille bleue" (Marguerite Bujard) whom we know about through Toussaint's confidences. They came often to Paris, where Jean and Franz courted them with walks and talks in the Luxembourg, with sonatas on the harpsichord in the flat of the rue de Condé. Toussaint has preserved a mock-rhapsodical letter they composed at the Tabarin, July 8, 1912, at 2 a.m.[6]

Giraudoux visited his family several times a year. He was home in the fall of 1913, and it is from there that he addressed his New Year's greetings the last of December, huddled over the new salamander to keep warm in the drafty house from which his parents were soon to move. Is it from the new house that he wrote the following July to arrange a code to communicate during the war? "My shoes are good" meant successful battle; "my soles are loose" meant battle misfortune, etc.[7]

The month preceding the outbreak of hostilities, Colrat, the director of *L'Opinion,* accepted Giraudoux's new book to appear as a serial under the briefer title, *Simon.* The war forced the paper to cease publication after several installments. In view of some ironical allusions to Germany in the novel, it seemed prudent not to have the manuscript about in case the Germans should enter the city. It was accordingly burnt. If Giraudoux possessed no other copy — as he seems to imply in a letter to Jacques Doucet[8] — he must have subsequently rewritten a very large part; for in 1915 he was offering it for publication in volume form. Before leaving for the Dardanelles, he wrote Morand: "Si l'on m'enterre à Eyoub, et si des *Nouvelles Revues Françaises* veulent publier mon roman, qu'il s'appelle *Simon le Pathétique.*"[9] By the time the novel actually appeared in 1918, Giraudoux must have done at least two versions. André Morize declares that in 1917 on the deck of the *Touraine,* which was taking them to America, Giraudoux redid it completely. The new editions of 1923 and 1926, which differ considerably from that of 1918, seem to hark back to earlier manuscripts.[10]

Mobilization, Campaigns, and Intervals

On the second of August, 1914, mobilization sent Giraudoux to the depot at Roanne as a sergeant with the 298th infantry regiment. A month later he was ready to leave for Alsace, full of hope, optimism, and good humor. His mother had come from Cusset in an automobile to see him off. Perhaps he told her how much he looked forward to being attached to the regimental headquarters as interrogator of prisoners, mayors, and spies — "Ce sera très intéressant."[11]

Giraudoux reached the front on August 15 in the Mulhouse area. The campaign is minutely recorded in "Le Retour d'Alsace" (*Lectures pour une Ombre*) — its marches and countermarches, the picturesque Alsatian towns through which the French troops passed on the heels of the Germans. Giraudoux's duties as interpreter were to interrogate the villagers and to requisition for the camp kitchens. After Ammerzwiller and Saverne, the division moved back to France, "sans trophées." It was then sent north of Paris to take part in the Battle of the Marne. The account of the trip north is given in "Périple" (*Lectures pour une Ombre*). This portion of Giraudoux's diary closes with the first casualties. "Les Cinq Soirs et les Cinq Réveils de la Marne"[12] goes on with the chronicle through the full fury of that great battle. In spite of the epic significance of the event, there are no dramatic effects, no horrible scenes, no departure from the author's own actual and intimate experience. The Battle of the Marne is recorded in accents of wistful melancholy by this sentimental Stendhal.

On the sixteenth of September, Giraudoux received a slight shrapnel wound and was evacuated to Fougères, where he was allowed to rest for several weeks. While enjoying sleep, wine, and hot meals, he wrote to Berthelot requesting transfer to Bordeaux with the government. Thus he hoped to avoid being sent back to Roanne. At the end of October, he found himself in Bordeaux as he had hoped, but in the Red Cross Hospital there. More shrapnel had been found in his wounds. He did not seem to be having too disagreeable a time of it though; the trip through France had been pleasant, and in Bordeaux he was finding many old friends. A jauntiness that is not uncharacteristic of the young soldiers of 1914 marks Giraudoux's letters. Note his remarks to Paul Morand, who had tried to enlist:

> Je serai bien attristé . . . de te savoir au feu, mais comment ne pas t'approuver. Tu verras d'ailleurs des choses si effrayantes et si fantastiques qu'on sacrifierait volontiers son bras droit pour les avoir vues. Tant pis aussi pour la vie! Tout serait si simple si nous n'avions pas de parents! Pour eux seuls la guerre est une calamité.[13]

For Giraudoux, as doubtless for many others, it was just a magnificent lark, and well might he have prayed, as he does in the colophon to *Adorable Clio:* "Pardonne-moi, ô guerre, de t'avoir, — toutes les fois où je l'ai pu, caressée . . ."[14] From Bordeaux to Pau for a short stay, then back to Roanne, where he received his "citation à l'ordre du Régiment." Giraudoux was decorated several times during the war and had the special distinction of being the first writer to receive *la Légion d'Honneur* for war service (July 31, 1915).

Although Giraudoux would have preferred to go to Italy instead of back to Roanne, he succeeded in passing the winter pleasantly. At least much of the time he was able to stay in his own Paris apartment, newly embellished by a fine mirror sent from London by Paul Morand. Mornings were spent writing, afternoons in the company of his young women friends. He saw a good deal of Suzanne Boland, particularly, whom he would marry before the war was over. He dined in society and kept in touch with his diplomatic and journalistic friends, being often in the company of Henri de Jouvenel, Edmond Jaloux, Mme. Edwards, Mme. de Messey, the Princesse de Polignac. He was a frequent guest at the Comtesse Murat's, where he met Henri Bergson. There were trips home to Cusset that winter and spring, perhaps by car, for Giraudoux had recently learned how to drive. At Easter he arrived bearing a coffeepot for his mother and a new table for his sister-in-law.

Meanwhile he had been pulling strings to be sent to the Dardanelles. His wish was finally granted. Through Berthelot's recommendation, Giraudoux — now a sublieutenant — was transferred to the 176th infantry at Riom, ready to head south. He wore the fine English belt that Paul Morand had sent him and announced his intention of filling its cartridge holders with candies to win over the Turkish harem. His parting word to Morand, one will remember, was for his new novel — if he should be buried at Eyoub, let it be called *Simon le Pathétique.*

At the Dardanelles with the Franco-British expeditionary force, Giraudoux was wounded again and had another bout with enteritis. Hospitalized at Vichy and then at Hyères, he was finally permitted to return to Paris, where he was attached once more to Philippe Berthelot. His duties, if any, were not very heavy. Much of *Lectures pour une Ombre* and of *Adorable Clio* must have been written at this time.

In the summer of 1916, at Berthelot's instigation, Giraudoux was sent with a mission of French officers to Portugal. The record of his trip is to be found in the "Journée Portugaise." With his handsome sky-blue uniform, his monocle, and his gloves, Giraudoux was very much the dashing French officer. He lived "à la Larbaud dans un hôtel des Wagons-Lits qui donne sur l'Avenida" and ate "des nouilles dans un parfum de piment et d'huile."[15] Evenings he dined with ministers, mornings he watched military reviews, afternoons he took sightseeing trips by car in the company of an English secretary. He went to Coimbra and delighted in its lacquered libraries. Paul Morand was kept posted of his activities and was commissioned to transmit messages for Mme. Boland. Morand was informed, incidentally, that Giraudoux's book dealing with his war experiences would be called *Lectures pour Lydia* and that its publication date was set for December.[16]

In December, Giraudoux returned to Paris, but his stay was not a long one this time. Berthelot attached him to a mission of officer instructors to be sent to the United States.[17] "C'était le samedi matin. De chaque estuaire de France s'élançait vers l'Amérique, du milieu exact du fleuve, comme d'une couleuvre sa langue, un beau steamer et son sillage."[18] We may read a full account of his trip in the poetic reminiscences that make up *Amica America:* his impressions of America revisited, the impact of war upon the Americans, the reception offered the French delegation. Woven through the pages of events and impressions we find also a sentimental history of tender friendships formed by the young French officer with young Americans bound in a common cause.

The mission reached New York in April, 1917. Sublieutenant Giraudoux wrote Morand how strange this land appeared to one who had been in the war: "un monde où la guerre est inconnue, et où tout n'est que richesse, or et bien-être."[19] The mission proceeded quickly to Boston. It must have been with a certain emotion that Giraudoux, now engaged in a political apostleship, found himself back in this city he had known as a student. Here is a newspaper report of the appearance of the French officers before the Boston City Club:[20]

ROUSING GREETING TO FRENCH OFFICERS
HERE TO TRAIN STUDENTS AT HARVARD GIVEN
ENTHUSIASTIC RECEPTION BY THE BOSTON CITY CLUB

Such a demonstration of enthusiasm as has rarely taken place at an assemblage of Boston business men, was that last night at the Boston City Club when the company that filled the auditorium cheered and sang at the dinner given by the club to French officers, who have come here to train the young men at Harvard. When boy scouts trooped the tricolor of France and the Stars and Stripes the demonstration started, it was redoubled when the French officers marched in, and it broke forth at frequent intervals during the evening. "The Marseillaise" was sung and repeated whenever there was an opportunity.

James J. Storrow, president of the club, presided. "France is an old friend of ours," he said. "She stood by us in a very critical period of our career, and we are going to stand by her now." This brought long-continued applause, waving of flags and cries of "Vive la France." Continuing, he said: "Our guests typify that wonderful spirit France has displayed in the past two and one-half years, and the time has come when we've got to stand beside those men and make our record. They haven't asked our help, but they need it."

Major P. J. L. Azan was the principal speaker for the guests. Referring to the Germans, he said: "At heart a humane people, they will wake in horror from their nightmare. They have been perverted even by their professors. This is not a war of peoples, but of systems. Many pro-Germans fail to make the distinction. We rejoice at help because it is not enough for France to defeat the imperial government. We cannot treat with it at all. We must never make terms with the militarism which is still violating sacredly guaranteed Belgium, in a fashion that one would have thought impossible in this twentieth century among white men. At moments I doubt that the outrages which I myself have seen can be true.

"I look forward to returning here after the war and celebrating with you the victory not merely of the Allies, but of democracy — a victory for all the world. It is not merely the Allies that you have come to rescue; you are fighting for an ideal.

"We know that your soldiers will fight splendidly because you have sent us such heroic helpers already, like the Escadrille LaFayette; like the members of the Harvard unit who left with a flag blessed at your Cathedral of St. Paul."

Lieutenant L. Morize said: "O American friends thanks, thanks not only for your kindness to us, but for the joy which thrilled France on the day when a new nation arose to defend the honor of the world. I bring the thanks of the suffering, the wounded, the homeless and destitute; of those who see in the sky of France birds that have come from America; of those for whom, with outlook long limited to the trenches, you have opened infinite and splendid horizons."

Everyone rose and drank a toast, at the request of Lieutenant Jean Giraudoux, to a small flag which the Harvard ambulance unit had brought to France from Boston and he had brought back. "We come," he said, "not as representatives of the French army, but as representatives of the whole nation. We are proud to see that you think of us not as having come to teach war, but to try to teach, in our small way, how best you may finish the last and most dreadful of all wars."

Major J. de Reviers de Mauny and Captain A. Dupont rose and bowed appreciatively. Lieutenant M. de Varney is still unable to go out, owing to an old wound in his foot.

Other speakers, all of whom paid high tribute to France and the French were Lieutenant Colonel James T. Dean, chief-of-staff, northeastern department; Lieutenant Governor Calvin Coolidge, John J. Attridge of the City Council, Collector of the Port Edmund Billings, Acting Adjutant General E. Leroy Sweetser, Dr. Joseph Armand Bedard, president of the Franco-American Historical Society, and George W. Kyte, a member of the Canadian Parliament.

It is interesting to compare this newspaper *compte-rendu* with the chapter of *Amica America* entitled "Discours dans le Massachusetts," which appears as an excellent example of literary transposition edited by caprice and whimsey.

Giraudoux described his life in letters to his friends at home — "vie de réceptions, de clubs, de banquets avec discours. Réceptions souvent émouvantes, mais épuisantes."[21] It must have been just as exhausting, if less moving, to drill 800 students every morning and teach military tactics besides. May and June went by. His book, now called *Lectures pour une Ombre,* was going to appear in an English version, and Giraudoux worked with his translator, Elizabeth S. Sergeant.[22] It was a well-earned vacation that he wrote about to his friend Morand:

> Je reviens de la campagne, près du Canada, où j'ai été me reposer six jours. Mes couleurs sont revenues, mais, comme toujours, condensées sur mon nez. J'ai vu des oiseaux-mouches et, cela pour Poupette, quatre petits blaireaux. Il y avait aussi un rat musqué qui nageait tous les jours dans le lac. Mais il sent encore.[23]

The literary account of this holiday at Squam Lake makes up another chapter of *Amica America:* "Repos au lac Asquam," and a piece contributed to the *Ecrits Nouveaux* entitled "Vacances sur un chagrin." Brief vacations were not sufficient, however, for a man whose health was still delicate and who was overtaxing his strength. Before leaving Harvard, Giraudoux once more was hospitalized. He was discharged, he says, to spend his last weekend with the Appletons, descendants of the first family off the Mayflower ("On débarquait sans doute par lettres alphabétiques!").[24]

In August, Giraudoux was on his way back to France for joyful reunions with family and friends. He was soon promoted to lieutenant and transferred to the 26th *chasseur* regiment. But most of the fall and winter his chronic enteritis kept him in hospitals. When finally discharged, he was made liaison officer with the American army in Paris, an assignment which seems to have left him leisure to write and to pursue a nonchalant social life for the remainder of the war.

André Beucler says of him at the time:

> On le signalait à Montparnasse, chez Baty, entouré de condisciples, de camarades; on le signalera au premier *Bœuf sur le Toit,* prenant sa place exacte par rapport aux snobs. On l'apercevait sur les quais, aux Puces, chez les bouquinistes, dans les endroits célèbres du sixième arrondissement entre lesquels Roques, un de ses amis, graveur sur médailles trop tôt disparu, assurait la liaison. Il était élancé, nous disait-on, mince, un peu glabre, un peu distant, mais très beau, et bien pris dans un bel uniforme de capitaine de chasseurs à pied.[25]

It is probable that the gay and frolicsome *Elpénor,* published the following year, was now being composed. We may infer from all evidence that Giraudoux was finding life very delightful. Some time during this period, his marriage to Suzanne Boland took place.

Immediately after the Armistice, the Quai d'Orsay sent Giraudoux to Strasbourg to be present as the French troops entered the city. The following month he was ordered to Lisbon to see the new President. The trip was canceled, however, when news of the President's assassination reached Paris. Giraudoux's military career, which had been as glorious as his scholastic one, was closed with the following demobilization order:

> Le Lieutenant de Réserve Giraudoux, du 26ème Bataillon de Chasseurs à pied, détaché à l'Etat-Major général de l'armée (Bureau Franco-américain), est mis à la disposition du Ministère des Affaires Etrangères. Il sera considéré comme détaché de son corps. (Réponse à la lettre du 7 janvier 1919)[26]

His official "Adieu à la guerre" is dated July, 1919:

> La guerre est finie. Voici que je ne m'endormirai plus sur l'épaule d'un bourrelier, sur le cœur d'un menuisier; mes jambes ne se prendront plus le soir — qu'il était ardu de les démêler seules le matin — dans les jambes d'un charretier, d'un plongeur.[27]

Now that the war was over, Giraudoux was eager to resume his job, his literary career, and — being newly married — to establish a home in a world once more at peace. But for the time being he wanted just to look out of the window at Paris under the sun, and exult in the triumph of his country: "Ce que je fais? Ce que je suis? Je suis un vainqueur, le dimanche à midi."[28]

Moreover, his health, still precarious, demanded that he rest again. In May, after successfully competing in written and oral examinations, he was named *Secrétaire d'Ambassade, 3ème classe.* But he was put on sick leave, and spent many months — the last of his vacations — away from the Quai d'Orsay. He spent much of the time in the country at Cusset, and doubtless did considerable writing while waiting for his health to mend. Two works that would appear in the years that follow translate this last hour of adolescence and this pause before maturity: *Suzanne et le Pacifique* and *Juliette au Pays des Hommes.*

Suzanne et le Pacifique continues the history of Giraudoux's spiritual evolution, begun by previous books that had evoked his childhood and adolescence. Arriving on the threshold of adulthood, the Giralducian hero lets his place be taken by a *jeune fille,* a better subject perhaps to exemplify the drama of moving from a world of dreams and possibilities into reality and irrevocable decisions. In *L'Ecole des Indifférents* and in *Simon le Pathétique,* Giraudoux had already sketched the drama of the first encounter with life: the story of Jacques, Bernard, and Don Manuel. All are borne along in the ship of their ideals and illusions. None is brought safely into port, and one watches them disappear with the apprehension that they may soon meet disaster. Simon represents a sort of adolescent perfection. This perfect young man meets the perfect young woman, Anne. Together they form a pair destined, one would say, to live happily ever after. Yet the realities of life intervene, and they turn away from one another, wounded and bitter. Adolescence is the period of the ideal: to pass from it into maturity means renunciation and compromise. The story of Simon and Anne ends with their disillusionment. The transition into maturity is the story of Suzanne.

Suzanne knows that maturity, a life of routine and responsibility, awaits her, and she does not protest. But before she "meets her tiger," this young woman of Bellac must live for a moment intensely in her dream. She is granted a long respite on an enchanted isle in the Pacific. Then she returns to marry the *contrôleur des poids et mesures. Juliette au Pays des Hommes,* although not published until three years after *Suzanne,* likewise dramatizes the author's transition to maturity and the last "vacation" that precedes it. After her fling, Juliette, too, returns to marry and live in Bellac.

So Giraudoux, after an adolescence extended by many years beyond the average span, was finally ready for the next period in his life. When he returned, in April, 1920, to take up his work at the Quai d'Orsay, he was almost forty years old.

Siegfried and the Problem of Germany

The office that Giraudoux entered soon after his return to the Quai d'Orsay was somewhat equivalent to the division we know now as Cultural Relations. In the *Service des Œuvres Françaises à l'Etranger,* he found himself in a field to which he was well suited by both his past experience and interests. Perhaps by his temperament, too, for his native tendency to turn abstractions into concrete equivalents and his bold readiness to reduce complex situations to what seemed to him the essential or the fundamental facilitated his thinking in terms of nationalities and races. As he studied the questions of Germany and Franco-German relations, answers came in the form of symbolic personages, whose soul and body incorporated all that Giraudoux found typical and general in the two countries. The results of his investigations and ponderings, blended with his memories and first impressions of the country in which he had sojourned as a student, may be found summed up in *Siegfried et le Limousin,* which appeared in 1922.

We remember that the Germany Giraudoux had fallen in love with was the land his schoolbooks had represented — the land of Goethe and Schiller and Hoffmann, of medieval castles and flaxen-haired maidens, the land of fantasy. But when he crossed the Rhine, his poetic notions were severely tried by certain aspects of modern Germany. Like Renan, Quinet, and other Frenchmen before him, Giraudoux became unpleasantly aware of a new Germany quite at odds with the old romantic one. His actual distress at the time was probably less than it is represented to be in the novel. To establish his antithesis, he is doubtless attributing to himself in 1905-06 views and judgments which were far less categorical at the time. But to the Giraudoux of 1922 at least, modern Germany, with its architecture, ersatz articles, and rapacious instincts, appeared to have denied its heritage and to have become sadly disoriented.

We have already quoted the passage of *Siegfried et le Limousin* in which Giraudoux fancies himself in a landscape at dawn which has somehow escaped the blight of modern Germany: "J'étais, non dans un pays, mais dans une aube de conjuration, de pillage, et qui s'obstinait à ne rien révéler de l'Allemagne moderne."[29] To go with such landscape, Giraudoux creates a character embodying the "défauts superbes et voyants"[30] which once adorned all Germans. His name is Zelten. He is handsome with his blond, curly hair, and charming with his moods and caprices, his generous and instinctive behavior. Every moment of his life seems given over to delightful chimeras: "Il descendait habillé dans les bassins pour poser la main sur le jet d'eau ou remettre sous la bonne aile le bec du cygne endormi . . ." In contrast to Zelten, the modern German is "chauve, rapace et pratique."[31] His chief delight seems to lie in ornamenting his person and his surroundings with tasteless and useless paraphernalia. Siegfried, the victim of amnesia, has acquired an appearance characteristically German: "Je vis un être orné de tous les appendices que confère l'Allemagne . . ." His face is "embelli de deux lunettes en fausse écaille, d'une dent en or, d'une barbe allemande coupée en pointe."[32] This man, once a Frenchman by the name of Jacques Forestier, is now at home in rooms cluttered with cushions bearing sentimental mottoes, trophies, and metal knick-knacks — "ces pots d'étain et . . . ces bassets de laiton dont un seul exemplaire indique, à Sumatra ou à Iquique, qu'un bateau allemand a passé."[33]

Giraudoux's mockery of German manners and personal traits can be taken as just saucy burlesque. His indictment of modern Germany as a nation, however, is unmistakably serious. Germany is charged with betraying her mission in the world. She has forsaken her proper functions which made her universally beloved, to assume others for which she is ill-fitted. She has stubbornly refused to be natural, to arrange her life simply. Instead of heeding her instincts, the advice of her soil and her past, she has made a gigantic superhuman model for herself. Instead of giving, as she has many times in the past, a new form to human dignity, she has given this time only a new form to pride and misfortune. Her present ambitions will lead to disaster, Giraudoux prophesies. Every time Germany has attempted to be practical she has failed, but every time she has turned a great thought or a great deed into symbol or legend, her genius has triumphed. "L'Allemagne n'est pas une entreprise sociale et humaine, c'est une conjuration poétique et démoniaque."[34] With Zelten, Giraudoux would like to believe that true Germans still retain a love for little kingdoms and great passions.

This is Giraudoux's summary of Germany — after years of study of German culture, his sojourn in the country, his contact at Harvard with German intellectuals abroad, his experiences during the war. His vision is completely dominated by this idea of old and new — the old Germany of his books and his dreams and the new Germany, to which he is instinctively hostile. *Siegfried et le Limousin* thus — by its nostalgia for the past and its reminiscences — seems to be, like *Suzanne* and *Juliette,* another farewell to youth.

Some may find that here Giraudoux is less courageous and less commonsensical than the young women of Bellac, who put aside their sentimental fiddle-faddle to accept the blunt facts of life. Rather than face the fact of modern Germany, Giraudoux calls upon that country to refashion itself in the image of a romantic past which may never have had much reality outside the minds of poets. The Germany of gingerbread houses — like the Japan of temple bells and cherry blossoms, like the France of Versailles — is chiefly a fond national symbol. Giraudoux fancies two great civilizations situated side by side: one mature and stable, which is France; the other in turmoil and growth, which is Germany. As they are diametrically opposed, they need each other to complement and complete themselves. One may think that to predicate the ultimate concord and reconciliation between France and Germany upon such parallels and antitheses is little else than a poet's dream — too simplistic, too literary to offer practical solutions to very real problems. Yet we know that a pretty, although inexact, picture of the past can turn into a mirror of the future, and that nature can copy art. The poetic solution can be, in the long run, the true solution. Giraudoux, at least, never believed otherwise.

Although in interviews Giraudoux stressed the intellectual intention of his book,[35] its ideas, which in themselves were indeed not particularly revolutionary, were found less exciting than its style. A novel so unconventional in form — such a potpourri of harangues, sketches, and anecdotes — was bound to excite strong comment. When it received the Prix Balzac, Paul Bourget declared that it seemed to him singularly inappropriate to have crowned with this prize a novel so completely outside the Balzac tradition: "Il y a trois choses à considérer dans un roman: l'action, les caractères, la composition. M. Giraudoux les ignore, et je crois qu'il n'en a nul souci."[36] Henri Massis called it a Chinese puzzle,[37] and an anonymous writer for *Le Correspondant* exclaimed, "Si une pareille littérature devait triompher, ce serait tout simplement la fin de notre culture."[38] These sour judgments were in the minority, however, and the general reaction in the press was delight before the spectacle of an original and uninhibited talent.

For several years after the publication of *Siegfried et le Limousin*, Giraudoux's diplomatic duties were directly associated with the German question, which remained acute. In 1924 he went to Berlin as Embassy Secretary, but was soon recalled and shortly afterwards assigned to another service. The subject of *Siegfried* was not done with, however.

Giraudoux had already published a piece the year previous that had probably been intended originally for the novel — "Visite chez le Prince."[39] Then, in 1924, for a *Festschrift* volume to be presented to Professor Andler, he recast a scene from the novel in dramatic form. This initial step towards the theater eventually led him to Louis Jouvet and the Comédie des Champs-Elysées, where the play *Siegfried* was presented on May 3, 1928.

The path of Giraudoux's progress from the sketch for the Andler volume to the final text as presented by Jouvet is marked by a profusion of sketches and rough drafts, which tell an interesting story of the discipline and purifying process to which Giraudoux submitted his art to adapt it to the theater.[40] The most important of these early versions is the full-length play called *Siegfried von Kleist,* one of the opening scenes of which appeared in 1927 in a magazine,[41] the entire text ultimately being published in the *Théâtre Complet.*[42] It is longer than *Siegfried,* with many farcical *hors-d'œuvre* that later had to be sacrificed in the interest of sustained tonality. There are also greater changes in scene and a very loose construction in general.

The numerous transformations effected to bring *Siegfried et le Limousin* to the stage were obviously prompted chiefly by artistic considerations. The ideas remain basically unchanged except for the implications of the last act. In *Siegfried von Kleist,* the man without a country, who lives only for and in an idea, dies when he has to abandon Germany. Such a tragic denouement to the debate on Franco-German relations was deemed too pessimistic for 1928, and the fourth act that was given the audience to applaud showed Siegfried returning to France, full of optimism, charged with the noble role of intermediary between the two countries.

During the early 1930's, variations on the *Siegfried* theme continued to appear in magazines and in separate *plaquettes.*[43] The subject of Franco-German relations remained for Giraudoux among his lifelong preoccupations. In 1939 he returned to it in his political essay, *Pleins Pouvoirs.* Finally, during the war in his capacity as Minister of Information, he reiterated his views in a series of radio broadcasts to his countrymen, again at war with the people with whom he had, practically the entire length of his career, sought to effect a reconciliation.

The Years from *Siegfried et le Limousin* to *Siegfried:* Early Maturity

In Giraudoux's life and career, the year of *Siegfried et le Limousin* (1922) was a year of both culmination and promise, a summit year from which Giraudoux could look back with satisfaction upon the distance covered, and, looking forward, view the future with confidence. He would know years of greater triumphs, but never without the experience of defeats and frustrations that in 1922 he had yet to encounter. True, his failure to obtain the *agrégation* after long years spent as a student may have represented more of a defeat than Giraudoux would ever admit. But now he could feel that the closing of one door had only opened far more attractive ones to him. In his professional career, in his personal life, and — most important of all — in his writing, Giraudoux could feel that everything was turning out for the best. The crowning of his work by the Prix Balzac meant arrival and far broader success than he had known previously. The monetary significance of the prize in itself was not negligible, and it could doubtless be put to good use by the young husband and father.

In his family life, what scant information we possess suggests that Giraudoux was enjoying with his wife and infant son a typical middle-class felicity. From Pierre Lestringuez, whose friendship with Giraudoux dates from 1922, we learn that Jean and Suzanne Giraudoux were admirable hosts and set a good table. When Mme. Giraudoux said, "Il n'y a rien à dîner," it meant a green and red tablecloth covered with cold cuts and shell fish, salads with truffles and nuts, choice wines.[44] Alex Madis, too, remembers that the Giraudoux had a good cellar and that the meals the cook Marie prepared under the capable direction of Mme. Giraudoux were excellent.[45]

Besides entertaining at home, Giraudoux continued to take pleasure in the company of friends in places about town. He could frequently be seen at the popular Bœuf-sur-le-Toit, where he would meet Jean Cocteau, the musicians who made up the famous *Groupe des Six,* and his old friend Morand. Everything inclines us to see the Giraudoux of the early twenties as leading the thoroughly normal life of a man happy in his work, his home, and the company of his friends.

It is therefore amusing to run across a newspaper "profile" dating from this time which represents Giraudoux as an eccentric, writing his books in a sort of cell, dressed in black and wearing a top hat![46]

> Le "cabinet de travail" de M. Jean Giraudoux est d'une simplicité remarquable: il se compose purement et simplement d'une immense table en bois blanc sur laquelle il étale ses papiers et où il travaille à toute heure du jour et de la nuit.
>
> Les murs sont nus, sans ornementations, sans papier, sans livres; il n'y a pas de bibliothèque: on se croirait dans une cellule de bénédictin ou de prison.
>
> Voilà pour l'aspect du "paysage."
>
> Quant à l'habitant, il n'est pas moins estomirant *[sic]*.
>
> L'auteur de *Juliette au pays des hommes* est assis à sa table de bois blanc et il écrit.
>
> Mais pour ce faire, il a pris soin, au préalable, de se vêtir d'un costume noir et de se coiffer d'un chapeau haut de forme, d'un *gibus*.
>
> M. Jean Giraudoux ne saurait écrire sans son gibus, sans son habillement noir, c'est sa livrée. Il ne peut pas s'en passer, et, quand il écrit, l'écrivain ne reçoit personne.

Some jovial friend had sent the clipping to Giraudoux, for across it we read in handwriting: "Du 'Carnet de la Semaine'. Que nous cachais-tu! Serait-ce une indiscrétion d'Eric?" A Cuban critic was blamed for the invention,[47] but we suspect that a spoofing ex-*Normalien* had a large part in it!

In the year of *Siegfried et le Limousin,* Giraudoux was still with the *Service des Œuvres Françaises à l'Etranger,* the office that he had entered with enthusiasm and optimism after his demobilization. He had risen from the ranks to become its chief. But if fortune seemed as smiling here as in the other aspects of his life, her countenance was soon to change. It is here, in his professional career, that Giraudoux had soon to feel that he stood no longer upon a pinnacle of general good fortune. In 1923, a campaign of criticism against the *Service* was launched in the press, Henri Béraud, writing in the *Eclair* of April 27, starting things off. His primary target appears to have been André Gide and the *Nouvelle Revue Française* group of writers with whom Giraudoux had associations. According to Béraud, the *N.R.F.* group was being favored by the *Service,* and he called upon Giraudoux to justify his actions. Giraudoux finally made reply in an interview with Frédéric Lefèvre, on the second of June;[48] Béraud, after a sarcastic rebuttal, let the matter drop.

The Béraud affair appears little more than an annoyance. A more serious matter, which already in 1922 could have given Giraudoux grave concern, was the political struggle that was going on above him between Berthelot and Raymond Poincaré. In the midst of his preoccupation with international problems, this domestic situation must have made a strong diversionary claim on his attention. When Berthelot, Giraudoux's friend and protector, saw that Briand's fall was imminent, he resigned even before the new ministry was formed. This did not save him from Poincaré, however, who brought him before a tribunal on a charge of having shown favoritism while in office towards the Industrial Bank of China. As a result, Berthelot was placed on the inactive list, and Giraudoux had no one to shield him against the severe and juristic Poincaré, whose animosity towards Berthelot extended to his protégé.

In 1924, when Herriot returned to power, it was Poincaré's turn to resign. Before doing so, however, he had the office on the rue François Ier closed and Giraudoux sent to Berlin as Embassy Secretary. After a few months Giraudoux was recalled to take charge of the *Services d'Information et de Presse,* an unhappy assignment for him since it made severe demands on his time and energy. All government communications to the press went over his desk. He edited the information released for telegrams, radio broadcasts, etc.; held press conferences; compiled the analysis of the domestic press; and was responsible for the *Bulletin de presse française.* Not until the end of 1926 could Giraudoux escape. He then succeeded in having himself placed *hors cadre* at the disposition of the *Commissariat d'Evaluation des Dommages Alliés en Turquie.* Incidentally, he was now an Embassy Secretary, first class, and had recently been made *Officier de la Légion d'Honneur.* Giraudoux would remain *hors cadre* until 1934, although he was promoted to *Conseiller d'Ambassade* in 1928, and in 1932, for a few months, was charged with a mission in the Herriot cabinet.

If renouncing all ambition and burying himself at the Turkish Commission meant a stalemate in his diplomatic career, it permitted Giraudoux, on the other hand, to pursue his literary career without harassment and, moreover, lead a casual and elegant personal life.

Friends who dropped in on Giraudoux at the quiet office on the Avenue Malakoff were more likely to interrupt him in the midst of a novel than an official report. Many of his manuscripts bear the letterhead of the Commission, suggesting that, seated before the Louis XV table, between the austere lamp and the telephone, Giraudoux had found the ideal retreat in which to compose his works.

Juliette au Pays des Hommes had already appeared, first in installments in the *Revue de Paris* during Giraudoux's short stay in Germany, then in volume form. The book was widely discussed in the press during the autumn and winter of 1924. Its author was doubtless already at work on *Bella,* which was written to score Poincaré and avenge Berthelot. Portrayed in series of deft and pointed parallels, Poincaré is easily recognized in the character Rebendart, and Berthelot in Dubardeau. Although the work was directly inspired by the bitterness and rancor Giraudoux was feeling at the time, its mood is conciliatory. He sees behind the two great political adversaries two great families serving France, and on an allegorical level, "les deux honneurs, les deux courages, les deux générosités du caractère français."[49] In internal affairs, Giraudoux's thinking follows the pattern he formulated in *Siegfried et le Limousin* for international disputes: the two opposing forces must somehow be brought into harmonious cooperation. The agent he invents for this reconciliation is Bella. She is the widow of Rebendart's son and becomes the fiancée of Dubardeau's son, the narrator. Like Siegfried of the first version of the play, this mediatrice dies in a desperate attempt to bring the adversaries together.

The world of the Rebendarts and the Dubardeaus, depicted in the novel, is the world Giraudoux had come to know through his association with the Quai d'Orsay. His heroine, Bella, is no small-town girl like Suzanne or Juliette, no Bohemian like Geneviève Prat — she derives from the oldest nobility of France and the powerful landed gentry. As Berthelot's protégé, Giraudoux had been introduced into the circles of diplomats and first families, to which his birth, or even his literary reputation, would normally not give him access. It is from them that he would draw the characters of the novels he wrote during the next few years.

The "Histoire des Fontranges" (subtitle of *Bella*) is pursued through *Eglantine* (1927) and *Aventures de Jérôme Bardini* (1930), of which portions had appeared already in 1926 and 1929 in *plaquette* form. We find the same group of characters in all three novels — as well as in the peripheral publications, *Je présente Bellita,* etc. There is the old country nobleman Fontranges with his twin daughters Bella and Bellita and his son Jacques. Then there are Eglantine, a girl of humble origins but brought up with Bella and her sister, the banker Moïse, and Jérôme Bardini, a civil service officer. Although these characters represent the social elite and the powers that govern France — the landed aristocracy, Jewish high finance, government officialdom — the novels do not constitute social history to any great extent. To be a "secretary of society," as Balzac described himself, presupposes a studious documentation entirely incompatible with Giraudoux's natural gifts or with his fundamental esthetic. He was a declared foe of Realism.[50] *Eglantine* has been described as a psychological study. But the characters are little more human types than they are social types. Their motives and behavior are too schematic, and whereas they stand for humanity in several of its aspects, they bear little resemblance to living persons. What life they possess is blown into their lungs by the author's lyrical talents. They really exist only to serve such themes as love, youth, and old age.

If Giraudoux had any sociological or analytical intentions for the Fontranges series, he abandoned them entirely in *Jérôme Bardini,* where he develops a theme purely lyrical or metaphysical — that of revolt and escape. But one doubts that he was ever concerned with painting a social fresco. The social stratum in which he set his poetic divagations was simply very close at hand.

Giraudoux, who in life must have known many Bellas, Fontranges, and Moïses, who knew his way about in drawing rooms and ministers' cabinets, looked himself to the manner born. We have seen him as the proud, aloof pupil in a provincial *lycée,* as a scholarship student, as a carefree young man about Paris, and as a dashing young officer. Now we see him as the very picture of the career diplomat — well-groomed, elegant, and urbane. He possessed a distinction that Frenchmen are wont to call British. "Un homme du monde raffiné, et qui crée la sympathie," declared an interviewer who visited him at his office in 1927, "une odeur de savon anglais, et une fraîcheur de santé, due aux sports, qui ramène à la trentaine ses quarante-cinq ans." The interview continues:

> Un buste gris clair un peu frêle, mais au maintien assuré, une cravate de teinte paille: une figure de chair rose, soignée, entière-

> ment rasée. Une bouche serrée aux lèvres pâles, un front bombé, des cheveux plaqués en arrière. Et l'armature des lunettes d'écaille, les célèbres "lunettes roses," à travers desquelles deux yeux foncés, couleur de mer, enchâssés profondément, vous dévisagent avec bienveillance.[51]

This is the classic picture observers give us of the mature Giraudoux — "simplicité, élégance, réserve britannique."

We have said, however, that what we know of his life bespeaks a comfortable, convivial, and thoroughly middle-class existence. The Giraudoux apartment for many years was at number 8, rue du Préaux-Clercs, in a neighborhood that still possessed a sober, provincial sort of charm. It was spacious, comfortable, casual, and from the windows one could see the greenery of the garden. There were interesting canvases and Rembrandt engravings on the walls, trophies of Giraudoux's browsing in the shops to and from work and on free afternoons. A modern lamp in glass stood on a center table, and upon a chest of drawers (doubtless the famous Boule chest from the rue de Condé) there lay a Baedecker of Germany to remind Giraudoux of his student travels.

As Pierre Lestringuez has told us, the Giraudoux were genial hosts, but their entertaining seems to have been largely informal and reserved for a few close friends. The poker parties with Paul Morand and Edouard Bourdet were one of the joys of Giraudoux's existence. No one recalls ever having heard literature come up for discussion at them. But of songs and horseplay there was plenty.[52] The tradition of Sunday dinners with friends dates back to the early days at the Morands'. Later, the choice of a restaurant would give rise to lengthy discussions in which Giraudoux would try to prevail by exhibiting remarkable knowledge of the relative merits of the various restaurants' cellars. No doubt he usually prevailed, for it was he who set the pace and thought up the little games that enlivened the Sunday dinner parties. He was particularly addicted to little bistros, but in restaurants or at home, Giraudoux took a very dim view of anyone's missing the weekly reunions.

In summertime he often went down to Cusset to visit his family. Jean-Pierre would go with him, and his father took him fishing in this region which still boasts of its well-stocked streams.

One would say that during the years at the Turkish Commission Giraudoux indulged himself fully in the joys that family and friends can bring. And indeed he chose to represent himself in life as fortune's darling. This is — the slightest reflection forces us to conclude — a pose or a part that his pride and his private code of conduct demanded that he assume. For it would be strange indeed if he did not suffer deeply from the frustrations and setbacks in his professional career. And it would be strange also if the story of Jérôme Bardini, part of which appeared as early as 1926, did not reflect, in some measure at least, urges and conflicts that Giraudoux himself was experiencing.[53]

Novels of the 1930's and Miscellaneous Prose Pieces

Giraudoux's triumph with *Siegfried* in 1928 marked a turning point in the history of the French theater. It also marked a turning point in the author's career. Henceforth his primary interest would be the theater. And as a successful playwright, he would be asked to deliver lectures on literature, write prefaces and articles, engage in the various activities of an *homme de lettres.* Nevertheless, in the decade that followed his debut in the theater, during the period of his major plays, Giraudoux wrote the novels that stand as his greatest. Let us consider them, as well as the various prose pieces that make up *La France Sentimentale,* before turning to Giraudoux's career in the theater.

Aventures de Jérôme Bardini appeared as a complete novel in 1930. It is the story of a successful, well-to-do man, friend and neighbor of Fontranges, who one fine day takes French leave of wife and infant son to go roaming. His life had become too stifling in its routine and its comforts; he longed for novelty and renewal. During his holiday — until Fontranges brings him back — he will remain anonymous and unclassified, move over the world as an unfettered being wholly *disponible.* In New York's Central Park he meets Stéphy and enjoys a brief idyll with her. But he is soon ready to rove again. Eventually he encounters a human being who is even more independent than he, the vagabond Kid, a veritable incarnation of revolt and self-sufficiency. Critics who reviewed the novel in the newspapers confined most of their remarks to style. The escape theme, which in retrospect seems of particular interest, evoked little comment at the time.

Giraudoux's preoccupation with the subject of escape from routine, from "embourgeoisement," goes back to the mid-1920's, since the first part of the novel, "La première disparition de Jérôme Bardini," dates from 1926. By 1928 Giraudoux had already hit upon the idea of using a vagabond child to depict total freedom. The Kid is prefigured in the short piece entitled *La Grande Bourgeoise ou toute femme a la vocation.* He is the little urchin discovered in the automobile, a runaway from a foundling home, a "voyou de race" such as the Kid that Bardini would encounter. One may have already reflected on the commonness of the escape theme during the 1920's and beyond. André Gide's *Faux Monnayeurs,* the Bible of revolt, appeared in 1926. The similarity between his child characters and the Kid is apparent — it would have been even more so, perhaps, had Gide adhered to his original idea of a nonrealistic presentation. Are we wrong seeing in the Bardini revolt something more than treatment of a theme in vogue? No, despite the popularity of the theme, it must have had deep personal significance for Giraudoux, just as it had for Gide. It is, after all, the basic theme of Giraudoux's mature novels, all of which constitute some sort of escape from daily reality. But its prevalence in the between-wars period does remind us to handle thematic material prudently. As evidence of specific and concrete personal problems, it is never conclusive.

"Fontranges au Niagara" (1932) constitutes a rejected chapter of "The Kid." It records Fontranges' visit to Jérôme and the sick child he has adopted. Why Giraudoux deleted it can only be a matter of conjecture, but he probably felt that these pages, which deal particularly with Bella's father, were an intrusion and would pointlessly distract the reader's attention from Bardini and the Kid.

During the same year, Giraudoux republished "Fontranges au Niagara" in the volume entitled *La France Sentimentale,* a miscellany of pieces which had not been included when the novels were put in definitive form. Only three are *inédits,* however. All save one of the items belonged to the *Siegfried* or the *Bella* cycles. The exception is "Sérénade 1913," which harks back to *Simon le Pathétique.* A *dépit amoureux* by letter, this pretty piece had been published separately in 1926 under the title of *Anne chez Simon.*

To *Siegfried et le Limousin* belongs "Visite chez le Prince," first published as a *plaquette* in 1924. It describes a visit to a Prince von Saxe-Altdorf whom the narrator had known fifteen years previously (the Prince von Saxe-Meiningen whom Giraudoux tutored during his student days in Munich). The ostensible reason for the visit is to disclose Siegfried's true identity — a Frenchman from the Limousin. Accordingly, we are treated to a mock-heroic evocation of the glorious past of that province which Giraudoux never tired of extolling. The generals, descendants of French Protestants who emigrated after the revocation of the Edict of Nantes, make an appearance and are analyzed with amusing poetic invention. Giraudoux dealt with them again in the various dramatic versions of his novel.

"Le Signe" had also been published separately (1922) and had been partially utilized in *Siegfried et le Limousin.* It describes the author's strange affliction at the news of the death of a man whom he had known but slightly during his year of military service. In the past, he fancies, Nature had always made him a sign to indicate that the end of a mourning period was approaching, but this time she remains stubbornly silent. The piece is embroidery on this theme — a prolonged state of grief fancifully interpreted as the work of a cruel, capricious Nature, which eventually exasperates her victim to the point where he stops looking to Nature for the sign. And that is the sign! Of this very elegant and mannered bit of writing, only the account of Dumas' death was chosen to embellish *Siegfried et le Limousin.* It turns up, wholly arbitrarily, as one of Forestier's newspaper articles.[54]

The obsession described in "Le Signe" is very much like Fontranges' state of mind as described in *Le Cerf* (1926). Because of this similarity, I speak of *Le Cerf* here, although it does not figure in *La France Sentimentale.* In this episode, which was however republished as part of *Eglantine,* the aristocratic old gentleman is grieving for his son Jacques, who has just died. He neglects his horses and his pack. One night he comes upon a stag in the forest, an encounter which he interprets in the light of Saint Hubert's adventure. That very night he resumes his hunting and his normal pursuits. Fontranges is depicted as being in the possession of an evil spirit which must be exorcised. The appearance of the stag accomplishes just that. Here, as in "Le Signe," the commonplace manifestations of grief — the inability to find satisfaction in customary pursuits, the search for signs and omens — are subjected to a poetic transposition.

Another story of obsession, one that was picked up for *La France Sentimentale,* is "Mirage de Bessines," published separately the year before the collection appeared. Rémy Grand, a painter who has done a portrait of Bellita, appears to be haunted by his native town. His well-being has been invaded by a disturbing presence which he finally identifies with Bessines, a little town near Bellac. There follows an account of how Grand tries to exorcise his demon, a story we would interpret as an allegory of the mysterious compelling force that a subject can evoke in an artist. But it may be just a little spoofing of Freud and psychoanalysis. With its atmosphere of hallucination and *Poltergeister,* it comes close to being a *Phantasiestück* in Hoffmann's manner.

The Bessines piece, with its allusion to Bellita, may have been intended for a novel devoted to Bella's twin sister. Such a novel could have begun with "Je présente Bellita," a chapter of bewildering thematic richness in which we meet a personage reminiscent of Bella and Eglantine. Like "Bessines," this work was published separately in 1931 before appearing in *La France Sentimentale.* It may be assumed that "Bellita" was actually composed much earlier, for 1920 is mentioned in the text in such a way as to suggest that it was written in that year. We lack evidence to determine the chronology of composition for these pieces; but, as in the present case, it often seems that Giraudoux held sundry manuscripts for extended periods of time before deciding to present them to the public.

The remaining items in *La France Sentimentale* are more in the *Bella* constellation. They are presumably episodes that Giraudoux did not see fit to include in the final work or are in the nature of embroidery upon a theme. "Le Couvent de Bella," a chapter probably from an early version of the novel, appeared first in 1925. It relates a visit to the school where Bella had gone as a girl. The name could have been any other, for the heroine does not appear at all, and there is no integral connection with her story, at least in its definitive, published form. "Hélène et Touglas," also from 1925, opens and closes with prophetic allusion to the Dubardeau-Rebendart combat, but otherwise possesses full autonomy. It covers about thirty-five pages of whimsical meanderings in which Francophiles are delightfully and somewhat cruelly made fun of. The young man narrator for these pieces can be readily identified as the young author of the Quai d'Orsay, and Philippe Berthelot is surely the model for the father alluded to. One *hors-d'œuvre* on the *Bella* theme not picked up for *La France Sentimentale* is *A la Recherche de Bella,* which appeared the same year as the major work.

All three *inédits* belong to *Bella,* more chapters — one might suppose — from an unpublished version. "Palais de Glace" plays on the theme of the generations, a *leitmotif* in the Fontranges stories. The narrator, finding himself isolated from Bella and bereft of companions of his own generation, tries first to fit in with a younger group, then with an older, finally renounces both in the presence of a third generation represented by the elderly Fontranges. In "Français amoureux aux Jeux Olympiques," Bella is back. The two are in the chief stand at the games watching the performance of athletes from many nations. "Attente devant le Palais Bourbon" is another whimsey spun while Bella is somewhere else. Beginning with "Le Couvent de Bella," it becomes evident how conducive to creative writing Bella's absences were! These half-dozen pages were doubtless written under the circumstances Giraudoux describes. When the young woman whom Giraudoux was waiting for in his sports car finally appeared, he closed his notebook.

The new major fictional work of the mid-30's is *Combat avec l'Ange,* a novel about happiness and its foes: pity, jealousy, ambition. The Bellas and Bardinis are done with; this is about Maléna, a beautiful rich Brazilian woman who loves Jacques, another of the elect. But Maléna is not content with herself as she is. She wants to know life outside her charmed circle. Accordingly she turns to the sick and unfortunate, eventually succeeding in making herself miserable. Of her love for Jacques she wishes to make something sublime. At first modest and simple in her love, she becomes gradually enamored of an idealized, heroic Jacques, who of course cannot live up to this grandiose conception of himself. She ferrets in his past and makes herself needlessly jealous of girls he has long since forgotten.

Maléna is cured, delivered of her obsession just as Jérôme Bardini was delivered of his. She eventually accepts her happiness and struggles no more against it. Someone has asserted that the model for Maléna was a South American woman whom Giraudoux actually knew. He may well have used a real person for the situations and detail in his novel, but the pattern of Maléna's spiritual adventure is a basic one in Giraudoux's narrative writings. An individual, before submitting to his destiny, must have a look around. Suzanne and Juliette indulge themselves in a romantic escapade before settling down to modest bourgeois happiness. Jérôme and Maléna wish to break away from their humdrum felicity, court risk and unhappiness to feel more keenly alive. Like all Giraudoux's men and women, they have been showered with blessings. And blessings cannot be tolerated for long.

Whereas most novelists have concerned themselves with man's quest for happiness, Giraudoux gave his attention to the contrary impulse — the perverseness of man, who, in a state free from want and fear, must render his life precarious. The destructive urge of Giraudoux's people does not carry them far — it turns out to be just a spree — and at the end of the novel they return, refreshed, to take up their burden of blessings where they had thrown it down. Like Edmée, of Giraudoux's last novel, they are all of the elect.

In Edmée's story, *Choix des Elues* (1939), Giraudoux pushes his basic fictional theme to its richest development. Edmée has a husband, Pierre, and two children, Jacques and Claudie. It is a happy, model family; but soon after her thirty-third birthday, Edmée leaves her husband and children to seek a destiny alone. Then one day many years later she returns, taking her place at the table the day Claudie's baby is christened. Her own adventure over, Edmée watches her daughter anxiously because Claudie, in her turn, is ready to depart. What is new in this novel is the attention given to the second generation. Jérôme Bardini's son was too young to play a role in that novel, and the Kid's role was episodic. But Claudie, as a child, aids and abets her mother in her flight, and, as an adult herself, is about to repeat her mother's adventure.

What of *La Menteuse,* the unfinished novel which was written in 1936 but not revealed to the public until 1958? Nelly is another young woman trying to find her niche in life and not quite ready to marry the adoring Gaston. Her encounter with Reginald has made Gaston seem odious. She does not break with him, however — no heroine of a Giraudoux novel ever burns her bridges — but seasons her bourgeois existence by a liaison with the stranger. It is her *fugue,* her escape. Scrupulously she avoids carrying into her relationship with Reginald anything of her routine self — no reference to her daily life, no revealing labels in her clothes — in fact, for her rendezvous with her second lover Nelly has a special wardrobe quite unlike her usual costumes. The novel is fragmentary and incomplete, but enough exists to remind us of Maléna, Edmée; and in the anonymity of their affair Reginald and Nelly resemble Jérôme Bardini and Stéphy. The two male characters have a family resemblance to all Giraudoux's heroes, Reginald closest perhaps to Bardini and Gaston to all the *contrôleurs des poids et mesures.*

Beginnings in the Theater: From *Siegfried* to *Judith*

After the war, as increasing acclaim reassured Giraudoux as to his literary vocation, he must have been often tempted to try his hand at a play. He could think back on his first essays in playwriting as a schoolboy and, as a student in the Latin Quarter, his plans for doing a play with P.-J. Toulet. Not until 1926, however, did he actually take a step in the direction of the stage, when he dramatized a portion of *Siegfried et le Limousin* for the *Festschrift* to honor Charles Andler. The piece constituted only five pages in all, but the critic Maurice Bourdet declared it indicative of rare dramatic talent.[55] Bernard Zimmer and Benjamin Crémieux urged Giraudoux to go on. Paul Morand's father, too, was insistent. According to Paul, Giraudoux admitted that it was his father's promptings that decided him to turn the entire work into a play.

But we can be reasonably sure that Giraudoux would have found his way eventually to the theater even without the encouragement of others. It is common enough for novelists to dream of a triumph in the theater, particularly those, like Giraudoux, who have been limited to a relatively small public of *raffinés.* A play is a way of making money, of assuring one's fame, and of speaking directly to the public. The seriousness of Giraudoux's themes — the fundamental problems of man's nature and his adventure on earth — indicates that he had a message to communicate, an ethical and didactic purpose in writing. Morand, who declares that Giraudoux remained a teacher all his life, suggests what appeal the stage would hold for him:

> J'ai dit que Giraudoux était resté toute sa vie un pédagogue; je ne voudrais pas alourdir ce qui est aérien en disant que la scène fut pour Giraudoux une chaire idéale, mais je suis certain que s'il a tant aimé le théâtre dans la deuxième partie de sa vie, c'est parce qu'il a su s'emparer du public d'une salle, comme un bon professeur sait s'emparer d'une classe; un auditoire est une source d'énergie vivante qu'il faut savoir capter; il est bien différent, avec ses qualités renouvelées chaque soir, de ce qu'est la foule anonyme des lecteurs, pour un romancier.[56]

One remembers that *Siegfried et le Limousin* was conceived as a sort of pamphlet. But in its fictional form, despite its prize and the success it obtained, it did not reach the public Giraudoux could have hoped for. He confesses: "Je souffrais de ne pouvoir exprimer à des groupes denses le résultat de mes méditations, de mes observations, de mes réflexions sur les causes qui divisaient deux grands peuples."[57] For this author with a message, whose success as a novelist was not entirely gratifying, a try at the theater was exactly what one might anticipate.

In 1927, Louis Jouvet, having left the Vieux-Colombier three years before and trying his own wings at the Comédie des Champs-Elysées, was on the lookout for new authors. He had already enlisted Jules Romains and Marcel Achard when the kind gods arranged that he should come across Giraudoux with the freshly written stage version of *Siegfried* in his brief case. Tradition has it that this historic meeting, a decisive one in the careers of both young artists, took place under a flowering linden on the Champs-Elysées, not far from Jouvet's theater and the Café Francis around the corner on the Place de l'Alma, which is the scene of Act I of *La Folle de Chaillot.* Bernard Zimmer insists, however, that the first discussion of *Siegfried* that took place between Giraudoux and Jouvet was at a lunch table in the Parc Montsouris![58] However that may be, the following spring *Siegfried* was presented to the *Tout-Paris* of letters and the theater.

The news that Giraudoux was about to present a play had caused astonishment and general misgivings. Mme. Arletty is reported to have said, "On va jouer du Giraudoux. Ça fera cinq représentations."[59] No author could seem less adapted to the theater. His poetic improvisations and sentimental souvenirs bespoke an art wholly incompatible with the prevalent notions of requirements for the stage. Did not Giraudoux himself describe his work as merely a sort of poetic divagation?[60] Moreover, the play was to be a dramatization of *Siegfried et le Limousin,* a curious allegory of postwar Germany. Plays made out of novels are proverbial failures, and there was no reason to suppose that this one would be an exception. The problem of the play was purely intellectual, a comparative study in Franco-German psychology; the characters were unblushingly creatures of Giraudoux's imagination without any resemblance to human beings; the plot was nonexistent; and the work an unorganized array of high-flung rhetoric, witty and poetic sallies. Truly, unfavorable predictions were natural enough.

To comprehend fully the dismay of the dramatic critics, one must recall the state of affairs in the French theater during the first decades of this century. The boards had been monopolized by authors such as Bataille, Bernstein, and Porto-Riche, who offered a fare of society dramas, triangle plays, and the like, scarcely relieved except by the light comedies of Flers and Caillavet or the Symbolist poetic drama of Maurice Maeterlinck. The esthetic as well as the box-office formula seemed definitively established: the stage should be an exact duplicate of a drawing room or a bedroom, and the actors should behave like real people and converse in plausible, if not authentic, language. Even after the war, in spite of a general literary flowering, the dramatic art failed to renew itself. It was in vain that leading impresarios such as Baty, Dullin, and Copeau solicited foreign productions. Nor could the younger French playwrights — Vildrac, Lenormand, Saint-Georges Bouhélier — impose a new inspiring formula for the theater. Paul Claudel, of course, was deemed unplayable. Throughout the 1920's the situation grew worse. In 1928, the very year of *Siegfried,* the newspaper *Comœdia* ran a series of articles on the "crisis in the theater," in which prominent personalities connected with the stage were interviewed in an attempt to fix the blame somewhere.

The presentation of *Siegfried* was an electrifying event. Surely many in the audience had taken their seats with the idea of witnessing a perfect "four noir." But from the first scenes the cause was won, and as the play went on even the most incredulous had to admit they were witnessing an epoch-making triumph. The public, surfeited by the succession of Realism, Naturalism, slices of life, and adulteries in the theater, flocked to see the piece. Its enthusiastic response refuted the cynics of the *Comœdia* poll, who had ascribed the inferior quality of current plays to public taste. After seeing *Siegfried,* the critic of the *Journal des Débats,* Henry Bidou, declared, "[Giraudoux] a fait une pièce où le public s'empresse. Et ce public, sidéré, dompté et saisi, s'émeut à ces caprices comme aux inventions du plus bête des dramaturges." As people listened enraptured to the long tirades, for years considered intolerable in a play, critics were quick to hail the beginning of a new era. James de Coquet wrote for *Le Figaro* of May 4, 1928: "En écoutant Siegfried, on avait l'impression d'assister à une transfusion de sang. Monsieur Jean Giraudoux offrait sa meilleure veine pour sauver un art dramatique moribond. L'opération a réussi au delà de toute espérance." Overnight Giraudoux became an object of public discussion. Connoisseurs delighted at what they termed the return of letters to the theater. They recalled that the theater is basically one form of poetry, and that it is under no obligation to imitate life. There was no more question for the moment of Giraudoux's art being unadaptable to the theater. Rather did it seem to be the means whereby the theater could again affirm its true nature.

Yet the transformation of Giraudoux, precious and whimsical improviser, into the leading dramatic author of the between-wars period was not accomplished easily or alone. Between the manuscript of July, 1927, and the play presented on May 3, 1928, there was an enormous amount of rewriting. At least seven times Giraudoux did the play over, with Jouvet at his elbow to indicate what would and what would not get beyond the footlights. It may seen remarkable that Giraudoux did not fold up his manuscript and go home. It is to his credit and to the glory of the French theater that he did not. He heeded Jouvet's counsels, and he assiduously followed the rehearsals. Without the training Jouvet provided, Giraudoux's plays might be read today like the *Théâtre de Clara Gazul.* The friendly collaboration begun on the script of *Siegfried* lasted throughout the ten years preceding World War II, years made more brilliant for the lights of the Comédie des Champs-Elysées and the Athénée.

Giraudoux's second play, *Amphitryon 38,* was presented for the first time at the Comédie des Champs-Elysées, November 9, 1929. One does not know when Giraudoux began work on this comedy, but it must have been written more easily and quickly than *Siegfried.* The experience with the first play had taught him much about the theater and dramatic technique. Moreover, he now knew his actors, and could write with Valentine Tessier, Pierre Renoir, Louis Jouvet specifically in mind. As for the plot of the play itself, he had little to invent. He must have been familiar since early school days with the myth of Jupiter's visit to Alcmene. Since Latin antiquity the circumstances of Hercules' birth had been dramatized many times. The versions by Plautus, Molière, and Kleist were within easy reach for reference. All Giraudoux had to do was to let his pen trace its fanciful arabesques around the subject. Thus it is that we find little rewriting in this play. The first two acts remain virtually intact throughout the several versions, and the alterations of the third suggest more inventive facility than struggle with dramatic necessities.

The fact that Giraudoux used a ready-made story does not mean that he did not transform it into a play unmistakably his own. Besides exploiting all its possibilities for burlesque and even inventing, to add to the general hilarity, an episode to bring in Leda, who had known

Jupiter as a swan, Giraudoux turned the ancient myth into a most noble defense of connubial felicity and of the human conditions. Alcmene becomes the chief personage in his play, a model of wifely virtue and of bourgeois "solidarity with her planet." Giraudoux's heroines are always offered an escapade — Suzanne on her island and Juliette in the "pays des hommes." Alone among them, Alcmene rejects the offer. She could have had an affair with the lord of creation, but she preferred her mortal husband; and to assure the birth of Hercules, she had to be duped. No promise of immortality or deification can tempt Alcmene. She symbolizes the most perfect adjustment to life that Giraudoux can imagine.

The critics feared that Giraudoux's precious style was excessive — that he risked parodying himself. Vaudeville and operetta elements threatened to engulf the play as Jupiter and Alcmene addressed each other in witty madrigals. Not that it was not charming, they said, but was it really theater? The public happily felt no such compunctions and pronounced the play a great success.

Judith, on the other hand, pleased the critics and left the public indifferent. One of the three great tragedies of Giraudoux, it deserves a popular success which it has never yet enjoyed.

The traditional story is well known. The Apocryphal *Book of Judith* relates how Bethulia, besieged by the Assyrian army of Holofernes, is delivered by a young widow of that city. Judith goes alone to the enemy camp, beguiles Holofernes by her charms, and decapitates him while he lies sleeping. Between the date of the manuscript which records this story, placed generally in the first century A.D., and the Giraudoux production, the legend had been treated many times in all the European literatures — in prose, narrative verse, drama, and oratorio form. Friedrich Hebbel's version is the only one to which Giraudoux's appears particularly indebted, naturally enough in view of Giraudoux's familiarity with German writers. But, as with *Amphitryon,* the story of Judith is turned entirely to suit the French author's talents, and to convey his own preoccupations. We find in *Judith* already all of the main dramatic themes to which Giraudoux is drawn.

Giraudoux's Judith, the elect of God, is not a widow but a girl on the verge of womanhood. She first refuses the role that destiny and her people demand she play, but is tricked into it by her pride. When she meets Holofernes, her pride has been humbled by the experience with Egon, and it is as a woman who has appealed to a protector that she enters Holofernes' tent. It is as a mere woman, too, that she gives herself to the enemy chief that night, and as such, in her shame and rage, that she kills him. Yet the rabbis see in Judith the savior of her people and the instrument of God's will. She is led back to Bethulia amid hosannahs of thanksgiving and to the glory of Judith. These transformations and interpretations of the old legend permit Giraudoux to ruminate upon the problems particularly dear to him — war, destiny, the nature of woman. They permit him, in addition, to demonstrate the tragic force of social pressures, the folly of religious fanaticism, and, through the speeches of Holofernes, to dream of a cleaner and more wholesome world.

Many explanations have been advanced for the failure of this play. The over-richness of theme, the complexities of motives, and the rapid passage from tragedy to comedy and back again must have left the audience at a loss. The finale was generally considered unsatisfactory, some believing that Judith should not have survived the play. Doubts were raised too about its construction, suggesting that it followed the German technique of *Entwicklung* rather than the French fashion of situating the action at a moment of psychological crisis. Perhaps the theater and the actors were to blame. Louis Jouvet's collaboration on the play was limited to the *mise-en-scène,* and when the curtain rose on November 4, 1931, at the Théâtre Pigalle, the audience could see only an unfamiliar group of Jewish actors assigned to the roles. Whatever the cause might have been, the public that had hailed the advent of Giraudoux to the theater with *Siegfried* now remained silent. And Giraudoux, who was not prepared for failure, was hurt most deeply.

Return to Favor: *Intermezzo, La Guerre de Troie,* and Other Plays

Perhaps it was because of the lack of public response to his tragedy *Judith* that Giraudoux decided that his next play should be a comedy. If strategy was behind the composition of *Intermezzo,* the author guessed right. When it was first performed on February 23, 1933, at the Comédie des Champs-Elysées, with music by Francis Poulenc, both the critics and the public received the play with acclaim.

Intermezzo is one of the few plays that Giraudoux cut out of whole cloth. His initial inspiration was a painting he possessed of a group of *commedia del arte* actors, the work of an unknown artist, dated 1577.[61] In contemplating these quaint figures ready to act out one of the stylized little plays of the period, he was moved to compose a play in something of the same spirit. For his own *divertissement,* he chose some of the stock characters of his novels and placed them in the familiar setting of rural France. Isabelle, the heroine of the play and a spiritual sister of Suzanne, is the teacher of a class of little girls in her home town. Her pedagogy is completely unorthodox. In botany, her pupils know nothing about monocotyledons and dicotyledons, but can tell you that the tree is the immobile brother of man. In geography, they have learned nothing of the injustice of nature, but lay all the great catastrophes — regrettable details essential however to a universe generally quite satisfactory — to one mischievous sprite called Arthur.

A small town in France, perhaps the prosiest spot on earth, is turned topsy-turvy by poetry and fancy. Isabelle has brought this all about, the young girl who is entitled to an interlude of enchantment and clairvoyance before accepting a flesh-and-blood husband. In her exalted state she has summoned up a handsome young ghost, who promises to tell her about the great beyond and the life of the dead. The town in alarm moves to put a stop to these goings-on. It is represented by the government inspector, standing for law and order and no nonsense; the druggist, a mediator between the forces in conflict; and the *contrôleur des poids et mesures,* into whose arms Giraudoux's heroines eventually fall.

So Isabelle's flirtation with mystery and magic comes to an end — likewise the poetic idyll lived by the entire town is over. The interlude has been just a spiritual tonic. Without it, life is "une aventure lamentable": for men, "des traitements de début misérables, des avancements de tortue, des retraites inexistantes, des boutons de faux col en révolte"; for women, "bavardage et cocuage, casserole et vitriol."[62] But healthy people must return to a life of workaday reality. In the words of the *contrôleur:* the greatness of life "est d'être brève et pleine entre deux abîmes. Son miracle est d'être colorée, saine, ferme entre des infinis et des vides."[63]

Giraudoux never gets too close to the brink. He reaffirms his stand with humanity and the life it has chosen to live. Yet it must escape from time to time into a purer and quieter zone. Such is the purpose of this play, and, in effect, of all Giraudoux's plays. "Il y a des peuples qui rêvent, mais pour ceux qui ne rêvent pas, il reste le théâtre."[64]

Before going on to new plays of his own, Giraudoux next turned his attention to the adaptation of an English work that had enjoyed a great success in New York and London, *The Constant Nymph,* taken from the novel of Margaret Kennedy. With his collaborator, Basil Dean, Giraudoux generally followed the composition of the original play. Here and there a passage was interpreted differently, and one character, the heroine's brother, was added from the novel. Where Giraudoux showed his greatest inventiveness was in the piquant dialogues, which rendered the play thoroughly French.

Before *Tessa (La Nymphe au cœur fidèle)* was presented in November of 1934, Giraudoux had let it be known that he was at work on a new tragedy. Apparently the success of *Intermezzo* had completely restored his self-confidence and he was eager to try his luck again in the most difficult of dramatic genres. But the subject of *Brutus,* which he had announced in June of 1934,[65] must have soon lost its appeal or proved troublesome. At least no *Brutus* was ever presented, and the second in chronological order of Giraudoux's tragic masterpieces is *La Guerre de Troie n'aura pas lieu* (November, 1935). The subject is the familiar story of the abduction of Helen by Paris and the dire consequences of this act. The paradoxical title indicates the themes — the hope of avoiding war and the fatal advancement towards it. War and destiny, persistent preoccupations of Giraudoux, here combine in a great poem of despair.

Hector is Giraudoux's noblest creation. He has loved glory and battles, the intoxication of victory and the excitement of risk. But during his last triumph a great horror of war has come over him, bringing with it the conviction that peace is the only good in life — to be bought at any price. All the while at home in Troy a new war is preparing, one brought on by his brother's outrage towards the Greeks. Helen has already become a symbol and a slogan. Old men and poets are beating war drums. The entire city is delirious. Hector strives grimly and heroically to prevent the war — in vain, because destiny will have its way, and forces greater than individual wills or reason govern the course of events:

> Si toutes les mères coupent l'index droit de leur fils, les armées de l'univers se feront la guerre sans index . . . Et si elles lui cou-

> pent la jambe droite, les armées seront unijambistes . . . Et si elles lui crèvent les yeux, les armées seront aveugles, mais il y aura des armées, et dans la mêlée elles se chercheront le défaut de l'aine, ou la gorge, à tâtons . . .[66]

Around this bitter theme Giraudoux wove his habitual verbal embroidery. Witty sallies, precious duets, comedy and spoofing decorate the piece. The observations of solemn critics never made Giraudoux renounce his capers. We can be grateful, for his linguistic virtuosity is an essential part of his genius and his lightness of touch an essential part of his charm.

The topical pertinency of this great play escaped no one in 1935. All Europe had bitter memories of World War I and knew that another was in the making. When the Chancellor of the Reich ordered the occupation of the Rhineland, an apprehensive French public felt that Troy's Gates of War must surely open again.

On the same program with *La Guerre de Troie,* Giraudoux offered a one-act adaptation of Diderot's *Supplément au Voyage de Bougainville.* Diderot's work, one may remember, is an amusing attack upon ecclesiastic celibacy, an exposé of *philosophe* ideas on marriage and the advisability of free unions. Giraudoux's *Voyage de Cook* is not quite the same thing. As it opens, the expedition has just stopped at a south sea island. The natives are eager to receive the Englishmen in their pagan, uninhibited fashion, but Mr. Banks, the God-fearing taxidermist and deacon, is determined to spread morality and English virtues in the wake of colonization. His adventures with the native belles are paralleled by those of his strait-laced spouse, to whom handsome young savages offer their hospitality. The pathetic mingles with the ludicrous as the middle-aged English couple gets a whiff of a tropical night. It is regrettable that this little play has not been taken up again. In itself it is a sprightly curtain-raiser. Developed with music and dancing, it could make an excellent musical comedy.

After *La Guerre de Troie,* Giraudoux turned his thoughts back to Roman history for the subject of a tragedy — not to the story of Brutus, however, but to that of the Gracchi. The play was never completed, and the text that appeared in 1958[67] is only a compilation made by the editors of the numerous drafts for one act. Ostensibly Giraudoux intended the work to be about civil war, the only kind of war — we are told — that may offer the trophies of truth and beauty. In

La Guerre de Troie he had depicted the stupid pointlessness of war: did he intend in this play to justify revolutions? Caius, supreme iconoclast and blasphemer (who anticipates the Caligulas of the postwar theater), is plotting against the Roman state. Under its mask of order, propriety, and sanctimoniousness, Caius sees only hypocrisy and corruption. His plan includes the destruction of his brother Tiberius, who is returning to Rome as champion and perpetuator of the status quo. The text ends on a *coup de théâtre,* for Tiberius reveals himself as his brother's ally, and the two are presumably reconciled. In theme, *Les Gracques* would seem to be a link between *La Guerre de Troie* and *Electre,* the topic of war being retained from the one and the theme of righteousness, of purity, anticipating the other.

The Plays of the Late 1930's

Giraudoux utilized the Electra legend to write his third great tragedy. It concerns justice and an uncompromising conscience. As the play opens, twenty years have gone by since Aegisthes and Clytemnestra have murdered Agamemnon. All trace of the crime seems to have disappeared, and Aegisthes, as regent, reigns over a peaceful and prosperous country. Yet there is Electra, a strange fragile girl, whose countenance reminds criminals of their crimes and brings sinners to the point of confession. She does not yet know that her father was murdered; but, since childhood, she has borne within her an undying hatred for her mother and the certitude that her mission in life is to avenge and punish. Aegisthes, who has taken elaborate precautions to insure his tranquility, wishes to marry off Electra to a gardener. In an inferior social position she would be less dangerous. Clytemnestra protests at a mésalliance for her daughter.

When Orestes arrives the tragedy is ready to break forth. Electra, to whom the truth has been revealed, tracks down the guilty. The fact that the city is besieged and can be saved only by Aegisthes will not deter her in her mission. Clytemnestra and Aegisthes perish, the city falls, and Orestes flees, followed by the Furies. But Electra is satisfied. She has fulfilled her destiny: "J'ai fait la justice, j'ai tout." The old beggar woman asks her, "Comment cela s'appelle-t-il, quand le jour se lève comme aujourd'hui et que tout est gâché, que tout est saccagé et que l'air pourtant se respire?" The reply brings down the final curtain: "Cela s'appelle l'aurore."

Does this mean that the play ends with a great hope and the tacit approval of Electra? Or that life goes on in spite of such human folly as she symbolizes? Those who would approve Electra interpret the play to mean that half-truths and connivance may maintain the security of a country, as Aegisthes, the eloquent champion of expediency, claims. Absolute truth may bring disaster. Nevertheless, disaster is preferable to security obtained by lies, and out of the wreckage a greater and purer nation can be built; but this interpretation implies the sort of intransigent thinking that we should hesitate to attribute to a writer who was also a professional diplomat. Giraudoux knew that uncompromising consciences bring misfortune, and that in the world of practical affairs the Aegisthes are right and the Electras wrong. He could not have approved of his heroine.

Although some have seen the play as a commentary on between-wars political policies, its implications reach beyond the political to the metaphysical, where it attains its highest significance. Here Electra becomes simply a great tragic figure, a human being forced out of her condition to become justice incarnate. She, like Judith, is one of Giraudoux's "femmes à histoires," a creature chosen by destiny to accomplish its ends. We shall have occasion to return to Electra and her role in the scheme of things when we discuss in general Giraudoux's conception of the universe.

L'Impromptu de Paris, presented at the Athénée on December 4, 1937, is a short curtain-raiser dedicated to the defense of the theater. Inspired by Molière's *Impromptu de Versailles,* this play is as revealing of Giraudoux as its model was of the great comic author. It constitutes Giraudoux's most explicit statement of his dramaturgy. The situation is as follows: a government representative of touching good will comes to the Athénée theater to make direct inquiries about the purpose, merit, benefits to society of the dramatic art. This enables Giraudoux to develop in brilliant metaphors and maxims his views on the theater. They are parceled out to Jouvet and his troupe, who stop rehearsing long enough to explain to M. Robineau what the theater is all about. The discourse ends on a discussion of the relationship between the government and the theater of a country, and the possibilities of collaboration between them. Rather than a play, this little piece is a debate on a stage or a dramatized lecture. It accompanied a revival of *La Guerre de Troie n'aura pas lieu.*

Cantique des Cantiques is another curtain-raiser, first presented at the Comédie Française on October 12, 1938. Giraudoux developed it out of the situation he described in *Eglantine,* even availing himself of some of the conversation contained in the novel. In his retelling of the Biblical love poem, King Solomon has become a government official, one M. le Président,[68] the Sulamite is a modern young woman, and the shepherd, any young man. A restaurant in the Bois de Boulogne is chosen for the scene in which the young woman bids farewell to her elderly lover and greets her young man. This eternally beautiful story comes to us through the lovely fanciful atmosphere that Giraudoux knew how to create. Typical spoofing breaks the tension created by the fundamentally grave and poignant theme of age and renunciation. With its ironical banter and melancholy lyricism, it is a little masterpiece, worthy to introduce its author into the House of Molière.[69]

In a note on the program for *Ondine,* put on at the Athénée April 27, 1939, we can read as follows:

> En 1909, Charles Andler, qui dirigeait les études de littérature allemande à la Sorbonne, chargea son étudiant Jean Giraudoux de lui apporter, la semaine suivante, un commentaire d'*Ondine.* Une excursion à Robinson, puis un siècle et une carrière particulièrement occupés ont retardé jusqu'à cette année ce commentaire qui a pris, grâce à Louis Jouvet, la forme d'une pièce, et qui est donc dédié, comme le fut *Siegfried,* à la mémoire de ce maître.

It is not quite exact to suggest that such a theme was never written, for among Giraudoux's papers there is an essay — still in rough draft to be sure — entitled *Die Einheit von Fouqués Undine.* In it Giraudoux takes the German author to task for certain flaws in construction.[70] In the late 30's, prompted by Jouvet and Madeleine Ozeray, Giraudoux set out to redo Fouqué's old *Märchen* and turn it into a play.

The story of Ondine was recorded by an unknown author as early as the fourteenth century in a poem entitled *Der Ritter von Staufenberg.* It concerns a water nymph who leaves her element and acquires a human soul through marriage to a mortal, only to be forced, through her husband's infidelity, to return to her own kind. La Motte Fouqué's claim to fame rests upon the *Märchen* he composed on this legend, although its sentimentality and numerous moral digressions may not appeal to the modern reader. Bourgeois virtues and piety stand out rather ridiculously against the background of magic and *Schaudern.* The fisherman's hut is an altar to cleanliness, godliness, hospitality. Homely and realistic elements weigh heavily on the tale. Fouqué could be thinking of any rural wedding as he describes the nuptial chamber being made ready for the knight and the nymph. Next morning the company greets Undine with lusty jokes which cause her to blush in her modesty as she sets about her household chores. In the midst of such *Gemütlichkeit* one is apt to forget that right behind the hut is an enchanted forest!

Giraudoux, as one would expect, seized upon these incongruities and exploited them for comic effect. Thus he would have Ondine consenting to do the family ironing only on craggy peaks, and to recite her prayers only with her head under the water. But his play develops into something more than a parody of the old *Ritterstück.* Throughout all the clowning there persists one note on a level of high seriousness. That is Ondine's love for Hans. The lyric theme grows stronger as the action progresses, and although Giraudoux's wit constantly wards off all impression of sentimentality, the play closes as a beautiful love poem.

There is no more question of a water nymph marrying a man to obtain a soul. Giraudoux took Ondine out of the sea and out of the kitchen to represent love as perfect as man can imagine it. No elemental spirit, she is a glimpse of a better and purer world. But if man dreams of such love which turns life into paradise, he cannot endure its reality. Hans, an ordinary male, deceives his wife with Bertha, whose character is just as grossly human as his own. Therefore he must die. The tirades that close the piece constitute a remarkably poignant lovers' farewell, and the piece itself deserves a high place among the love dramas of our age.

Plays of the War Years, Posthumous Plays, Giraudoux's Films

L'Apollon de Bellac was presented first in Rio de Janeiro on June 16, 1942, under the title *L'Apollon de Marsac.* Giraudoux had sent the little play from Switzerland to Jouvet, who was on tour in South America during the war years. Jouvet himself took the role of Monsieur de Bellac and Madeleine Ozeray that of Agnès. She was replaced by Dominique Blanchard when the play was put on in Paris.

Agnès is a girl looking for a job in an office, but completely lacking any of the conventional qualifications. Moreover, she is very much afraid of men. To her aid steps Monsieur de Bellac, who imparts to her a magic formula to cure her fear and obtain anything she desires. All she must do is to exclaim before any man, "Comme vous êtes beau!" The phrase works like a charm and becomes the mainspring of subsequent action in the play. With such a silly theme it is difficult to account for the popularity and critical esteem the play has enjoyed. One would say that Giraudoux is here just parodying himself. But its dramatic construction has been lauded and, on the whole, it is considered an elegant, witty, and intelligent comedy. We are asked to interpret what at best seems a demonstration of the incurable vanity of men as a bitter reflection of the persistent nostalgia for beauty in this life. Compared to another *pochade, Cantique des Cantiques,* about which little good has been said, this play strikes us as being inferior on all points.

Sodome et Gomorrhe, the last of Giraudoux's great tragedies, takes its theme from Vigny's famous lines: "Et se jetant de loin un regard irrité/ Les deux sexes mourront chacun de son côté," and unequivocally refutes the optimism of *Amphitryon 38.* In place of Alcmene and Amphitryon, the happy couple, we have Lia and Jean, who, no more than the ghostly couple in Sartre's *Les Jeux sont faits,* are capable of loving each other. In Giraudoux's earlier play, the felicity and the solidarity of the human couple could defy the gods; in *Sodome et Gomorrhe,* the world must be destroyed because men and women are congenitally incapable of understanding each other. What a distance Giraudoux has traveled from the confidence of his youth, when he showed us undeluded young women who knew how to make the best of life's bargain, and, reconciling themselves to reality, found happiness through compromise and renunciation. *Ondine's* bitter theme of the couple was softened by wit and idyllic poetry. In 1943 Giraudoux neither smiles nor hopes, and one can only surmise what tragic personal experiences he passed through to arrive at such pessimism.

The play is as stark and blunt as its theme. Dramatic technique is reduced to a minimum, and comic relief is almost totally lacking. It is tantamount to a philosophical dialogue. Jean and Lia carry most of the burden of the play, with the other couple, Jacques and Ruth, mimicking the gestures of the protagonists in the "mirror" scheme often resorted to in Giraudoux's plays. It rests with them whether the world will be spared divine wrath: only the existence of a happy couple can save it. Jean is an ordinary mortal, patterned after all Giraudoux's heroes, who wants an ordinary wife. But Lia is one of these "femmes à histoires" with aspirations that do not stop before the seduction of an Archangel. Perhaps they just have the wrong partners; they exchange with Jacques and Ruth. All are deceived in their hopes and return to their original mates no happier than before. A reconciliation is attempted, but is fruitless. Jean stands with the men of the two towns, Lia with the women, and together the couples of Sodom and Gomorrah perish in the destruction of the world.

Sodome et Gomorrhe was presented for the first time at the Hébertot, October 11, 1943, with settings by Douking, music by Honneger, costumes by Christian Bérard. Lia was played by Edwige Feuillère, who achieved in her extremely important and exacting role a great personal triumph. As for the general critical reaction, wonder and perplexity mingled with admiration before this great apocalyptical poem of despair.

It was in a far different atmosphere from the gloom of the Occupation which enshrouded *Sodome et Gomorrhe* that *La Folle de Chaillot* was produced. Louis Jouvet, back from exile, was eager to reestablish his theater in Paris with a dazzling presentation. Giraudoux's new play, with optimism bubbling through the whimsy and poetry that had captivated so many audiences, seemed to him eminently suitable to the times and the occasion. All Paris thought so too. To his public appeal for costumes which would complement the superb sets Christian Bérard was planning, the response was overwhelming. To his request for government assistance, the Beaux-Arts Division replied with adequate funds; this enterprise, combining some of the finest talents of France, seemed an ideal way to demonstrate to the country and to the world that French prestige in the arts was as great as ever. The staging of Giraudoux's first posthumous play became an object of general piety and pride.

At the opening on December 19, 1945, with General de Gaulle in the audience, it was hailed as a national event. Marguerite Moreno received the crowning ovation of her long career for her interpretation of the role of Aurélie, the *Folle,* and it was a triumph for all concerned. The play ran for 297 performances, longer than any other play Jouvet had ever staged, except for the perennial *Ecole des Femmes.*

La Folle de Chaillot is generally described as a philosophical comedy about modern mercantilism. This is quite accurate if one does not imply that it is just a diatribe aimed at capitalism. Giraudoux defends more than he attacks, and his aims are surely not just political. The cause here in question is the very unspecific one of poetry and idealism, a just measure of which is necessary to keep materialism and practical astuteness from disfiguring the earth.

Thus the *Folle,* an eccentric old woman frequenting the Chaillot district, represents the sort of madness that turns things of this world into objects of goodness and beauty. We do not see her until we have first met the president, the baron, and the broker — sinister persons who have convened at the Café Chez Francis to form a corporation aimed at destroying Chaillot in order to exploit the oil the prospector assures them is underneath it. As they plot, a typical Paris street scene is enacted before them: singers, beggars, flower sellers pass by, chatting with the waiter and with Irma, the dishwasher, who incarnates youthful innocence, love, and right attitudes. The excitement caused by the entrance of Aurélie, decked out in all her preposterous finery, has scarcely died down when a young man, fished out of the Seine, is laid down before the café. His attempted suicide was brought on by his association with the villains of the piece. As Aurélie restores him to life by her own whimsical praise of life, she formulates a plan to rid the earth of the prospector and all members of the new corporation.

To seek counsel she summons several other *Folles,* who meet together in a mad scene in Aurélie's cellar apartment. After their conference and confabulations the exploiters arrive. Ostensibly to permit them to examine the soil beneath the city, Aurélie lets them all pass through a trap door and then closes it upon them. This symbolic execution of the forces of evil resuscitates the forces of good in the persons of great benefactors and other deserving among the dead. A new order of love and justice is inaugurated, and grass grows on the Champ de Mars.

The first performance of *Pour Lucrèce,* the second posthumous play, took place at the Marigny theater, November 4, 1953. It was probably written in 1943, while Edwige Feuillère was playing in *Sodome et Gomorrhe.* One evening of that year Giraudoux read to her parts of his new manuscript, a drama inspired by the Lucretia fable. On at least one other occasion Giraudoux spoke to Mme. Feuillère of the role he was creating for her. Then, on January 31, 1944, Giraudoux died at the Hotel de Castille, and for two years nothing was done about his play. In 1946 Jouvet initiated inquiries, but Mme. Giraudoux refused to release it. As she explained, by delaying the performance of her husband's last play, it was as if she were prolonging his life. Only in 1952 did Suzanne Giraudoux lift her veto. Jouvet was now dead, and it was to Jean-Louis Barrault that the production was confided.

Whereupon rumors began to circulate that Giraudoux had never done more than outline a play, that the piece to be presented was of another hand, probably that of the playwright's son. Barrault put a stop to these insinuations by exhibiting the manuscript — three of them in fact.

The existence of three manuscripts of course indicates merely that for *Pour Lucrèce,* Giraudoux composed in his usual fashion. After committing his first inspiration to paper, he might lay that manuscript aside and write a second version entirely from memory. For his plays sometimes Giraudoux made several fresh starts before he was ready to collate and edit for a definitive text. This technique accounts for the quality of spontaneity and fortuity that his work exhibits. He composed, like a musician, variations on a chosen theme. The final text would not necessarily be established before rehearsals. *Pour Lucrèce* never got that far during Giraudoux's lifetime. But there seems no reason to suspect that it is not entirely his own.

Barrault's production was one of the brightest jewels of the 1953 season. A particularly brilliant cast was assembled to do Giraudoux honor, notably Barrault himself, Madeleine Renaud, Edwige Feuillère, and Yvonne de Bray. Its triumph, like the highly successful revival of *Siegfried* the year before, indicated that Giraudoux had lost none of his charm.

Pour Lucrèce is about virtue and vice in Aix under the *Second Empire.* The *procureur impérial,* seconded by the beautiful prude, Lucile, his wife, has determined to take severe measures to combat the easy licentiousness which prevails in the Paris of the *Midi.* While his duties take him away from the city for a short time, Lucile begins by exposing to Armand that his wife, Paola, is deceiving him. Paola avenges herself by having Lucile drugged and carried to a house of ill-fame, where she regains consciousness in circumstances designed to convince her that she has been attacked. By this odious trick Lucile has not only been dishonored in the eyes of the world but also destroyed in her essence, in the conjugal purity that she symbolizes. She permits Armand to avenge her. In killing Count Marcellus, Armand kills a man innocent of the crime imputed to him, but by so doing avenges his own honor, for Marcellus was Paola's lover. Lucile recounts her shame to her husband upon his return. She could not live with a lie or a sin of omission between them. He, alas, reveals himself to be an ordinary husband with an ordinary sense of honor. Hearing that she has been defiled, he rejects her and flees. The revelation of her husband's mediocrity, plus the sense of impurity which his attitude has infected her with, makes her take her own life.

On the basis of internal evidence, there can be little doubt as to the authorship of the play. One recognizes in Lucile one of Giraudoux's heroines and their uncompromising idealism; in the male characters, his heroes, as well, made of lesser stuff. One recognizes Giraudoux's language, which transfigures the world and lends to everyday acts the significance of great symbolic gestures. Without it we should have here a mediocre melodrama in the style of Alexandre Dumas, or, with its lachrymose theme of wronged virtue, something like an early movie plot.

Since *Siegfried,* with each succeeding play Giraudoux's dramaturgy has always come up for impassioned discussion. It was apparent from the first that his theater was essentially one of style and ideas. What action there is exists to serve the development of the ideas. It does not spring from lifelike situations or proceed with the continuity of daily experience. Cerebral in origin, it follows rather a pattern of logical or fanciful ideas wholly arbitrary in nature. The characters also exist only to serve ideas. They remain undeveloped and unparticularized in any concrete sense, standing for abstract qualities, or, at most, the young girl, the young woman, or the male of the species. Yet, although action and character are subservient to ideas, it was equally apparent, from *Siegfried* on, that what is said in Giraudoux's plays is less important than how it is said. The importance of style was repeatedly stressed by the author himself, whenever he had occasion to present his views on the theater.

Such a conception of the theater, running counter as it did to all prevailing notions of what the theater demanded, could not fail to provoke suspicion and criticism. Through the years the same question has been asked: are Giraudoux plays really theatrical pieces? Edouard Bourdet, whose own dramaturgy is poles apart from Giraudoux's, nevertheless formulates the best reply:

> Si, pour qu'une pièce soit du théâtre, il faut que tout y soit subordonné à la fiction et que l'auteur, pour la créer et l'entretenir, consente à ces grossissements, ces approximations de la pensée, ces simplifications du style, toutes ces "humiliations joyeuses" selon l'expression de Colette, qui caractérisent, pour certains, le véritable homme de théâtre, alors Giraudoux n'en est pas un. Mais si le théâtre comporte avant tout ce goût du merveilleux, d'un certain merveilleux, la recherche des situations touchantes ou pathétiques, l'attente de la surprise, d'une certaine surprise, du hasard intelligent ou spirituel, alors on doit reconnaître que Giraudoux a, plus que quiconque, le goût de ces choses et qu'il est instinctivement attiré, dans ses pièces, par ce que l'on ne saurait nommer autrement que l'aspect théâtral de la vie.
>
> Cette question d'orthodoxie théâtrale chez Jean Giraudoux a-t-elle, au surplus, un si grand intérêt? Je pense au mot, si joli, d'Horace Walpole à propos de Marie-Antoinette et, le transposant ici, je propose cette conclusion: "On prétend que ce n'est pas du théâtre? Alors c'est le théâtre qui a tort."[71]

With *Pour Lucrèce,* the perennial question narrows somewhat. It is now less whether Giraudoux's plays are plays than whether Giraudoux's tragedies are tragedies. Pierre-Aimé Touchard, the former director of the Comédie Française, declares that Giraudoux, who felt deeply drawn to tragedy and in whom a whole generation put their hope for a revival of the tragic theater, failed to create a real tragedy because, in his plays, a spirit of preciousness and fancy intervenes at the crucial moment.[72] No one would deny this striking ambivalence of Giraudoux's genius that M. Touchard points up. He might have gone on to say that the intellectual control that wit and fancy imply is incompatible with the sentiment of real tragedy. But the question is whether these elements are present in sufficient quantity to give the impression that it is the author and not his personages or fatality that control the course of events. Back in 1940, Georges-Albert Astre said no, Giraudoux is a tragic writer because he shows man in the grip of the gods: "Toute œuvre ici suppose l'archarnement des dieux sur les hommes, la domination du destin."[73] Jean-Louis Barrault indirectly dismisses the threat that preciousness and fancy might constitute to tragedy by ruling out verbal expression as any criterion. For him, *Pour Lucrèce* is a tragedy because of the *démesure* of the characters:

> Ce n'est pas la mode d'expression verbale qui caractérise une tragédie, c'est la manière dont se conduisent ses personnages. Quand les personnages, dans leurs conduites, n'hésitent pas à agir au delà de leur instinct de conservation, il y a tragédie. Autrement dit: une tragédie commence là où l'instinct de conservation disparaît. C'est le cas des personnages de *Pour Lucrèce* . . . tragédie non par l'expression, mais véritablement par l'action.[74]

Another proof for Barrault that here is a tragedy is that the play proceeds on a plane that excludes all sympathy for the characters. The only question is one of being right, of justice: "*Pour Lucrèce* appartient encore à la famille des tragédies car elle existe sous le signe de la Justice." In sum, Barrault believes that in spite of the honeyed atmosphere that envelops the play all the laws of tragedy are respected: "règlement de comptes, questions de droits, démesure passionnelle des principaux personnages, fissure réelle du héros." He would even call it a classic tragedy, and, on the basis of structure and language, place it close to Racine.

Very well, is Giraudoux's theater really theater? Is he a tragic author? Many of the impassioned and sweeping affirmations that have been uttered on these questions are easily refutable. But it is not really important for us to refute them or decide these questions, since we are less interested in classifying Giraudoux's work than in obtaining a deeper appreciation of it. To this end we turn a sympathetic ear to widely divergent opinions, for, in developing his argument — whatever tack he takes — each critic affords us new and interesting insights.

With *Pour Lucrèce,* we have completed our review of Giraudoux's career in the theater. At the time of this writing the revival of *Tessa* (1958) demonstrates once again the enduring popularity of his plays and reminds us that they are not revived often enough on Paris stages. Before turning to quite another phase of Giraudoux's literary career, let us look briefly at his work for the cinema.

The film *La Duchesse de Langeais* brought Giraudoux, in 1941, to the threshold of a new career. One can only presume what brilliant achievements his untimely death prevented, since the cinema, which finds its most appropriate material in works of fancy and pure imagination, seems a medium ideally suited to his genius. The happy encounter of Giraudoux and the films makes one think of the "Image de Préface," which opens *La Duchesse de Langeais* by showing the Duchess and Montriveau being brought together ultimately and inevitably.

Giraudoux's scenario follows essentially the plot of Balzac's story, although Giraudoux discards the flash-back narrative in favor of a forthright chronology, cuts, organizes, and offers alternate endings. Perhaps in regard to plot detail, he depends a little too much on Balzac, for, as in the case of *Le Voyage de Cook*, he wrongly assumes that everyone knows the original, and therefore does not get across some witty parodies. For example, those who do not remember Montriveau's nonchalent cigar in Balzac's abduction scene — the climax where the Duchess acknowledges her wickedly frivolous treatment of Montriveau — will not understand the ironical reference. In the scenario, the righteously indignant lover threatens to brand the Duchess on the forehead. Whereupon she cries out at the sight of the branding iron: "Pourquoi ce fer! Brûle-moi de ton cigare, Armand, de ce feu qui vient de ton souffle!"[75] Such an allusion would seem appropriate only in a pastiche, and Giraudoux's film is far more than that. He has made it, on the whole, his very own. By submitting Balzac's novelette to a sort of purifying process, he has dissolved all the heavy realism of the original and let the protagonists emerge crystal-clear in their essential natures. Their family resemblance to the heroes of Giraudoux's plays is unmistakable, and as masculine passion and feminine coquetry engage in a pretty combat that ends most tragically we know we are watching one of his dramas.

The film *Les Anges du Péché* (1943) represents the collaboration of Giraudoux with the Dominican father Raymond Bruckberger and Robert Bresson, the *metteur-en-scène*. We may assume the dialogue is exclusively Giraudoux's. One wonders what attracted Giraudoux in such an assignment. Why should the professed partisan of this life and this world compose a canticle to the glory of the Béthanie nuns; the master of preciosity and irony be content to forgo his habitual expression to employ a language of monastic simplicity? The attraction may have been in the character of Anne-Marie, the luminous soul dedicated to the salvation of the murderess Thérèse. Anne-Marie's extreme purity, her proud conception of her destiny, make her a sister of all Giraudoux's heroines of election.

Realizing that one can give only in giving oneself, Anne-Marie has taken leave of her bourgeois life to enter this order, which is particularly charged with the salvation of women gone astray. She finds her mission in Thérèse, a young woman serving a sentence in prison. Immediately upon her release, Thérèse buys a revolver and shoots her former lover, then seeks a hiding place in Anne-Marie's convent. The nun hopes to continue to work for Thérèse's regeneration, but is soon forced to leave the convent, where her uncompromising honesty has made her enemies among the other sisters. Refusing to return to her family, Anne-Marie wanders aimlessly until one stormy night she is found in a dying condition at the tomb of Père Lataste, the founder of the order. Thérèse is summoned to take care of her. The presence of her former *marraine* slowly releases Thérèse from the evil that has held her so long. As the death knell sounds for Anne-Marie and the sisters begin to sing the *Salve Regina,* Thérèse makes ready to give herself up to the police.

These two scenarios mark the extent of Giraudoux's collaboration with the films. By utilizing new devices that are purely cinematographic and by adjusting his style to the exigencies of a new art, Giraudoux proved that even just before his death, his genius remained as supple and adaptable as it was when he effected his remarkably successful transition from fiction to drama.

Chapter 3

THE ESSAYS

Literary Criticism and Theory

Giraudoux's career divides itself fairly neatly into decades. Personal reminiscence characterizes the writing done from 1910 to 1920; the 1920's make up the period of concentration on fiction; in the 1930's the theater dominates. The period of the theater is also the period of Giraudoux's largest contribution to literary criticism and theory. From 1927, when the preface to Gérard de Nerval's *Aurélia* appeared, to 1941, when *Littérature* collected many articles in one volume, Giraudoux composed twenty or so brilliant and provocative literary essays.

The Nerval study sets the pattern for Giraudoux's critical approach and shows him already in full possession of the intuitive gifts that make his comments unique. Tendencies discernible even in the early paper on Fouqué's *Undine*[1] have here evolved into a characteristic manner to which Giraudoux will henceforth consistently adhere. We may not expect of him erudition or comprehensive treatments. What interests Giraudoux the critic is what a writer or a work seems to stand for, the essence or the fundamental characteristic. When he feels that he has detected the ultimate significance of the object of his scrutiny, he proceeds to try to convince his readers by a series of bold affirmations sustained through paradox and antithesis. His method is not remarkably informative, but it is stimulating to the highest degree.

This first essay is constructed on the theme of the absolute necessity of Nerval's presence in French literature, necessity due more to

Notes to Chapter 3 begin on page 220.

his personality than to his works. Strange, Giraudoux observes, that the lives of these personalities of absolute necessity should be made up only of chance, accident, and dream. Thus he continues to develop his thought by associations and contrasts, moving from one brilliantly stated paradox to another. The mediocre personalities among the artists of France are the real priests of art. In France, great sorrows are not necessarily borne by her greatest men. Nerval has become the symbol of the unhappy life. Yet we know everything about his life except its misfortunes! The nature of Nerval's melancholy must be sought not in specific misfortunes but in the contact he habitually maintained with a dream world. In France intimate writing of the sort Nerval practiced is rare, because the rites of the Catholic Church have canalized introspection and the *examen de conscience*. The reader may protest at every one of Giraudoux's generalizations. The slightest documentation exposes them as overstatements at least. But they captivate our attention by their vigor and picturesqueness, and refresh our vision by sudden and unexpected illuminations.

The year of *Siegfried*, 1928, Giraudoux issued a eulogistic essay on Emile Clermont, the young novelist of *âmes d'élite*, shot down during the war. The conceit which Giraudoux develops is stated in the opening line: "Il y a, dans toutes les âmes grandes, un grand génie ex-tensible qui donne à leur vie, qu'elle soit brève ou longue, conclue normalement ou brisée, l'équilibre et la perfection."[2]

During the next year, he made numerous minor contributions here and there, as well as publishing one major essay. Among the minor items are several more eulogistic pieces. The preface to P. Frayssinet, *Poèmes* would not appear until 1931, although the text (in *Littérature*, under the title "Tombeau d'un jeune poète") is dated 1929. It is built on another conceit typical of Giraudoux's turn of mind; i.e., that a person — in this case, a writer — somehow symbolizes an area, a place in the world. For the book of travel reminiscences by Emmanuel Chaumié, *La Belle Aventure de Robert de Flers*, Giraudoux offered a few polite prefatory remarks. Again for Marcel Valotaire's study of Laboureur, the book illustrator, he wrote a letter-preface, presented in manuscript facsimile. He is listed as one of the writers contributing an introduction to an edition of Stendhal's *Ecrits intimes*, but it is doubtful if such an edition ever appeared. In 1929 Giraudoux offered his first remarks on the theater: "Sur le Théâtre contemporain" (*Le Temps*, July 22). The views that he expresses here will be reaffirmed in subsequent essays. "Racine" (*La Nouvelle Revue Française*, December) is the important piece of the year. Its introductory sentence reads: "Il est satisfaisant de penser que le premier écrivain de la littérature française n'est pas un moraliste, ni un savant, ni un général, ni même un roi, mais un homme de lettres."[3] The tack Giraudoux takes is that Racine's inspiration was largely literary, that his plays do not depict his personal crises at all. With evident pleasure he demonstrates the purity and abstraction of Racine's heroes, qualities that they share with Giraudoux's own creatures. On this basis, critics who have called Giraudoux the Racine of our times may be justified. We may note finally in this essay the concern Giraudoux habitually shows for defining a period, for establishing the relationship of an author with his times. If Nerval had seemed to him at odds with his times, Racine, on the contrary, appears in perfect harmony with the epoch in which he lived.

Subscribers to the Parisian lecture series known as the *Université des Annales* could read Giraudoux's name on the program for 1930. His *causerie* on March 7 of this year which marked the anniversary of *Hernani* was hardly what they might have expected from a commemorative address, or even from the title: "D'un romantisme à l'autre." It amounted to a repudiation of official Romanticism and Victor Hugo. Giraudoux, who, in his youth, had discovered the German Romantics, declares that the French revolt of 1830 was nothing but a counterfeit. The *cénacles* were too bourgeois to merit the name Romantic. If Hugo is a Romantic, Giraudoux does not understand. For him:

> Un romantique est celui qui n'a plus aucune complicité avec chaque homme et chaque institution humaine, et qui en cherche une avec tout le reste de la nature . . .
>
> Le mouvement romantique d'un pays est celui, en effet, où tout a cédé devant l'exigence et la nostalgie du cœur . . . Le romantisme est le panthéisme des époques civilisées. Chaque divinité est remise par lui à chaque citoyen, qui en devient à la fois le prêtre et le démiurge. C'est une époque de maladie et de droiture morale, d'insatisfaction et de clairvoyance, la seule époque où le rôle de l'homme de lettres l'élève jusqu'à être la conscience du siècle.[4]

After defining what he feels is true Romanticism, Giraudoux undertakes to define the role or mission of the writer today. Not political or moral guidance surely, but two things we should expect of him: a sensitivity and a vocabulary. Form and genre do not matter. There should be no distinctions between poets, prose writers, essayists, or dramatists. "Ce que le monde, en effet, cherche en ce moment, c'est beaucoup moins son équilibre que son langage." "Le secret de l'avenir, c'est le secret du style."[5] This ringing conclusion uttered by a writer so often accused of being just a stylist, a verbal acrobat, constitutes a proud defiance and a declaration of principles. No other pronouncement of Giraudoux's has incited so much discussion. What reaction the audience had to his speech, on the whole, is hard to say. Someone has reported that he spoke too rapidly to be fully effective. There can be no question that, as with any Giraudoux text, the printed version enhanced its comprehension and appreciation. The lecture was published in *Conférencia* in December.

Going before the *Université des Annales* again on March 4, 1931, Giraudoux spoke on the theater. The lecture is a comparison between postwar trends in Germany and France, and a tribute to Louis Jouvet. It may be read *in extenso* in *Conférencia* and, altered and abbreviated, in *Littérature* under the title "Le Metteur-en-scène." It appears also as a preface to the book *Louis Jouvet et le théâtre d'aujourd'hui,* by Claude Cézan. What we notice especially here is the evidence it offers of Giraudoux's sustained interest in the German stage. We remember his enthusiasm while a student in Munich. He doubtless kept abreast of what was going on in the German theater during the years that followed and renewed his contacts with it directly whenever he had occasion to be in that country again. How often he went back to Germany after 1924, when he did a stint in Berlin as Embassy Secretary, we cannot be sure, but it is not unlikely that he returned rather frequently. His *plaquette* on Berlin appeared in 1930.

On November 19, 1931, two weeks after the première of *Judith,* Giraudoux spoke again on the theater. The failure of his play had been a hard blow, and the invitation by the alumni from Châteauroux gave him an opportunity to vent his feelings publicly and strike back at his detractors. He begins by affirming his belief in the high spiritual calling of the theater and by scoring the commercial forces that have corrupted the Parisian stage. He blames the critics for misunderstanding the true function of the theater and for adhering to the outmoded conception of a play as an agreeable accompaniment to after-dinner digestion: "Théâtre, roman, critique même, au lieu d'être les accessoires d'une vie superficielle et tranquillement bourgeoise, sont redevenus, dans notre époque comme dans toutes les époques amples et angoissées, des instruments de première nécessité."[6] He defends himself against his judges who, on the basis of a spurious distinction between "good theater" and "literature," have labeled him an unprofessional, a *littérateur*. One remembers how eloquently Edouard Bourdet will support him in his position: "On prétend que ce n'est pas du théâtre? Alors, c'est le théâtre qui a tort."[7] Giraudoux ends his speech to the alumni by the slogan he launched in his *Hernani* address: "Notre époque ne demande plus à l'homme de lettres des œuvres; . . . elle lui réclame surtout un langage."[8]

The year of *Judith* is important in Giraudoux's criticism for these two studies on the theater. Also for 1931, one should mention two prefaces written for special editions of *Suzanne et le Pacifique* and an introduction to Musset's *Contes et Nouvelles*. Since this last work is not to be found even with some searching, one may suspect it never appeared. The *Suzanne* prefaces were published also in the *Revue Nouvelle* in February. One is the "Jeune Fille nue dans une île" that Charles Murciaux will append to his *Jean Giraudoux ou Prospero vaincu* (1954), and the other is the "Dieu et la Littérature" of *Littérature*. "Dieu et la Littérature" is in the form of a letter to Daragnès, who did the illustrations in the edition especially printed for the "Bibliophiles de Lyon." Suzanne explains with characteristic Giralducian eloquence why the subject of God never entered her book. She shares the anti-metaphysical feelings that Holofernes expresses with equal eloquence in *Judith*. The two statements, formulated about the same time, show interesting similarity.

The preface to *Les Liaisons dangereuses* (1932) constitutes one of Giraudoux's major critical essays. It presents Choderlos de Laclos as the exposer of a wicked and frivolous century, and implies that without his novel the eighteenth century might never have been found out! This "angle," which Giraudoux may owe to Balzac,[9] is very cleverly sustained throughout. The essay abounds in subtleties such as the distinction we are asked to perceive between Laclos, "un homme vrai," and Rousseau, who merely "possessed" truth. *Les Liaisons dangereuses* shares with *Manon Lescaut* the honor of being the "truest" novel in French. In praising Laclos for his sensitivity and his style, Giraudoux affirms here again his faith in the lofty role of the writer: "C'est à la poésie, à elle seule que seront toujours réservées la navigation et la découverte."[10]

In "Sur la caricature" (1932), irony is equated with poetry. Giraudoux begins this article for *Les Nouvelles Littéraires* by expressing sorrow at the decline in caricature and satire, which he calls the two great arms against stupidity and pride. Caricature is a religious art, he asserts, invented by man to ward off the wrath of the gods. If we make ourselves ugly and ridiculous, the gods will not be jealous! Even though satire does not treat humanity so harshly, it also is not well thought of by modern society. Society is made too uncomfortable by satire or irony: "cette ironie . . . dont l'autre nom est la poésie."[11] This interesting piece of whimsy was reprinted to preface *Diablerie,* the translation of a work by Evelyn Waugh, and was subsequently collected in *Littérature.*

In another lecture at the *Université des Annales,* given November 18, 1932, Giraudoux traced a fanciful history of Bellac and developed the theme that it is the comfortable people of such a town who have a real taste for tragedy. Nietzsche had sustained something of the sort in his essay on Greek drama where he declares that comedy is the product of decadence, but a healthy civilization produces tragedies. The text of Giraudoux's address appeared in the October 1, 1933, issue of *Conférencia,* and in *Littérature* under the title "Bellac et la Tragédie."

The invitation to preface a translation of the German novel, *Catherine soldat,* by Adrienne Thomas (1933), gave Giraudoux the opportunity to return to a favorite subject — the comparison of France and Germany. His theme is war and the different attitudes taken towards war by the French, the English, and the Germans. One has the usual impression of highly interesting and suggestive generalizations, but the suspicion, as well, that they are not demonstrably sound.

By 1934, at the age of 52, Giraudoux had reached a point of full and diversified accomplishment. In the theater, he had just presented *Intermezzo,* and would soon present *La Guerre de Troie n'aura pas lieu.* In the meantime, *Tessa,* the English play which Giraudoux had adapted for the French stage, was playing to full houses. In the novel, to the public which had not had a major work of fiction by him since 1930, he offered *Combat avec l'Ange.* From January on, this novel began appearing in the *Nouvelle Revue Française.* Giraudoux's name appeared many times during the year in magazines and newspapers.

His journalistic activities, steadily growing in recent years, now were in full swing: articles on urbanism, sports, public instruction, etc. Three articles appearing in *Marianne* deal directly with literature. They are all essays in definition: "L'Ecrivain journaliste" situates the writer vis-à-vis the newspaper; "Les Ecrivains, gardiens du domaine national," vis-à-vis the nation; "Sur la Nouvelle" suggests some distinctions between the novel and the *nouvelle.* In addition to his many other activities, Giraudoux had addressed the *Annales* audience the previous December on another subject for definition — the writer vis-à-vis the theater, and how the dramatist's relationship with his play differs from the novelist's relationship with his novel. Giraudoux ventures the paradox that the greatest names in the theater are anonymous — we have no manuscripts of Shakespeare, Molière, or Racine — and develops his point by frequent citations from the classic French theater and that of the *siglo de oro.* What he means to say is that in the theater the writer as a person is effaced by his play; that plays, representing as they do the participation of producers and actors, acquire an autonomy that other literary forms do not possess. A portion of this speech is devoted to an exchange of letters between the repentant Racine and his stern judge, Bossuet, which dramatizes, with pathetic eloquence, the close of the most brilliant period in the French theater. Giraudoux's lecture appears, in shortened form, in *Littérature* under two titles: "L'Auteur au théâtre" and "Un duo." Towards the end of 1934, Giraudoux began his series of lectures on *La Française,* also at the *Annales.*

If we include in the discussion of criticism the little polemic that Giraudoux published in *Le Figaro,* April 2, 1935, on the occasion of Paul Claudel's failure to be elected to the French Academy, it is because his defense of Claudel indicates his own taste and his conception of the role of the writer. Giraudoux had, since student days, been an ardent admirer of Claudel and had made allusion to him in his writings and conversations. One may remember the reference in *Suzanne et le Pacifique.* For the girl on the desert isle, Claudel, Rimbaud, and Mallarmé are "les seuls à visser maintenant notre pauvre existence contre le monde et ses mystères." Older writers like Renan and Barrès have become "beaux écrous un peu desserrés." Although Suzanne's musings take the form of strange images — "je sentais que c'était sur ces trois réseaux neufs qu'il fallait brancher ma pauvre tête-ampoule"[12] — her meaning is clear. Claudel is one of the three great modern poets who have given the world a new sensitivity and a new language, exactly what the world requires of its artists.[13] Paul Claudel, "ce créateur d'un langage nouveau," as Giraudoux hails him in his *Figaro* article, thus receives the highest tribute Giraudoux can pay. Incidentally, whether he knew it or not, Giraudoux's laudatory article on Claudel was payment for a personal debt of gratitude, for it was Claudel who had, we remember, many years before, first pointed out to Berthelot the talent of the young *élève vice-consul* who was working in his department.[14]

The most extensive single critical work of Jean Giraudoux is the series of lectures he gave at the *Université des Annales* during the months of January and February, 1936. His subject was La Fontaine, a choice due perhaps to the kinship Giraudoux himself felt with the seventeenth-century writer. He must have recognized that La Fontaine's gift of transforming banal reality into something delightful was similar to his own. And that the keys that he found to La Fontaine's literary personality in general — style, distraction, innocence — would fit his own equally well. Each of the five lectures was devoted to what Giraudoux was pleased to call one of La Fontaine's temptations: namely, the temptation of the bourgeois life, of women, of society, of literature, of skepticism and doctrine. Again the lecturer might have been speaking of himself.

It goes without saying that we cannot expect here an erudite study. Giraudoux had not dug very deeply into scholarship to prepare his remarks, nor taken much heed of previous opinions. Rather did he choose to present a wholly personal conception and defend it with a graceful dialectic. In short, the lectures constitute a witty and charming *causerie,* constructed with a minimum of information and a maximum of poetic fancy. La Fontaine's life appears to Giraudoux as a series of tests, each ultimately passed with success, by means of such sterling virtues as laziness and absentmindedness. The five tests passed, or the five temptations withstood, La Fontaine is at long last in a position to compose his great work, the *Fables.* It is hard to keep from musing on what Giraudoux would have found for the sixth temptation, had he been asked to deliver six lectures instead of five!

The text appeared in book form in 1938 (*Les Cinq Tentations de La Fontaine,* Grasset) and was given generous praise by the press.

After the lectures on La Fontaine (1936), Giraudoux returned to the subject of the theater. Previously he had presented his point of view in lectures, chiefly those given at the *Université des Annales.* Now, following Molière's example, he decided to incorporate his ideas in a play. *L'Impromptu de Paris* (1937) argues them out in light and witty dialogue. We have already noted the topics which come up for discussion and the numerous maxims which stud the conversation.[15] "Le théâtre c'est d'être réel dans l'irréel." "C'est une heure d'éternité, l'heure théâtrale." "Le mot comprendre n'existe pas au théâtre." "Ceux qui veulent comprendre au théâtre sont ceux qui ne comprennent pas le théâtre." Such phrases as these constitute a sort of capsule dramaturgy as entertaining as it is provocative of serious reflection upon the aims and accomplishments of the dramatic art.

Other than *L'Impromptu de Paris,* before *Littérature* (1941) there is little else to note. In 1937, Giraudoux made a speech in honor of Alain Fournier on the occasion of the naming of the boys' *lycée* in Bourges after this author: "Et moi aussi, j'ai été un petit Meaulnes." It was printed subsequently in the *Nouvelles Littéraires* and as a *plaquette* (Emile-Paul, 1937). In "Charles-Louis Philippe," first appearing in the *Nouvelle Revue Française* (1937), he returned to one of the favorite authors of his youth. The uniqueness of this writer, we are told, lies in his being the first nonbourgeois writer. Developing this theme, Giraudoux considers the effect on modern literature that bourgeois domination has had. All this, we must decide, is highly speculative if we have really never had anything but a bourgeois literature!

Littérature collected most of Giraudoux's short critical pieces into a convenient volume, the only *inedita* being the "Tombeau de Lavedan" and the epilogue, "La France et son héros," which has nothing to do with literature. The "tombeau" was written in 1940 in Portugal, where Giraudoux had gone in search of his son.[16] Noting the prominence the newspapers there gave to the death of a "mediocre" French writer, Giraudoux composed a few pages of praise to a country in which such an event is not relegated to a place far behind the war news. As for Lavedan, he comes out rather badly as a "mediocre" dramatist, the homage to him consisting of an evocation through a series of rhetorical repetitions which are sustained a little too long. "La France et son héros" is a message of patriotic exhortation, which Giraudoux wrote on the last day of December, 1940, back in his mother's house in Cusset. He would remind all Frenchmen that their traditional hero has been the incarnation of reason, lucidity, and measure. Other nations have peopled their mythology with extra-human creatures and monsters, but France has never conceived of her national saints and heroes except in very human terms. During the last thirty-five years, however, she has lost sight of this symbol of noble and generous values to pursue in all her activities (the arts excepted) a policy of ugliness and cowardice. As Giraudoux depicts for his countrymen the ideal from which they have strayed, he is again affirming his own personal ideal. The national hero he paints here and the ideal land he describes are exactly what we find in all his novels and plays.

What we know under the title *Visitations* (1947) is a group of lectures given in Lauzanne in 1942. Giraudoux's delight in being, for a moment, outside Pétain's France gives these talks a very jovial tone. He will speak on the theater, he says, but not on subjects such as the danger that is threatening the dramatic work by overemphasis on the *mise-en-scène*. He will speak, for the first time, about himself and his own writing, but not about what he has already done. He will not discuss either what he plans to do. Rather, on this little vacation, he will speak of the charming and fanciful things he would like to do but probably never will. Then, with a graceful bow, Giraudoux raises the curtain. What we behold is, for the most part, what he certainly has done or will do. Here is a scene from *L'Apollon de Bellac.* It is followed by a *Samson et Dalila,* which will later find a place in *Sodome et Gomorrhe,* and several scenes where he lets personages that "haunt" him have their say. In the bit devoted to the young consular attaché, the Madwoman peeps in. The gardener and the Archangel give us another foretaste of *Sodome et Gomorrhe.* These scenes are choice dramatic morsels which Giraudoux must have thoroughly enjoyed presenting. Between times he makes interesting remarks about the theater and the playwright, much in the manner of *L'Impromptu de Paris.* He would recall the theater to its former state — a troupe of wandering actors, playing in one town after the other an ever-changing repertory. The author he sees as a member of the troupe, always ready with a new text. Improvisation is for Giraudoux the essence of the theater, and he reminds us that Calderon and Tirso de Molina wrote hundreds of plays. As in *L'Impromptu de Paris,* his remarks here turn often to apophthegm: "La vie théâtrale n'existe que par la diversité. Le monde de l'inspiration doit être, lui aussi, comme le monde réel, chaque jour renaissant."[17] Giraudoux finishes by mentioning again his notion of the relationship between the play and its creator — how it detaches itself from the dramatic author to live a life of its own[18] — and then has a word on the role of "écho sonore" which the playwright takes in society and in his times.

For the 255th anniversary of Marivaux's birth, the Comédie Française commissioned Giraudoux to write a tribute to the eighteenth-century writer which would be read from the stage. The spiritual affiliation between Marivaux and Giraudoux, frequently observed, lends particular interest to this *hommage.* For indeed what Giraudoux says about Marivaux can be applied to himself: "Il avait cette honnêteté qui consiste à ne pas être importun, ennuyeux, à ne pas être mal tenu, à ne pas dévancer son âge . . . C'est un des hommes dont le passage dans la vie a causé le moins de trouble, d'équivoque, de mal." With a boldness typical of Giraudoux the critic, who above all likes to take an unconventional stand and defend it with dazzling verbal skill, he declares Marivaux's theater without artifice or artificiality:

> Qui a cherché l'imaginaire chez Marivaux? Ses scènes sont les scènes de ménage ou de fiançailles du seul monde vrai. Qui a vu la fausseté dans son style? Les paroles en sont neuves, subtiles, parce qu'elles affluent de la zone des silences, parce qu'elles sont la voix des deux sentiments qui jusqu'ici se sont tus, l'amour-propre et la pudeur, et elles sont nuancées, capricieuses, agiles, fleuries, parce que les héros s'approchent dans un goût de l'amour qu'ils n'ont pas trop de tous les secours du ramage et du langage pour aviver et contenir.[19]

Nowhere better than in this essay does Giraudoux display his special talent for introductions and prefaces. His humor and wit, his suave and polite fancy whet the appetite like *hors-d'œuvre.* To sustain a long study these qualities may seem insufficient, but for an article or a talk before a sophisticated audience they are unexcelled.

We need not, I think, concern ourselves over-much about possible inconsistencies. For example, we note that Giraudoux goes on from Marivaux to praise the eighteenth-century concept of love. He finds it great, even perhaps the most perfect, because love is regarded as neither slave nor magician but as a normal daily companion. Elsewhere, we remember, he has said harsh words about this century on the basis of its cult of reason and its rejection of poetry.[20] Yet the concept of love he admires is surely a product of the general attitude of which he disapproves. Repeatedly Giraudoux professed adherence to the most extreme sort of Romanticism. Yet his essays on Racine, Laclos, and Marivaux show that he could and did admire writers in quite different traditions. The problem is discussed by R.-M. Albérès, who suggests that Giraudoux may have worked out an ingenious formula to reconcile his taste and his principles.[21] One cannot be sure that the matter ever occurred to him, however; and if charged with inconsistency, Giraudoux would doubtless have replied that his enthusiasm for Romantic principles and his deprecation of the limitations imposed by the eighteenth-century rationalistic tradition in general did not preclude his admiration for individual geniuses, whatever spirit animated them. In this connection, a remark Giraudoux made during the course of an interview should be cited: "XVIIIe siècle — période d'amaigrissement du langage, mais encore, malgré tout, période de merveilleux langage . . ."[22]

Now that we have reached the end of our survey of Giraudoux's critical writings, we may pause to try to articulate a general estimation of this aspect of his work. First, some basic reflections on the problem of authors turned critics. It has become fashionable in some circles to place the criticism by creative writers higher than that of those who make it their main business to analyze works of literature. Baudelaire, we have read, is the greatest French critic of the nineteenth century. The observations of Proust and Gide on other writers are praised to the skies. And yet, lest we risk being absurdly excessive, we must remember that what great writers have to say about other writers and writing in general is enhanced, in the reader's eyes, by their reputation earned on quite other grounds, and to place their random or incidental remarks above the careful and methodical analysis of a professional critic may not be a cool, objective judgment. Moreover, the creative writer and the professional critic usually approach a work of art in such a dissimilar fashion that any qualitative comparison seems inappropriate. Jean Giraudoux, as a critic, exhibits the same qualities and limitations as his great senior, Proust, or any other creative genius who, from time to time, expresses his views on a literary subject. The richness of Giraudoux's criticism lies in its novel insights and its engaging presentation; its insufficiencies, in its subjectivity and incomprehensive character. Needless to say, he is weak where the literary historian is strong, and vice versa.

Most of Giraudoux's criticism is written "for the occasion." It comprises a good number of prefaces, addresses, and the like. With a given subject to write on, Giraudoux has only to develop his first intuitive flash — Gérard de Nerval, the symbol of a writer whose life is greater than his works; Laclos, the exposer of the eighteenth century; La Fontaine, the poet who overcame five temptations. The thesis is brilliantly stated and developed with all the power of poetic fancy. But the finished article may have told us nothing really accurate in a factual sense about Nerval, Laclos, La Fontaine, or their works.

In Giraudoux's theoretic writing, his originality and importance lie almost wholly in his expression. Many times he spoke on the theater — how brilliantly one can judge from the samples we have perused. The appeal of his lectures is how, rather than what, he says. Consider two of the points he belabors: one, the supreme importance of style (he himself is his best illustration); another, the inadequacy of realism on the stage. Neither assertion is very novel, yet the formulas Giraudoux invents to express them are without equal.

Alexandre Arnoux has composed the following laudatory description of Giraudoux as an essayist:

> Lecture et observation infatigables; regard toujours en alerte, enregistrant; oreille tendue; vocabulaire innombrable d'allusions et de traits; répertoire de détails et l'art de les fondre, de les estomper dans l'ensemble, de les marier et de les tresser avec une négligence savante et innée; génie de la broderie verbale, et non pas gratuite, mais soumise à une loi stricte en dépit de sa profusion, subordonnée à une armature ferme, intérieure, linéaire, qui en commande le foisonnement; maîtrise du thème, et toujours grand, que la variation ne dissout pas; perpétuelle invention de rapports qui étonnent d'abord, que l'on trouve bientôt évidents, dont la nouveauté, le saugrenu parfois, ne masquent pas longtemps la logique aventurée, la justesse; vérités qui enchantent d'autant plus qu'elles débouchent de sentiers inattendus, qu'elles sourdent de puits non forés encore, et non pas sans voiles, ces vérités, mais parées, qu'il faut les dévêtir pour voir enfin leur nudité pure; don de persuader sans recourir à l'éloquence, par une certaine magie travaillée, improvisée et impalpable.[23]

We should quarrel on a few points. Among writers, Giraudoux is not remarkable for his reading or his observation. In spite of numerous literary allusions — particularly in his early works — he was never a bookish author, and his critical studies suggest little or no documentation. They reveal, moreover, power of invention rather than indefatigable observation. What of composition? Fanciful development or variation on a theme is essentially what it amounts to. The "armature ferme, intérieure, linéaire" is rather rudimentary, and the "broderie" more than seldom is gratuitous. The rest of Arnoux's praise we subscribe to with less reservation. We would not deny that the particular qualities of a creative writer engaged in criticism show off to splendid advantage in the pieces Jean Giraudoux dedicated to literature.

Miscellaneous Essays

Besides criticism and literary commentary, Jean Giraudoux produced a considerable amount of writing on other subjects, which demonstrates equally well the qualities Arnoux ascribes to him as an essayist. Political essays and essays on urbanism constitute the most important part, but we shall consider first a miscellany of articles, prefaces, *plaquettes* devoted to other matters. If we give them more space than their importance merits, in relation to Giraudoux's great creative works, it is because they are not readily available in the text and frequently have not been described in other studies on Giraudoux. We need not, however, tarry over each and every one, for some in themselves offer little interest, and their existence has already been noted in my bibliography of Giraudoux's works.[24]

The author of *Siegfried* returned to Germany for a visit in May of 1930. *Rues et Visages de Berlin* (La Roseraie, 1930) records his impressions of the capital. If they are more favorable here than in *Siegfried et le Limousin,*[25] it is chiefly because Giraudoux finds the Germans far ahead of the French in sports and city planning. However, his treatment of modern Germany and her "ersatz civilization" remains, on the whole, strongly ironical.

Les Hommes Tigres (1926) may be attached loosely to the *Siegfried* cycle because it is in the novel that the subject of *hommes tigres* is first mentioned[26] and because the narrator's friendship with Dagot, whom he meets at a café every four years, seems like the relationship with Zelten. But the situation is here just a frame for a strange account of cannibalism in Africa. Dagot is a colonial administrator, and his official report on the matter constitutes the text. Mrs. Agnes Raymond, who gives considerable attention to this work in her dissertation, *La Pensée Politique de Jean Giraudoux,*[27] is convinced it is a *canular* invented by Giraudoux and friends to while away the time at the Quai d'Orsay. In her eyes, the piece is a disguised pamphlet against capitalism. Her contention is ingenious and elaborately presented, but remains without factual proof.

Le Sport (1928), a collection of maxims in praise of athletics, is a little monument erected by a writer who never forgot that he excelled in track as a youth. Occasionally, in the late 1920's and early 30's, an article on sports signed Jean Giraudoux appeared in the newspapers and magazines. Students of Giraudoux's style are interested to find them written in an easy, even racy, journalistic manner. Many appeared in the *Annales Politiques et Littéraires,* for which paper Giraudoux "covered" important athletic events. His contribution to the collective work, *Tableaux de Paris* (1927), was "Paris sportif." Never did he miss an opportunity to encourage his countrymen to take a more active interest in physical culture of all sorts. During the Occupation, at Vichy, he composed a short essay, *L'Art et le Sport* (Presses de Savoie, 1942), designed to commemorate an exhibition on this theme which was held at the City Hall. The text was reprinted in *Sans Pouvoirs.* At the end of his life, he took up his pen once more in praise of athletics to preface a collection of stories published by the *Fédération Française de Football.*[28]

A reminder of Giraudoux's fondness for bridge is his preface to Gaston de Bellefonds' *L'Essentiel du Bridge* (1934). He was pleased to do this for the man who had, years before, handed him a pass to attend German theaters.[29] Another preface (J. Reignup, *L'Esprit de Normale,* 1935) lets him speak in loving terms of his alma mater and define what distinguishes graduates of the rue d'Ulm: "serviteurs de l'esprit, c'est-à-dire les adversaires de la matière. Ils n'acceptent pas le poids du monde, ni sa contrainte physique en vertu d'une poche aérée qui leur permet de se mouvoir à l'aise dans cette vie sans espace — et qui est l'esprit." This preface reappears in *Littérature.*[30]

In the midst of the Occupation, Giraudoux addressed himself to the students of another great French school in his preface to *Portraits de la Renaissance* (1943), a volume that the Ecole des Sciences Politiques had printed exclusively for its students.[31] By invoking the splendors of the sixteenth century, that other period of stress and trouble, Giraudoux composed a message of hope for the recent war generation.

Giraudoux speaks on one of his favorite musicians in the preface to the French translation of Annette Kolb's book on Mozart (1938).

He speaks on artists in the "tombeau" to Vuillard,[32] his personal friend and portraitist; in the letter-preface to Marcel Valotaire's study of J.-E. Laboureur;[33] and in the catalogue for an exhibit of the works of Daragnès, another of his illustrators. We find here elaboration of Giraudoux's idea of the versatility required of an artist and the liberty he should be accorded. The last sentence of the following passage is particularly interesting as a comment on the spontaneity which Giraudoux always claimed for his art:

> Un peintre est comme un écrivain. Il doit l'être partout, et en tout. Celui qui n'exploite pas son talent comme une clef à résoudre tous les problèmes de lumière qui se posent à lui n'en est pas digne. Un peintre doit être un graveur, un graveur doit être un aquarelliste, un aquarelliste doit être un imprimeur. La recherche des thèmes, le cloisonnement des genres sont des attentats directs à tout art et à sa liberté, mais les mains seules savent rendre naturels ces passages. L'inspiration n'est pas dans la tête, elle est en elles, et sur ce point les peintres sont comme tous les autres et comme le Créateur lui-même, les plus illuminés ne créent que par tâtons.[34]

The *plaquette* entitled *Combat avec l'Image* (1941) is inspired by a painting by Fujita which represents the head of a woman asleep. Pierre Lestringuez tells how Giraudoux bought the picture in Vichy, during the war, when Giraudoux and his wife were living at the Hotel Trianon.[35] Giraudoux kept it in his hotel room, unframed, leaned against the wall, where it often caught his eye. The picture seemed to symbolize an attitude towards life which gave him comfort and pleasure: 'Un être humain ne peut vivre à l'aise dans une attitude, dans une vertu que s'il a près de lui un objet qui en soit le symbole même."[36] As the characters he created are simplified, reduced to an attitude towards life, so living at ease in an attitude seems to be for Giraudoux the perfect adjustment, the supreme good.

The supreme virtue and the supreme vice — Giraudoux's essays throw light on his position in basic ethical and philosophical matters. The vice which is most often spoken of in his works is pride. It is the vice of his Simon, his Judith, his Electre, and — one has reason to suspect — the vice that Giraudoux ascribed, not without indulgence, to himself. Significantly, his contribution to the book of essays entitled *Les Sept Péchés Capitaux* (1927) is the article on pride. Vanity and pride must not be confused, he warns. Pride is all we have left of original sin, the struggle against God. Beside it, the other deadly sins are insignificant. In pride, Giraudoux distinguishes two degrees: the desire to vanquish God and the desire to bring about one's own defeat. The proud man has only one arm against God, and that is scorn for God. He refuses to find life good and looks to death as a deliverance. For him:

> La mort est une propreté. Elle seule nous sépare vraiment des autres êtres, nous épargne d'être un pauvre bassin de vie communiquant avec les milliers d'autres, fait de nous un être étanche. Pour peu qu'on ait la chance d'être orphelin, quelle impression de merveilleux lavage, que de sentir, à quelques années au delà du présent, l'autre borne de sa vie. La mort est la seule originalité. La mort seule enlève à l'être cet aspect confection qu'ont les hommes qui ne croient pas mourir.[37]

The bitterness and blasphemy of these lines are unparalleled in Giraudoux's essays. As if a man on the verge of destroying himself, he adds reflectively, "Le monde est borné, est stupide. Il est plein d'enfants." By what we read here we can better define those ambivalent attitudes towards life that are dramatized in Giraudoux's creative writing. The wisdom of accepting the human condition or the intoxicating glory of standing apart — each of his books reopens the question. But now let us return to essays in a lighter vein.

We have noticed what seem to be subjects of predilection — sports, bridge, music, and art. Most of Giraudoux's miscellaneous essays are tributes, large or small, to his various hobbies and enthusiasms. Although Jean-Pierre Giraudoux has declared that his father was not an animal lover, at least not in the usual sense of the word, his attachment to his brown poodle, Puck, is a well-known fact, and some of the most delightful pages he ever wrote were on the subject of animals. One remembers the charming animal that Giraudoux invents in the last lines of *Simon le Pathétique:*

> O amis, si l'on permet jamais aux hommes de se créer un nouvel animal, un nouveau compagnon, au pelage noir le jour et blanc la nuit, qui sourira, qui pleurera, — ne trouvez-vous pas qu'il manque? — et pas infécond, comme tous ceux qu'ils ont formés jusqu'ici, hippogriffes ou licornes, et tel que parfois vous l'imaginez sûrement, dans une île ronde d'Océanie, au bord du lac intérieur où cuit au bain-marie une eau douce délicieuse, veillant sa petite femelle endormie et pensant aux hommes d'Europe . . . un animal qui vous parle, qui chante . . . — qu l'on me charge de la tâche![38]

He once lectured to the *Société Nationale d'Acclimatation* on the subject: "Les animaux rapellent à l'homme d'aujourd'hui la vie naturelle."[39] His greatest tribute to animals, however, may be found in the text he composed to introduce a book of fine photographs. He contends that for the first time in history, animals today are allowed to be themselves! In this essay, reprinted in *Littérature,* Giraudoux is at his fanciful best. Listen to his concluding sentence:

> Pour moi, terriblement verrouillé dans mon compartiment de mammifère non volant, dénué à un point incroyable de la faculté de pondre des œufs et de dissimuler des piquants dans ma fourrure ou des dents dans mon bec, je n'ai guère qu'un titre à faire précéder de l'écriture humaine le nouveau visage des bêtes: je n'ai jamais humilié un animal devant ses petits.[40]

As we noted, many of Giraudoux's miscellaneous essays are difficult to find. Some are buried in collected works of a very limited edition. Such is the case for *L'Ambassadeur* (1931) and *Le Diable à Paris* (1938), which cannot be tracked down. One may find, however, the rare *D'Ariane à Zoé* (1930) at the Bibliothèque Nationale. It consists of a gallery of feminine portraits, young women whose names take us through the alphabet. The second one, "Barbe," is by Giraudoux. Doubtless there are more bits of writing which we do not know about. In *Marianne,* the newspaper for which Giraudoux was doing various *reportages* in the early 1930's, we might discover other pieces like the *Jouets* we find on the front page of the 1932 Christmas issue. The article, flanking a picture of children playing with toys as parents think they should, and another showing what children actually prefer to play with, is a precious little spinning on a theme. The following August, one could read in *Marianne* a very witty report on France's great spa, Vichy.

It is regrettable that the miscellany of writings which we have reviewed here is not more easily available. They are *hors-d'œuvre,* to be sure, but delight by their exquisite expression; and some, such as the article on pride, possess a significance in relation to Giraudoux's thought that far exceeds their modest *cadre* of circumstantial essay. The implications of "L'Orgueil" and *Combat avec l'Image* reveal a seriousness that the public was very slow to recognize in this author. Perhaps here, as we turn to the political essays, is where we should look a bit closely at this long-persisting misconception of Giraudoux's fundamental nature.

Political Writings Prior to World War II

How many critics have considered Giraudoux beneath their serious consideration! His frivolity in treating even the gravest of themes explains the attitude of many of the earlier critics. One does not discuss the law of gravity with a juggler. Moreover, his reiterated statements regarding the importance of style disposed critics to ignore his claim of lofty intention. One cannot take seriously a writer who declares that how one says something is more important than what one says.[41] The stand taken by the later critics of the postwar "engaged" period, like Sartre, was a matter of principle — they could not take seriously a writer who refused to come to grips with the problems of the day, who refused to sweat and groan through his prose like a wrestler on the mat. From principle, too, they could not approve of a writer who proclaimed the primary importance of style.

Most of Giraudoux's partisans feel no compunctions about defending him in a position that he is far from the first to take in the arts,[42] but there have been those who, not willing to take him at his word, find all sorts of concealed "engagement" in his work. We think they are wrong. In spite of a certain joy in mystification, Giraudoux never buried his views very deeply, never wrote his plays and novels as prudent vehicles to convey dangerous political ideas to a happy few, all the while laughing in his sleeve that the vulgar saw in them only plays and novels.[43] To suggest he did so seems patently absurd. Yet no more absurd than to conclude from Giraudoux's views on the primary importance of language and style that he can be dismissed as a mountebank.

This said, let us try to elucidate the problem of Giraudoux's "participation" by isolating some of the elements which, in most discussions of the subject, tend to become confused. In the first place, no one will contest the seriousness of the themes which inspire Giraudoux's creative writing in general. What has often been criticized is rather the frivolity of his treatment of them, the frivolity of his manner. We shall not debate this question here, for it would take us too far afield into Giraudoux's philosophy and esthetic. Suffice it to observe that treatment and subject matter are two different things, and on the basis of theme, no writer has dealt with more fundamental problems than Jean Giraudoux. Furthermore, in defining the writer's mission in terms of language and style, he is in no wise diminishing the importance of his role. To the writer is entrusted the heavy charge of articulating an attitude towards the fundamental problems, the serious work of offering in an art form a mirror of basic human situations. There can be no question that Giraudoux meant what he said when he declared to Frédéric Lefèvre, "J'ai même . . . des intentions morales."[44]

But it is only in this sense that Giraudoux's creative writing can be said to be "engaged." Dedicated to eternal problems, it avoids, on principle, "burning questions." One thinks of Giraudoux's own phrase by which he describes the tendencies of French literature as a whole: "sujets théoriques fixés à l'avance depuis des siècles, et retirés de l'humanité contemporaine."[45] The topical, the specific — no matter how important — have a place in his main writing only incidental to the general and the everlasting. Thus even *Siegfried et le Limousin*, described by its author as a pamphlet,[46] broadens out into a symphonic poem on the French and German soul; *Bella*, inspired by a political quarrel, broadens out into a contrapuntal depiction of two types of statesmen, two concepts of life. *La Folle de Chaillot* is only very incidentally an indictment of capitalism. It is rather an indictment of materialism and — even more than that — a hymn to a life of generosity and lovely make-believe.

Proponents of "engaged" literature could reproach Giraudoux for not writing his novels and plays as propaganda. Here it is his concept of literature that is up for debate. But they could not say that Giraudoux remained entirely aloof from "burning questions." He merely chose to deal with them in the essay or on the lecture platform. Besides Giraudoux the creative writer, there was Giraudoux the diplomat, the citizen, the Frenchman, who spoke out emphatically on a variety of topical subjects throughout his entire career. One may disapprove of his stand on many issues, but no one can contend he never took a stand. In summary, to criticize Giraudoux in the matter of his "participation" one should make clear exactly what is being criticized: his treatment of theme, his concept of art, or his political views. Lumping them all together confuses the question exasperatingly.

Today, when "engagement" is a much less vital issue, critics are apt to see more clearly. Yet one may wonder if their focus is even now quite exact. The notion that Giraudoux turned to matters mundane and immediate only towards the end of his career, for example, seems to persist. Those who recognize that the bulk of Giraudoux's work is dedicated to the contemplation of man and the universe see here the last stage, so to speak, of a spiritual evolution. This is an oversimplification if not a misinterpretation of the facts, for there does not appear to be any point in Giraudoux's career that marks a break or a radical change in orientation. True, essays of "participation" multiply in the late 1930's and in the 40's, but there are external reasons to explain their profusion — Giraudoux's reputation and prestige which would make him now more outspoken and would make his opinion more sought after by reporters and editors; his habit of holding essays written over the years to publish them in a collection; the critical times; and his duties with the government. The necessity of taking into account such factors makes us wary of defining a stage of spiritual development. Did he ever stop contemplating man and the universe? It was during the war that he wrote the "inactuel" *Apollon de Bellac. Sodome et Gomorrhe* was playing when he died. *La Folle de Chaillot* and *Pour Lucrèce* were in his posthumous papers. And do not his topical writings stretch back over many years of his career?

The first is probably the article he wrote on the Franco-German conflict at Harvard (1912),[47] which shows that while a fledgling author, composing the precious portraits of "Indifférents" and the rollicking travesty of Homer called *Elpénor,* Giraudoux could wield a pen like a rapier and was already the master of ironical thrust that he would be in later writing of a polemical nature. He began haranguing his countrymen on the subject of athletics at the same time *Suzanne et le Pacifique* was appearing (1920). In "L'Olympiade de 1924" we read: "Il s'agit de donner aux Français le goût des sports, du grand air, de les pousser du café ou de la salle d'étude vers les terrains de sport, avec le but d'améliorer la race."[48] He inaugurated his campaign for urbanism the year following his debut in the theater.[49] In 1932 he discussed his interest in civic matters with a reporter from *Le Jour.*[50] By 1933 and 1934 his voice was loudly heard. Editorials for *Marianne* and *Le Figaro* protest against what he considers civic disfigurement. "Place Saint-Sulpice"[51] protests against a project to put a grass plot before the church. "Promenade de printemps"[52] attacks the ugliness of highways and the foolish building projects which sully Paris. "Fêtes et expositions"[53] deplores the government's lack of imagination in such matters. The plight of the elementary teacher is the subject of "Institut et instituteurs"[54] and the inadequate techniques of French propaganda abroad are denounced in "La Propagande."[55] Persons surprised at Giraudoux's nomination as head of

Information in 1939 apparently did not know of his long experience, dating back to his post-World War I assignment at the Quai d'Orsay.[56] Towards the end of 1934 he elaborated his views on many civic subjects in the series of lectures he presented under the title of *La Femme française.*

In three lectures that would not be published until 1951,[57] Giraudoux took up the subject of the Frenchwoman at home and in the world. We observe him to be a moderate feminist as he traces the Frenchwoman's gradual emancipation and foresees the franchise for her. Yet he notes with sly facetiousness that the progressive woman in America has abused her gains. Claiming all the rights of the strong, she relinquishes none of the rights of the weak. It must be said that in these lectures, the ladies present in the audience did not hear so much a description of themselves as an appeal to support the reforms Giraudoux wished to see carried out in French society. His opening speech indicts the government for excluding writers from any active function in the state. Then he passes to another complaint which he will return to many times — that is, the discrepancy between what France stands for and what the behavior of present-day Frenchmen is actually like. The subject of urbanism is touched upon, and, in describing the excellent publicity Germans give themselves abroad compared to the creaky machinery of the French, he alludes to another favorite topic — propaganda. In sum, several of the civic themes that are near and dear to Jean Giraudoux are taken up in these addresses at the *Université des Annales* under the title *La Femme française.*

As to form, these lectures deserve study as models of rhetoric. In elegant, graceful language Giraudoux balances his parallels and his paradoxes, formulates his conceits and exquisite definitions, just as he does in his literary criticism. Hear him define French culture:

> La civilisation française, comme la grecque, à un degré plastique égal et dans un élan moral décuplé, réside en ceci qu'elle a trouvé la raison de l'homme dans l'homme. Cela ne veut pas dire qu'elle attribue à l'homme la responsabilité et les mérites de son existence et l'existence du monde; au contraire, c'est une conception modeste, sensible et en même temps pleine de réserve, vis-à-vis des êtres géants ou des êtres minuscules auxquels cette civilisation reconnaît pleinement le droit d'exister.
>
> Elle n'est pas une formule métaphysique qui consiste à faire de l'homme un dieu et lui conseille une vie d'ambition et d'effort.

Elle n'est pas une formule matérialiste qui consiste à faire de l'homme un néant et lui dicte une vie de renoncement. A mi-chemin de ces deux extrêmes, tout en réservant tous les droits d'un être supérieur ou d'un chaos fondamental, de la religion ou de la philosophie, elle a, par la dignité et par la variété de ses distractions morales, l'agrément de ses loisirs, la conscience apportée à ses occupations manuelles, trouvé le rapport exact de l'homme par rapport à la planète.[58]

The years between 1935 and 1939, at first sight, seem barren of writings with political intent. His next course of lectures at the *Annales* was on La Fontaine. But the reason for his choice of subject was not purely literary. This is what he says:

L'un de vous . . . s'étonne que, dans un après-midi consacré aux problèmes modernes, et alors que moi-même, les précédentes années, j'avais délibérément orienté mes auditeurs vers l'urbanisme, le vote des femmes, ou l'hygiène sociale, je les dirige tout d'un coup vers celui qui semble être le plus inactuel des poètes . . . Je réponds à ce censeur inconnu qu'il se trompe. A la réflexion, il me semble que c'est un souci d'actualité, plus profond peut-être encore que les autres, qui m'a inconsciemment mené cette année à La Fontaine.[59]

He proceeds to argue that solutions to national problems can be found only in a deeper recognition of national genius, in self-knowledge. He will say something of the same thing again to introduce the collection of his literary essays in 1941.[60] In a very broad sense, his portraits of writers are political essays.

In 1939, when Giraudoux went before the *Université des Annales* for the last time, there is no doubt about the nature of his subject:

Nous ne sommes plus dans une époque où l'orateur ou l'écrivain ait le loisir de choisir ses sujets. Ce sont les sujets, aujourd'hui, qui le choisissent. Ou plutôt le sujet, car il n'en est qu'un. Nous en sommes revenus à l'âge de pierre du sujet: la conservation de la vie, pour notre pays et pour nous.

This is his introduction to the lessons that will make up *Pleins Pouvoirs,*[61] Giraudoux's masterpiece of political writing. Paul Claudel describes it in these terms: "l'un des jugements les plus raisonnables et les mieux justifiés qui aient été portés par un expert sur les tares d'un régime qui s'abandonne, il serait plus exact de dire: qui s'avachit. C'est un document d'un intérêt capital et durable."[62] Mr. Gunnar

Høst, the author of the first major study of Giraudoux, declared it worthy to take a place near the *Dûne Royale* of Vauban, Fénelon's letters to Louis XIV, Turgot's to Louis XVI.[63] With severity tempered by tenderness, Giraudoux denounces the sins of his countrymen and enumerates the tasks before them — preservation of the race and increase in population, modernization of French living habits and conditions, plans for public works, strengthening of the nation's moral fiber. Although written when no one could foresee the extent of the debacle to come, today it seems dramatically prophetic, and in the period since the end of the war it has lost none of its pertinency.

As we have already pointed out in approaching the subject, when Giraudoux was moved to express his opinions on specifically political matters, he took to the forthright essay or to the lecture platform and reserved his plays and novels for more universal or more personal reflections. The difference between essay and creative work is, aside from the obvious difference in genre, chiefly one of subject matter. The human values and ideals set forth in Giraudoux's political essays we recognize as those which inspired him always — wholesomeness, harmony, dignity, and measure. R.-M. Albérès characterizes his social and political essays as only "une application pratique de sa pensée à des problèmes plus précis et plus concrets."[64] We recognize in them, too, the same magician of the word, conveying his message in terms ablaze with imagery and the most brilliant gems of rhetoric.

In considering the little esteem felt in some quarters for Giraudoux as a political and social thinker, we must take into account that this very beauty and originality of expression have worked against him. In the minds of many, honest and useful ideas can be set forth only in plain talk. And that is probably the most serious criticism. Giraudoux remained a poet — and a rhetorician — whatever his subject: he saw social and political problems in terms of antithesis, parallel, allegory. The validity of his argument is on the level of abstraction and poetical generalization, high over the head of the average politician, who could regard Giraudoux only as a dreamer and inventor of clever phrases. Even some critics without strong hostility believe that Giraudoux can be consulted only on the "plan de l'éternité":

> On peut faire sur Giraudoux toutes sortes de réserves, surtout au point de vue de ses idées politiques et de son activité diplomatique qui s'est insérée et dévelopée tout entière dans l'idéologie brian-

diste dont son chef Philippe Berthelot n'était que l'exécutant; idéologie généreuse sans doute, mais inopportune à l'époque. C'est qu'à aucun moment Giraudoux n'a été ou ne sera "actuel"; c'est seulement sur le plan de l'éternité qu'il faut le consulter.[65]

Perhaps this is true. Once at Bernard Grasset's, while he was doing the *service de presse* of his latest book, a group of young authors were vehemently asserting that a writer must "prendre parti." Giraudoux remarked that, although he was not at all indifferent to questions of the day, he preferred to "prendre position" instead of "prendre parti."[66] When war was declared and Giraudoux was mobilized — given a pen as a soldier is given a gun, for the specific purpose of defending his country — he changed nothing of his attitude or technique in his writing. His propaganda messages, ridiculed and denounced by some critics, passed over quickly as if a subject of embarrassment by others, still await publication in full and objective evaluation. We shall limit ourselves here to the task of defining their nature and scope. But let us pause first to assemble a general picture of our author on the eve of World War II.

In 1939 Giraudoux was undoubtedly at the height of his career. As a dramatist, his prestige was equaled by none. Working in close collaboration with Louis Jouvet, he had, for over a decade, made box-office triumphs of plays that were considered too intellectual, too poetic, for the general public. At the success of *Siegfried,* critics had declared their astonishment to see people flocking to a play that was over their heads.[67] In the years that followed, the team Giraudoux-Jouvet made this miracle a commonplace. At the rehearsals of each play, Giraudoux would take his seat next to Jouvet and listen:

> Détaché en apparence, et tendu à la fois, dès qu'un comédien commençait à répéter sur scène, une sorte d'effort respiratoire l'étreignait . . . Les bras croisés, presque souriant sans que son visage s'altérât sensiblement, sa respiration suivait le texte dans un rythme égal ou contraire, aisé ou malaisé, dans une cadence juste ou boitante par rapport à la diction des comédiens, et moi je surveillais cette respiration qui s'ajustait à la longueur d'onde de la phrase et son amplitude, égale ou dissemblable de celle des comédiens . . . Tout son être . . . se modelait physiquement sur le texte, avec plaisir ou contrainte suivant le moment.[68]

In 1939 Giraudoux was listening to the love duets of Hans and Ondine in the play he had made out of La Motte Fouqué's romantic tale. *Ondine* was the theatrical event of the year. As the text of the play appeared in the bookstores, it was joined by *Choix des Elues,* reminding the public that Giraudoux had been a prize-winning novelist before he had turned to the stage. This last novel was by far his greatest, the flower of his full maturity. During the summer, after the lectures at *Annales, Pleins Pouvoirs* appeared in volume form, the *summa* of his social and political thinking to date. In all three phases of his literary work, 1939 is a year of fulfillment.

Since 1934, when he was named inspector-general of Diplomatic and Consular Posts, Giraudoux's professional career had become increasingly important. Each year his duties took him abroad. In 1935 he went to the Near East, Iraq, and Palestine, then to Poland and the Balkan states. In 1936 he was in the Antilles, the United States, and Canada. Between 1937 and 1938 he made a great tour of the South Pacific posts. In 1939 he was back in the United States, taking time to visit friends in California and the Alfred Lunts on their Wisconsin farm. Upon his return from his numerous junkets, newspapermen eager for interviews flocked to his residence at number 89, quai d'Orsay, the apartment for which the Giraudoux had forsaken the rue du Pré-aux-Clercs. The reporters would wait in the spacious, rather cold-looking drawing room, which from its sixth-story windows offered a panorama of Paris from the quays to Sacré-Cœur. The study adjoining, into which they were eventually ushered, was cosier because it was smaller, but it, too, was a severe room. Giraudoux received them behind a broad, uncluttered table:

> Un homme grand, mince, élégant. Son complet de drap anglais clair lui donnait une allure sportive et jeune, ses cheveux étaient coupés si court que je les supposai d'abord blonds, et il me fallut faire effort pour remarquer les cheveux presque blancs, le teint rouge, la peau ridée.

The famous Giraudoux smile kindled the pale eyes behind glasses à la Chardin — the smile of a man who preferred not to argue, who, behind a barrier of charm and politeness, could keep his own opinion and remain unmolested — a smile, in short, that bespoke as much reserve as did the room. Claude Leroux, to whom we owe the picture of Giraudoux quoted above, remarks that "sa table de travail était nue, les livres de sa bibliothèque étaient neutres. Son point d'honneur était de ne pas être diviné et ses gestes, ses sourires étaient comme des concessions polies à l'idée qu'on pouvait faire de lui."[69] In the portrait that Leroux gives us here we can see a sort of culmination of all the earlier Giraudoux — the scholarship student, the young-man-about-town, the dashing officer, the diplomat of promise — each representing a stage along the way to the goal of elegance, reserve, and urbanity that Giraudoux had fully attained by 1939.

The War Years: Messages from the Continental and Giraudoux's Final Words to his Countrymen

Returning from the United States in July of 1939, after a short stay in Paris, Giraudoux was off to Vittel for a vacation. Puck, his adored poodle, of course went along. For several summer weeks he pretended to forget the war clouds threatening, as he rested in the sun and chatted with his old friends Charles de Polignac and Edmond Jaloux. He told them whimsical stories about his travels, such as the one of the seal in Australia that guided ships safely into port through dangerous reefs.[70] But soon after mid-August, a summons from Daladier put an end to the holiday. At the Hotel Matignon he received instructions to form a division of Information. André Morize tells us that Giraudoux received this appointment, made on the basis of *Pleins Pouvoirs,* with the utmost pleasure.[71] It gratified his long ambition to take an active role in civic matters, and he took up his duties with his head filled with great plans. Then on August 26, general mobilization was called. Giraudoux had been working for only three days when his office was put on a wartime footing. His orders henceforth came from the War Department, his services were only "attached" to Information. He exercised no control over censorship, the press, cinema, or the radio.[72] His situation now was not the one for which he had longed.[73]

The Hotel Continental, where for eight months Jean Giraudoux was, nominally at least, at the head of Information, symbolizes the tragic administrative bungling and public irresponsibility that preceded the collapse of France. From the description we have, it partook of the madhouse and the native bazaar, with countless bureaucrats tripping over themselves and a motley throng of visitors bent on gaining special favors or hobnobbing with important personalities:

> C'était un curieux spectacle que celui de ces bureaux éparpillés dans les chambres, les cabinets de toilette et les salles de bains ou dans de vastes salons rouges cantonnés de plantes vertes. Plus curieux encore le spectacle des gens qu'on y apercevait: politiciens, écrivains, artistes, hommes du monde. La personalité de Giraudoux attirait tous ces quémandeurs, déguisés en informateurs. On pensait au mot de Bernstein mobilisé à Chantilly en 1915 et disant à Edouard Bourdet, qui partait pour le front: "Comment? Vous allez dans les tranchées? Vous n'y rencontrerez personne." Tout le monde, à cette guerre-ci, était au Continental.[74]

Giraudoux had arrived there one September morning, on foot, without brief case or newspapers, accompanied only by Puck. He walked into an impossible job. Hostility and stupidity on the part of the majority of the functionaries assigned to the department, distrust and reluctance to cooperate on the part of the War Office and other government divisions. His reputation as a writer and a *mondain* was against him. People misinterpreted his unorthodox manner — if they saw him writing two speeches at once, they said he was criminally casual; if they saw him sneaking out the back way to avoid the crowd, they said he avoided his responsibilities. His quips and retorts, too, seemed proof of alarming levity. Soon he found himself gradually edged out of his position. The bureaucracy took over, and Giraudoux was alone with his entourage — Morize, Hazard, Joxe, Julien Cain, René Laporte, de Tarde and Guinle — all men, like Giraudoux, of a caliber to have accomplished great things. But little or nothing came of their efforts, and the bright expectations that Giraudoux had entertained when he was named to the post were most dismally deceived:

> Bien que l'on ne puisse prétendre affirmer que Giraudoux eût des qualités de chef ou d'organisateur, on ne peut, dans ces conditions, le rendre responsable de la gabegie du Continental. Il eût fallu un génie herculéen pour secouer, en quelques mois, l'encroûtement administratif, la force d'inertie qui s'opposaient partout à l'effort des bonnes volontés.[75]

The literary side of the fiasco of the Continental is represented by the radio speeches that Giraudoux made while there. They have been collected in a volume with the title *Messages du Continental;* but, although the page proofs were set up, the book has never appeared. The speeches are all bits of literary embroidery on the theme of Germany and France. Harking back to *Siegfried et le Limousin,* Giraudoux reiterates his condemnation of modern Germany (now Nazi Germany) and opposes to it a France of solid virtue. It is as unfair as it is pointless to judge these addresses except for what they were and had to be. But one may question how effective as morale-builder for the average person Giraudoux's literary fancywork could have been. For example, his talk *Le Futur Armistice,* dealing with the subject of luck, ends with the prediction that the Germans will be beaten because they do not believe in their luck. Someone reported Dr. Goebbels to have said that Giraudoux was the only Frenchman he feared. Such a statement could scarcely have been made on the basis of this sort of speech, as little apt to frighten the Germans as to hearten the French. However inept as propaganda, this speech does afford an indication of Giraudoux's fanciful notion of the universal order, interesting for the light it sheds on his plays and novels. Here is an extract:

> Mais il est un allié sans lequel nous ne réussirons pas, sans lequel échouent les meilleurs plans, les meilleurs chefs, et c'est la chance. Il nous faut cette complaisance des événements, cet ajustement des contraires, ce vent en poupe, cette souplesse du destin qui est la chance, et nul peuple ne peut l'avoir que s'il se fie à cette chance générale, cette chance des grandes causes, des grands moments, qui s'appelle la Providence.[76]

The radio speeches have been the butt of much mockery, witness the venemous remarks of Roger Peyrefitte:

> Du moins, le jour de la rentrée scolaire, les élèves de nos écoles eurent la consolation d'apprendre, par un message de Giraudoux, que les écoliers allemands étaient, à la même heure, tout sales, n'avaient pas de savon pour se laver. Puis, les écoliers allemands étaient près de mourir de faim, parce que l'Allemagne n'avait de vivres que pour deux mois. Puis, les écoliers allemands étaient près de mourir de froid, parce que les mineurs faisaient la résistance passive.
>
> Qu'un écrivain dont la France faisait gloire, débitât de telles insanités à la face du monde, était assez inquiétant. Ou la gloire de cet écrivain était douteuse, ou la France, en gardant "l'arme au pied," comme disait Daladier, était devenue insensible à l'arme du ridicule. Le plus regrettable était de la voir maniée contre l'Allemagne par un homme qui avait semblé favorable à une entente franco-allemande.[77]

Even R.-M. Albérès, in his erudite work on Giraudoux, is only kind. Granting that the broadcasts were admirably written, he feels that Giraudoux was out of his element and that during this time he was generally *dérouté*.

> Elles constituent une exploitation littéraire de la situation en 1939-40, mais ne l'éclairent pas. On peut dire que devant le problème de propagande qui lui est posé, Giraudoux ne le domine pas et ne se retrouve pas lui-même non plus.[78]

Giraudoux left his post when Reynaud came into power and presumably returned to the Quai d'Orsay, since we hear of him next in Bordeaux with the Ministry of Foreign Affairs.[79]

It is doubtless there that he composed the *Armistice à Bordeaux*, not published until 1945 but written just before the event of June 21, 1940. This address atones for some of his previous speeches and demonstrates his oratorical power at its finest. After evoking in moving fashion the distress of France, her immortal glories, Giraudoux proceeds to give quite practical advice to effect her regeneration. He does not preach repentance to his countrymen, the official exhortation of Vichy. Quite rightly he reminds the conquered nation not to confuse the judgment of sabers with the Last Judgment.[80] But he defends capitulation and reproves the outside world for urging France to resist to the death:

> L'univers, lui, voyait ailleurs ce salut. Il eut aimé qu'elle se sauvât par l'anéantissement . . . à cause de la haute idée qu'il avait d'elle, à cause aussi de cette certitude que lui serait capable, la France disparue, de la recréer par ses hommages, sa foi, par une étreinte avec le siècle souffrant et héroïque si puissante qu'une France en fût née, bébé nouveau. Toute une France qui résistait et succombait, à Lausanne, à Boston, à Bogota, surgissait depuis le 10 mai autour de la France qui cédait et vivait. Pour celle-là, la meilleure façon de conserver au monde ses villes, ces cathédrales, c'était de les laisser détruire . . . Quelle erreur![81]

France, he insists, cannot live just as a symbol, a glory, but must have a face and a race. She must seek her destiny alone and not accept one imposed from without. The crime of the between-wars period was to mummify her into an abstraction for the world, to make of her an old idol, instead of letting her live and develop independently. In bitter defeat she may be able to come back to life: "alors que la vie va nous être assurée par cette réalité à son comble: la défaite et l'humiliation." We may disagree with Giraudoux's argument, find him even in disagreement with previous assertions, find him rhetorical rather than sound. But let us not forget the circumstances: Giraudoux is not urging a people to capitulate; he is consoling a people for having capitulated, and only in this sense can his words be judged. He closes on a personal note, in the fashion of a testament to his son and of a challenge to him and to his generation.[82]

For Giraudoux the sorrow over his country's disaster was mingled with the personal anxiety over the fate of his son. Some recently published documents offer moving testimony. Jean-Pierre Giraudoux had deserted on June 19, 1940, made his way across Spain and Portugal, then reached London to offer his services to de Gaulle. Not knowing that he had already left, Giraudoux and his wife motored to Portugal to try to find him. While there, Giraudoux jotted down some impressions, just as he had once before when, during World War I, he had gone with a French mission to Lisbon. Again he feels the marvel of being in a little country at peace, while all around it there is war. But, although the inspiration is the same, the notes of the minister plenipotentiary of a nation in humiliation and of the father searching for his son contrast pathetically with those of the carefree young officer that Giraudoux had been some twenty years before. The poet's fancy, customarily at the service of the highest of spirits, now translates only grief and wistful complaint. Before Giraudoux's eyes rise visions of his son's trudging through Portugal, without money and in clothes grotesquely and painfully ill-fitting. He follows his trail, still marked by abandoned cars, abandoned persons — signs of the tragic exodus.

Giraudoux's Portuguese diary closes on the "Miracle de Viseu," a text which we recognize as one of the gardener's soliloquies in *Visitations,* now turned into a sort of little *Märchen.* At midnight in the moonlight, Giraudoux listens to a giant begonia tell him that the reason there are wars is that "les hommes n'ont jamais trouvé l'attitude humaine."[83] For the begonia, the only proper attitude is immobility and isolation: there will be no more wars for human beings "quand ils consentiront à être plantés, non mobiles, à être chacun planté à distance où ils ne s'atteignent ni par le goût ni par le toucher . . ."[84] The antithesis movement versus immobility, a favorite with Giraudoux, is particularly developed in *Pleins Pouvoirs* and elsewhere when he contrasts the German and French nations. Although he shows a preference for immobility (the wisdom of France and of begonias) it would be excessive to treat this figure of speech as evidence of a serious *parti-pris*. We should interpret the begonia's counsel not as serious political philosophy but as a sardonic whimsy prompted by the discouragement of the moment. It is to be compared with the epigram of Pascal: "Tout le malheur des hommes vient de ne savoir pas se tenir en repos dans une chambre."[85]

In publishing these Portuguese manuscripts in 1958, Jean-Pierre Giraudoux preceded the text with several letters that he had received from his father. The first was written as Giraudoux was making ready to return to France:

> Lisbonne, 19 septembre 1940
>
> . . . Je ne sais comment je vais retrouver la France en rentrant. Je n'ai pas l'impression que les changements apportés au Ministère le rehaussent beaucoup. Notre mission est de résister de tout notre cœur puisqu'il n'a pas été permis de résister de toutes nos armes. Dans tout le pays, l'énergie croît, la conscience monte, et il importe que ceux qui peuvent aider à cette rénovation ne s'éloignent pas. Tu as de la chance d'être encore dans une nation qui se bat, mais chez nous le combat est à reprendre et tu n'y serais pas, non plus, inutile . . .[86]

Thus Giraudoux, who missed his son keenly, gently chided him for not remaining in France. In the same spirit he wrote the following April a touching letter that begins: . . . "Tu ne saurais croire combien tu manques à tous et surtout à moi."[87] He tells him that he is putting the account of his journey to Portugal in form and that he is collecting his critical articles. He mentions, furthermore, that he is thinking of a novel and that he has taken up again his play on civil war.[88] Another letter, dated September 17, 1941, speaks of working on the urbanism essays, but that without the presence of Jean-Pierre all writing is extremely difficult.

We presume that these letters were sent either from Vichy or from Cusset. Giraudoux had joined the government at Vichy and, after refusing the post of minister to Athens, had served for a brief moment as director of historical monuments. But most of the time during the two years following the Armistice he remained in retirement in Cusset, occupying himself with his writing. His only major excursion was to

Lausanne to deliver the *Visitations* lectures, but apparently there were trips also to Paris, where he stopped at the Hotel de Castille, in the rue Cambon.

By the beginning of 1943 Giraudoux seems to have taken up permanent residence at this hotel and to have begun some clandestine activity:

> Et c'est dans une chambre d'hôtel de la rue Cambon, dès le début de l'année 1943, qu'il accepta tous les risques de la campagne clandestine contre l'invahisseur, qu'il s'exposa journellement à être abattu en plein travail. Cette petite pièce d'étudiant aisé, mais économe, devint rapidement le centre d'une organisation qu'il avait conçue dans son ensemble, une manière de tribunal, une bibliothèque de pièces à conviction.[89]

What Giraudoux's *resistance* amounted to seems to be three undertakings: a compilation of German war crimes together with their documentation, a sort of manual of practical propaganda (a little volume designed for officials abroad who might need facts and figures in handy form), and *Sans Pouvoirs.* In his heatless room Giraudoux stayed in bed, wearing a big gray sweater over his pajamas and writing on a board. Friends supplied him with the data he needed, according to Jean Blanzat and André Beucler, who visited him regularly.[90] Nothing of the first two projects has since come to light. What exists seems all to fit in the outline for *Sans Pouvoirs,* parts of which appeared here and there before the volume was brought out. *Ecrit dans l'Ombre* (1944), for example, is a compilation made by the publishers from several texts. Giraudoux himself had submitted the first one in the fall of 1943, asking that it appear anonymously on account of his connection with the government. His sudden death made this concealment unnecessary. Mme. Giraudoux authorized the publishers to go ahead with the work and sent them another version of the first text which had been arranged as a message to deportees. The publishers preferred to print the original, however, and added the fragment entitled *Avenir de la France.*

Sans Pouvoirs appeared eventually in 1946, Giraudoux's complete program for his country's future. It, too, is a compilation made by the publishers. The plan was clearly outlined, but a number of the chapters — "Finances," "Education nationale," "Le Sport" — had not been completely developed. One chapter is entirely lacking — "La Population et la Femme française." We may assume that it would have been a condensation of what Giraudoux had already published on that subject. As a matter of fact, this work, a companion piece to *Pleins Pouvoirs,* contains little that Giraudoux had not stated already elsewhere. We recognize his main themes. Their treatment is altered only in keeping with the national situation after the defeat.

In the "Avant-Propos," Giraudoux returns again to the distinction he makes between France and the French. He points out that the former has suffered more from the defeat than the latter. In analyzing the ills of his country, he stresses particularly two subjects for alarm: first, its "mummification," as he had spoken of it in *Armistice à Bordeaux;* second, the government-inspired *mea culpa* psychology, which he had also scored before. "Le Protocole" contains lashing criticism of the politicians and officials responsible for the France of the between-wars period. "Les Finances" attacks their financial policies and measures. "L'Information" preaches the necessity of establishing a permanent bureau to serve the country abroad. "L'Urbanisme" is an appeal for a council on urbanism. "Le Sport" reiterates Giraudoux's appeal to get French youth out of the study halls and cafés. "L'Education" deals with the problem of the national moral structure and incidentally exposes the plight of the teacher. In the concluding chapter, which summarizes much of what has gone before, "Avenir de la France," the situation of postwar France is foreseen between two great world powers: "D'un côté, tyrannie de la civilisation mécanique et matérielle, — avec une prime, la liberté individuelle. De l'autre, liberté dans l'exploitation du monde et de la vie par l'âme nationale, — avec une prime, l'esclavage."[91] It is Giraudoux's fond hope that France can be strong enough to keep the whole world from going to one extreme or the other, to maintain its historical role, and to be a force in rebuilding the world along the lines of wisdom.

We can imagine that in his room at the Hotel de Castille, Giraudoux wrote steadily. Besides his clandestine compilations and his essays that would make up *Sans Pouvoirs,* doubtless he was busy with his new plays and the scenario for *Les Anges du péché.* For *Sodome et Gomorrhe,* which opened on October 11, 1943, he must have had rewriting to do during the months of rehearsals. The final touches to *La Folle de Chaillot* may date from this time, as well as the several drafts for *Pour Lucrèce.* In addition to everything else, Giraudoux was working on his essays devoted to civic planning.

These texts on urbanism were collected, along with earlier ones, to make up the posthumous volume, *Pour une Politique Urbaine* (1947). In 1943 Giraudoux was planning a reorganization of the *Ligue Urbaine et Rurale* to launch a great campaign. France and her devastated cities had to be rebuilt. Now was the time to accomplish the reforms he had long advocated. His dream was for Frenchmen to create for themselves surroundings both lovely and healthful, adapted to twentieth-century living. They possessed the skill and the resources to do so. Only lack of imagination, vested interests, and administrative bungling stood in their way. Giraudoux called for drastic and dramatic action, a breadth of vision and a determination that, alas, has remained an appeal as yet little heeded.

The Apollonian ideal, which had enabled Giraudoux all his life to see radiating through persons and places their pristine natures, inspired him during his last months to envisage a regenerated France, its essence made substantial. His final words were a challenge to his countrymen to make the France that he had so often evoked through poetry and whimsy a living reality:

> Le devoir de remodeler, en la rebâtissant, la Patrie meurtrie, de faire de la nation vieillie une nation toute neuve dans laquelle chaque citoyen puiserait la force et le jeu de son caractère dans des leçons constantes de force, d'élégance, d'aisance, qui lui seraient données par le décor de la vie, dans une atmosphère aérée, par le séjour quotidien dans des villes et des maisons qui seraient dotées de tous les avantages de la civilisation.[92]

January 31, 1944, at 10:30 a.m., Jean Giraudoux died of an attack of uremia. By noon, the news had gone out over the radio. That evening, *Sodome et Gomorrhe* played as usual, but Jacques Hébertot appeared from behind the curtain to request the audience to refrain from applause: "A la fin des actes, le rideau ne se relèvera pas. Vos applaudissements, qui nous sont pourtant chers, nous demandons qu'ils ne viennent pas troubler l'émotion de cette soirée."[93] On February third, the funeral services were held in the church of Saint-Pierre-du-Gros-Caillou. The notables of diplomacy, of letters, and of the theater were present to pay their respects. Outside the church an immense crowd waited to see the cortege set out for the Montmartre cemetery. On March 4, a *matinée poétique* was held at the Comédie Française, at which scenes from Giraudoux's plays were given.

The news of Giraudoux's sudden death had come as a great surprise, so great in fact that it was bruited about that he had been poisoned by the Gestapo.[94] The reaction in the French press to the news of his death was complicated by political sentiment, reticence in view of censorship, and troubled memories of Giraudoux's participation in the "phoney war." In the allied countries, where Giraudoux's writings had never found great favor, the news stirred little interest. "His books survive him," wrote Harold Nicolson in the *Spectator* of February 11, 1944, "lovely petals from a tree that was sterile of all lasting fruit." For many at home and abroad, it seemed easy to dismiss this poet as just a *précieux* and this patriot as just a parlor diplomat. Even the *hommage* publications of the years immediately following his death contain much that is faint praise. Some time had to pass before the public and the critics would revise their judgment. But for over a decade now Giraudoux has steadily climbed in favor. Today, almost universally acclaimed, he occupies a position as one of the truly significant French artists and thinkers of the twentieth century.

PART TWO

The Testimony of Giraudoux's Creative Work

Incidentally to our presentation of Giraudoux's novels and plays, and whenever they elucidated the events of his life or his spiritual evolution, we have already discussed his principal themes. We have not avoided, moreover, alluding to aspects of his philosophy of life and of art, or to the characteristics of his style, whenever reference to them seemed pertinent. But since our aim in Part One was to trace his life and career, we preferred not to stop along the way to treat these matters comprehensively. To do so is our aim in Part Two. The facts of his life have been stated (as we know them) and his publications described, each in turn. Now we propose to look back over his creative work as a whole and, on the basis of the evidence it presents, summarize what we have already noted and attempt to arrive at a general statement of Giraudoux's reactions to the world and of the manner in which he expresses them. To make this statement fully complete, we must of course include the evidence of the essays, in which Giraudoux expresses his views on literary questions, the theater, politics, and civic matters. But they have already been too explicitly indicated in the chapter that closes Part One to require review or summary here. For this reason we shall concern ourselves in Part Two only with Giraudoux's nonexpository writing.

Chapter 4

HIS TEMPERAMENT: REFRACTIONS OF THE WORLD ABOUT HIM

The autobiographical nature of Giraudoux's books is apparent, particularly his first ones. Through them we have already been able to trace the reflection of his childhood and adolescence, his war experiences, the beginnings of his diplomatic career, etc. He himself is the central theme of these works, whether he is recording his manifold impressions of the world about him, giving vent to his joys and sorrows, or musing over the problems that man must face. In his later works of fiction and in his plays, the confessional nature of his writing becomes less direct. Symbolism, anecdote, and other literary devices transmit his message. But in the early pieces, there is little more than the diaphanous veil of the poetic imagination to come between the reader and the author's personal experience. To recapitulate their themes, we have only to look back with Giraudoux as he recalls the first part of his life.

Sentimental Themes of Youth

These words — Nostalgia, Spring, Love, and Friendship — the titles of the "Allégories," which comprise a section of *Provinciales* — point to the sources of inspiration for all Giraudoux's early books. Nostalgia for his province and his childhood, memories of seasons, of school days, and of tender sentimental ties pour forth as the young poet begins to write. First of all there is the little country town, the

Notes to Chapter 4 begin on page 225.

sort that Giraudoux grew up in, which is the setting for *Le Dernier Rêve d'Edmond About* and the *nouvelles* of *Provinciales,* which will frame, as well, the later novels *Suzanne et le Pacifique, Juliette au Pays des Hommes* and the play *Intermezzo.*

Memories of province and school.

"De ma fenêtre," which opens *Provinciales,* offers us a view of the little country town and its goings on from the bedroom window of a fanciful little boy of ten. He is ill, then convalescent; the sounds and impressions from the outside world reach him only indirectly through his lazy daydreaming. The leaves fall, the great winds blow, at times rays from the setting sun streak across the room, some days are uniformly dark and all the sounds are muffled by the quiet rain. He listens for the step of familiar passers-by in the street below — Uncle Voie and the other old men of the town, housewives on their shopping errands, the pharmacist's wife. From the window, one by one, we can make out the chief buildings of interest: the pharmacy with its apothecary bottles filled with colored water, the hotel at the entrance of town, the city hall, the post office. Across from the church with its statue of Christ on the Cross, where sparrows nest in the wound made by the Roman sword, stands the customs office, covered with jasmine and wisteria. Outside the town proper is the school, far from the sawmill and the forge, surrounded by cherry trees. The next story, "Sainte Estelle," is a child's portrait of Estelle Faguette, a visionary who actually lived in Pellevoisin. Through the child's eyes, we watch the religious procession in honor of Estelle go by; and, as the story of the reluctant saint progresses, the principal village characters come into view. We see the curé and the tax official, the innkeeper and the harness maker. In the bar there is the Millet boy, very man-of-the-world, giving the little narrator his first drink. The *Parisienne* is doing her washing. Some girls appear in the street — Adèle, Eléonore, and Valentine, the beautiful dressmaker "qui croit faire réclame à ses corsets en n'en portant pas"[1] — the same girls who will be described in more detail in *Suzanne et le Pacifique* — Victoria, Juliette — schoolgirls who dream and who flirt, who walk or run laughing together through the summer fields.

In the later piece of whimsy entitled *Mirage de Bessines,* Giraudoux translates his nostalgia into psychiatric terms. To deliver himself of the obsession of his birthplace (Bessines is near Bellac), a painter returns to the spot. He enters shops where his mother had sent him on errands, goes by the cemetery where he used to collect the beads that had fallen from funeral wreaths and make them into Inca headdresses, crosses the meadow where he played on Thursdays. As remembered in adulthood, all in the classic French village of one's childhood is charm, innocence, and tenderness.

A childhood, in fact, so linked with nature that to find it anything but pure "il aurait fallu convaincre arbres et animaux, ses vrais ascendants, de maladie et de faute transmissibles à un petit humain."[2] The image of the town cannot be evoked without the countryside that frames it or the weather that establishes its moods. The scenes of the *Provinciales* stories are alternately drenched with sun or soft summer rain. A ten-year-old lad's day is from sunup to sundown, each hour holding its particular savor. With his companions he lags through fields and brook-traversed meadows on the way to and from school, following the soggy prints made by the cattle. He knows where the brook begins, where the ponds are as green as frogs. He knows where the woodpeckers nest in the twisted elms and where hazelnuts are to be gathered. In "Le petit duc," he goes to the fair to meet his chum whose fine curls and aristocratic complexion have earned him his nickname. This is a story of boyhood rivalry and affection — and what must have been little Jean's first heartache. The "Allégories" are wistful evocations of seasons and scenes that shift from Giraudoux's boyhood village to his trip across the Atlantic to North America. But the long *nouvelle*, "La Pharmacienne," which closes the volume, takes us back to the French town to hear a gossipy account of rural adultery.

In *Intermezzo,* written in full middle-age, Giraudoux calls back all the inhabitants of his little town to act out an idyllic interlude — schoolmistress, mayor, druggist, government officials, even the two old gossips here presented under the names of Armande and Léonide Mangebois. A chorus of little girls assists in the performance. To revive Isabelle, whom the departure of the ghost has left in a swoon, all the familiar local sounds are played in her ear: housewives whisper, pinochle players start their game, the horn of an auto sounds, a passer-by whistles, the town band takes up, a canary sings. But it takes a discussion of dressmaking to restore the girl to consciousness and to her community.

The familiar scenes of Giraudoux's boyhood never quite left his mind, and, just as he always enjoyed motoring down to the country on a fine weekend, throughout his works there are frequent excursions back to the places he had known as a child. Usually the reference is specifically to the Limousin, but the implication is quite general. In depicting his own *patria chica,* he aims to paint the moral portrait of rural France. Siegfried and Geneviève are chatting with the customs official as they wait at the German frontier, looking over into France:

> *Siegfried:* C'est la première ville française qu'on voit là?
>
> *Pietri:* Oui, c'est le village.
>
> S. Il est grand?
>
> *P.* Comme tous les villages. 831 habitants.
>
> S. Comment s'appelle-t-il?
>
> *P.* Comme tous les villages. Blancmesnil-sur-Audinet.
>
> S. La belle église! La jolie maison blanche!
>
> *Geneviève:* C'est la mairie.
>
> *P.* Vous connaissez le village, Mademoiselle?
>
> *G.* Et à mi-flanc de la colline, ce chalet de briques entre des ifs, avec marquise et véranda, c'est le château.
>
> *P.* Vous êtes d'ici?
>
> *G.* Et au bout de l'allée des tilleuls, c'est la statue. La statue de Louis XV ou de Louis XIV.
>
> *P.* Erreur. De Louis Blanc.
>
> *G.* Et cet échafaudage dans le coin du champ de foire, c'est sur lui que les pompiers font l'exercice, le premier dimanche du mois. Leur clairon sonne faux.
>
> *P.* Vous connaissez Blancmesnil mieux que moi, Mademoiselle.
>
> *G.* Non. Je ne connais pas Blancmesnil. Je ne l'ai jamais vu . . . Je connais ma race.[3]

Giraudoux's tone is usually bantering, as in the passage where the narrator describes his part of the country to the German prince:

> Je décrivis la petite oseille qui annonce qu'il n'est pas un gramme de chaux dans le sol; la belle vallée transversale, si solitaire depuis que les Romains ne vont plus de Lyon à Saintes, mais toujours fréquentée par le soleil . . . Je décrivis toutes les roches tremblantes, car on peut faire osciller la moitié du Limousin avec la main. . . . Je décrivis ces petits bourgs, auxquels les moindres

> divinités avaient offert chacune une source, et les fils célèbres . . . une pompe.[4]

But no one could mistake the tender patriotism which inspires such passages. "Que l'on me redonne pour patrie," exclaims Siegfried, "un pays que je puisse du moins caresser."[5]

Early critics often charged Giraudoux with writing like an impenitent schoolboy. They were not wrong. Without the belittling and condescending implications, we can repeat today that even in his most mature works, his greatest attainments, Giraudoux remained the schoolboy of genius, the *fort-en-thème*. We can see furthermore in the mature man the adolescent who refused to grow old, addicted to the life represented by the neat, bare impersonality of a dormitory room, still fond of sports and sprees, restless and sentimental. We can say that the basic patterns of Giraudoux's character and talent were fixed during the years he devoted himself to his courses and his books.

After the little town, next in chronological order, and perhaps also next in importance as a theme in his early writings, is life in school. It is so vividly and amply depicted that in tracing Giraudoux's actual career at Châteauroux, we have been able to rely greatly on his pictures of the *lycée:*

> De briques et de ciment, . . . tout neuf. A tous les étages, la clarté, l'espace, l'eau. D'immenses cours sans arbres. D'immenses dortoirs dont les fenêtres donnaient sur le terrain d'une caserne. . . . Je trouvai tout en abondance: dans mes rêves les plus heureux ce que j'avais juste imaginé, c'était le lycée. Les poêles ronflaient à rouge. Chaque étude possédait des dictionnaires historiques, sa bibliothèque, son atlas. J'eus le jour même trente volumes, sur lesquels j'écrivis mon nom; j'eus d'un seul coup vingt professeurs.[6]

With tender albeit ironic indulgence, Giraudoux looks back upon the years of study there, of conversations with professors, of recreation with classmates. Although in reality we judge him to have been little gregarious at school, he lingers in his writing over the potraits of his companions. Simon's two best friends were:

> Gontran, inégal, paresseux, l'été, qui, par un devoir raturé, inachevé, parvenait à un quart de point, dans les compositions finales, de ma copie parfaite, . . . Georges, qui ne savait que dépein-

> dre les forêts, et dans toute narration parvenait à glisser la description d'un taillis, ou d'un étang entouré de futaies, à la rigueur d'une oasis.[7]

There was André Bovy, too, "blond, avec des yeux éclatants," who finally succeeded in sitting next to "Jacques l'Egoïste" in the classroom. From the windows they could look out upon the sunlit meadows where tawny spotted cows were grazing.[8] In time, the trees that were newly planted when the village lad arrived at school acquired all their leaves, and the provincial *lycéen,* now already a young man, was ready for Paris.

Paris and the world through student eyes.

In an anthology of Giraudoux's descriptions of cities that someone will compose someday,[9] Paris must have first place. Of all the cities that Giraudoux evoked in their characteristic attitudes and under characteristic skies, it is Paris that he knew best and loved most in the world. He never tired of strolling through its streets, contemplating its monuments, or visiting its shops. His mature novels involve the *mondain* Paris and the Paris of the Quai d'Orsay; but in the early books, which follow Giraudoux's own life step by step, we see it through the eyes of a student, whose Paris is the Latin Quarter with its schools and cafés. A student who, during hours of leisure, takes sentimental walks with friends and sweethearts. By day, with Etienne, Jacques visits the bird markets on the quays; by night, they watch the moon float along the Seine before the Tuileries. Sunset is the romantic hour. It is then that he takes Dolly to her streetcar: "Chaque maison, chaque objet n'est plus qu'un arc-boutant d'ombre dressé contre un arc-boutant de feu"[10] — and Madame Sainte-Sombre to the railway station: "Le soleil n'est pas couché. Mais il n'est plus qu'un clou doré auquel est suspendue une hirondelle. L'automobile, au long des quais, soulève l'ombre des platanes, en secoue les taches du jour, les rejette"[11] — again with Miss Spottiswood: "Des trembles, des bouleaux mélangent incessamment dans l'air les dernières clartés du soir. De grands jeunes gens affables se passent un angora qui guettait les feuilles agitées par le vent et que l'un d'eux a surpris."[12] As Jacques continues to saunter through the Latin Quarter with the American girl, he is thinking, "Je promène dans Paris, fringante et soumise, ma petite femelle."[13] They watch the sun disappear. "Voilà la petite nuit. Les boutiques se ferment. Entre les devantures, les glaces restent prises comme des flaques de jour encore trop profondes.[14] . . . La lune va se lever."[15]

In rain or fine weather, Bernard pursues his fancy along the sidewalks of Paris. He overhears bits of conversation, observes the laughing working girls and a tall young woman in blue ransacking a bargain counter. In the Luxembourg Gardens, facetious students have put red dye in the basin. A beggar draws his attention. Back in his little room, he waits for the dinner hour, watching night fall over the panorama of the city. Other days he sits with Dolores before the Medici fountain, talking of life and playing at love. Musings on life and death, his own nature, and what to do with the force that he feels within him are the constant preoccupation of Giraudoux's hero. But not to the point of anguish, for he is essentially a happy young man, happy at his reflection in the mirror and in the eyes of his friends, even while being reproved by them. He has no doubts as to the great things he will one day accomplish. Anticipating the serious interest Giraudoux would develop in urbanism, the student Bernard dreams of glorifying Paris:

> Reconstruire les vieilles maisons sur le pont Notre-Dame, les cahutes sur le parvis; planter de pins les hauteurs de Montmartre, flanquer Paris, les fortifications une fois démolies, de vingt palais qui seraient les pavillons d'été de chaque arrondissement, avec des théâtres pour ballets, avec des bains.[16]

The end of July, Simon makes ready to leave Paris for the summer vacation:

> Il n'y avait plus dans les jardins publics que les enfants de la campagne, rançon rose et joufflue des petits Parisiens épars dans les provinces. Les concierges, las d'être assis, supportaient debout leurs maisons vides. . . . On voyait passer solitaires les étudiants qui étaient deux au printemps, trois en hiver, — et passer à deux ceux qui étaient quatre, qui étaient six.[17]

But in the autumn he is happy to return and take up again the round of his flirtations and infatuations with Anne, Gabrielle, Hélène, and the others. *Simon le Pathétique* and *L'Ecole des Indifférents* are filled with winsome memories of a student's Paris, where ambition, learning, and love fill a young man's heart to overflowing.

As we know, Giraudoux's student years in Paris were interrupted by two sojourns abroad, first in Germany and then in the United States.

His impressions of the cities he visited and his memories of the life he led while residing in those two countries crop up frequently in his early books. Simon arrived in Germany after a roundabout sight-seeing trip through the low countries. The gaily painted and *gemütlich* Bavarian houses he lived in, the *Bierstuben* where he spent the evenings with jolly companions will be described at greater length in *Siegfried et le Limousin,* the thematic material of which is largely furnished by Giraudoux's year in Munich. The opera, the concerts, the carnivals, and the outings with Ida, Trude, Elsa, and Fredy all come back to the Frenchman who is visiting the city fifteen years later. Snow is falling on Munich when he arrives, and we have winter descriptions to match those of summer which fill earlier books:

> Quand je m'éveillai, la neige ne tombait plus, mais un grand vent soufflait, qui soudain, comme si le vent avait été le grand ennemi des hommes à leur naissance sur la terre, rendait attendrissante aux larmes l'invention des maisons, de la casserole de cuivre, du lit, et des doubles fenêtres. Les animaux, chevaux et bœufs, qui n'ont point la faculté ou le temps de changer leur couleur l'hiver, effarés d'être aussi visibles sur la rue blanche, s'y creusaient, en piaffant et grattant, un socle noir. Comme si la neige avait été le premier ami des êtres humains à leur naissance, les passants se baissaient là où elle paraissait le plus sensible, et la caressaient. Point de bruit de pas, les hommes semblaient tout au plus appuyer sur le monde, comme par un trolley, par leur rire ou par leur parole. . . .[18]

Don Manuel, of *L'Ecole des Indifférents,* pursues on an American campus the same sort of sentimental career as Jacques or Bernard in Paris, or as Simon in Munich. He observes with poetic eye his exotic surroundings, flirts with Mrs. Callie, and strolls with Renée-Amélie through the autumn leaves. Don Manuel travels during the school holidays, thus affording us, besides the pictures of Boston, Cambridge, and university life, some glimpses of Ottawa and New York City: "New York étrenne les saisons avec magnificence, les déforme en un jour, puis les passe à la province qui les ménage jusqu'au bout. L'automne, sur les pelouses de Wellesley, est déjà élimé et couturé de mille pièces de soleil."[19] The American scene is further evoked in two of the *Contes d'un Matin,* one may remember: Niagara Falls in "La Surenchère," and Texas in "Une Carrière," where Giraudoux imagines a bogus "Université Shakespeare": "W. O'Duffin ne pouvant diriger un collège sans l'autorisation du governement décida donc — tout citoyen en a le droit — de fonder une université. Ce fut l'Université Shakespeare, la 525e des Etats-Unis!"[20] With the other gay and irreverent little newspaper stories that make up this collection, we return to Paris, for they are vignettes of life in the French capital, where the student Giraudoux, jostled by the crowd, stopped to observe all the little comedies or tragedies of the city streets.

Reactions to the war.

The university student becomes a soldier, and war succeeds school life as a theme in Giraudoux's works. *Lectures pour une Ombre, Adorable Clio,* and *Amica America* take us from general mobilization to the Armistice, but anyone expecting to find in these books a picture of the First World War planned to scale would be disappointed. We know only what happened to one individual, and what constituted his personal impressions and musings, which suggest for the most part such a detached and playful attitude towards the events that to some critics of the time Giraudoux seemed a young smart aleck and his war just a "guerre pommadée"[21] or a "guerre en dentelles."[22] The experiences of the war seem to have altered neither the young man's attitude towards the world nor the writer's whimsical and lyrical style. This in spite of Giraudoux's personal heroism and patriotism — perhaps because of it.

However lightly Giraudoux seems to have taken the war, he could not have had any illusions about its fundamental evil. Scenes of the misery and horror occasioned by war are not so much avoided as underplayed. He shows us the swarms of refugees, choking the roads:

> . . . ils ont l'air d'émigrer par professions et l'on a seulement à se dire, devant leur jaquette à palme académique, devant leur bourgeron taché de couleur: voici l'instituteur qui fuit, voici le charron qui fuit, ou peut-être même le peintre. D'immenses voitures chargées d'enfants, dont on diminue à chaque arrêt, pour nourrir l'attelage, la litière de foin. Dans des carrioles à claire-voie, des arrière-grand'mères avec leurs petites-filles, les garçons ont passé au travers et suivent; sur des brouettes, une famille qui traîne ses matelas comme des fourmis leurs œufs.[23]

the soldiers in muddy trenches, haggard with fear and soaked in the freezing rain:

> Des camarades assoupis prennent soudain un air énergique; c'est qu'ils ont subitement décidé d'ouvrir, dès la première pause, leur dernière boîte de conserves; c'est que la mort, subitement, ne les effraye plus; c'est qu'ils ont sacrifié leur femme, leur mère, c'est qu'ils ont renoncé à boire encore du bordeaux, à pêcher encore les truites.[24]

> Il est trois heures. Il gèle. Un cheval de colonel regarde tristement l'ordonnance brûler son foin.[25]

the wounded in a field hospital:

> A mesure que l'escalier tourne j'aperçois, dans la grande salle, des têtes pâles, des têtes jaunes, des têtes sanglantes, et en vingt secondes il m'enfonce par ce pas de vis au centre de la souffrance humaine.[26]

cadavers in grotesque postures:

> On voit un mort assis, adossé au talus, son fusil écarté de lui par ses mains crispées, comme un aviateur surpris dans une vrille qu'il n'a pas voulue, et qui a tiré le levier à fond pour en sortir.[27]

When Giraudoux considers the general havoc wrought by war, he is moved by an intense feeling for humanity and a tender patriotism:

> La France, qu'on a éventrée comme une ville où les tuyaux de plomb ont sauté, — où le bonheur, l'amour n'arrivent plus à chacun par de vastes conduites, et doivent chaque matin se rallumer dans une chambre close comme un feu de bois; . . . la France, avec ses gares d'où chaque soldat en permission doit pour sortir écarter et bousculer des mères, des épouses, la chair la plus meurtrie et la plus sensible de Paris, qui le retient, qui le rejette, affreuse naissance à chaque retour du front; avec ses enterrements, dont la vue du moins soulage, car par chaque convoi la terre s'allège d'un témoin de la guerre . . .[28]

But Giraudoux's deep-rooted dislike of emphasis and his persistent refusal to dwell upon the unlovely aspects of life will not let him stay long in such a vein. Like Mlle. de Rambouillet "couvrant de sa blanche main tous les mots cruels, et nous les rendant ensuite, le mot Courroux, le mot Barbare, inoffensifs comme les détectives qui changent le revolver du bandit en un revolver porte-cigares,"[29] he pretends at times that war is make-believe:

> Trinqualard me donne un vrai prisonnier qu'il a ramené de Puisieux, avec lequel nous jouons une minute, qui s'apprivoise et ne

veut plus nous quitter. Mais quand un obus arrive, il gémit, déplore son aventure et nous lui crions de se taire: — Comment se taire, avec une guerre pareille! répond-il.[30]

In spite of being already thirty-three years old, Giraudoux was still an adolescent, with the adolescent's love of a lark. The war was a great adventure where one could give oneself up to the moment and to chance:

> C'est la guerre: on ne me fera pas travailler de l'après-midi . . . C'est la guerre, avec son ciel bleu, ses canons grondants, ses pigeons voyageurs qui s'entraînent autour du clocher sur la piste étroite et dure des martinets. Sous un pommier aux pommes vertes je m'étends . . .[31]

No one knew where he would be sent next: new landscapes, new villages, new faces. Giraudoux relished them all as his unit advanced or retreated, hailed by flag-waving civilians as heroes or conquerors. It marched laughing, joking, singing, through towns that could serve as sets for *The Student Prince:*

> Le 1er bataillon nous rejoint. Il est gai, et chante, car on l'a fêté toute la nuit. Aux fenêtres, tout ce qui se peut voir d'Alsace vivante à cinq heures du matin, quelques épaules rondes entre des rideaux noirs à fleurs roses, un sein à demi dégagé, un bras blanc qui relève un store, une petite fille entière, qu'on assied sur la fenêtre et qui lance des fleurs en papier.[32]

The inhabitants invite the men to dinner and bring out their hoarded bottles. And the girls greet them with enthusiasm:

> Ces notairesses blondes aux yeux de feu, angoisse, délices des notaires, ces bijoutières délirantes, loyales dans leur passion soudaine, car les soldats achètent peu de bijoux . . . ces jupes de velours bordées de rose . . .[33]

Between towns the countryside offers its vistas which the soldier on the march or during halts heightens with poetic fancy. Summer scenes at evening or dawn inspire rapturous apostrophe, such as the following:

> — Tendrement je t'appelle, amour des combats, qui secoues tes ailes pleines de rosée, et te coules dans la forme vide du génie de la nuit comme le ramier dans celle de la chouette! Voici la première haleine du jour; un vent chargé et son brouillard soufflent sur les cyprès, ensoleillés, et les attisent . . .[34]

The soldier Giraudoux is still the poet of spring:

> Vous êtes froissée, Gladys, d'entendre parler du printemps dans la première lettre que je vous écris de la guerre. Mais à mes pieds, découpée par un rayon, je vois soudain noircir la première ombre des feuilles nées ce matin, au flanc des collines, je vois des poiriers, des pêchers généreux contenir la sève des feuilles pour livrer plus tôt toutes leurs fleurs, c'est la guerre, sur des squelettes encore desséchés, et, dans le vallon, de hauts pruniers tout blancs, drus comme des choux-fleurs.[35]

Furloughs in Paris, where solicitous *marraines* were waiting for him, and special missions abroad — to Lisbon, where his splendid uniform caught all eyes in the street — to the United States, where he was welcomed not only as one of the "defenders of civilization," but as an old friend. No, in the picture Giraudoux paints of the life of the soldier and the officer in war not all is blood, sweat, and tears. Even life in the trenches seems sweet for the comradeship it fosters. Although in reality Giraudoux knew hard and grueling duty, was wounded, and lay ill for many months, he did not choose to remember these truths, any more than the general horror of war or the seriousness of the issues involved. The themes of the "Allégories" — Nostalgia, Spring, Love, and Friendship — can still be heard above the battle din in *Lectures pour une Ombre* and *Adorable Clio.*

Themes of Maturity

When Jean Giraudoux put away his uniform in 1918 to resume his diplomatic career, he discovered new sources of inspiration. Henceforth, his writing would reflect a more mature person, drawing his themes from his work at the Quai d'Orsay and the preoccupations it engendered, from his contacts with the ruling classes of society, and from his personal life as a settled man with a family.

Politics and international relations.

First among the important new themes is the political — primarily on the level of international relations. It is conspicuous in the novels *Siegfried et le Limousin, Bella, Eglantine, Combat avec l'Ange,* and in the peripheral *plaquettes.* Among the plays (besides *Siegfried* of course), we usually think first of *La Guerre de Troie n'aura pas lieu,* although *Judith, Electre,* and *La Folle de Chaillot* have political implications. In these works we encounter heads of state, high government officials, financiers, corporation presidents, etc., who move their chessmen across an international board and who affect the fate of nations by their every decision. The student who wrote the account of an imaginary interview with Bismarck was to view at close range a great many statesmen during his career. The pictures he draws of some of them indicate his sympathy or his aversion for the school of thinking they represent. To help us formulate Giraudoux's political point of view, let us open his books again at these symbolic portraits.

The first sketch of a political personage is that of Jacques de Bolny in *Simon le Pathétique*. Presumed to be that of the famous editorialist Bunau-Varilla, it shows a thoroughly unscrupulous, hypocritical politician who introduces his young secretary into a world of stupidity and corruption:

> A tour de rôle, il invitait, pour me les présenter, les hommes d'Etat. Il organisa pour moi le dîner des ministres malhonnêtes, des ministres sots, et celui des néfastes, dont chaque assistant avait, avec la meilleure volonté, perdu une administration. Il me montra le monde politique tel qu'il serait plus tard, distribué dans ses treize cercles.[36]

In the political allegory *Bella*, the personage Rebendart (presumed to be Poincaré) incarnates the faults of insensitivity, malice, professional patriotism; Dubardeau (presumed to be Berthelot), on the contrary, represents everything a statesman should stand for — "Mon père était, si l'on excepte Wilson, le seul plénipotentiaire de Versailles qui eût recréé l'Europe avec générosité, et le seul, sans exception, avec compétence."[37] Another sympathetic statesman is Brossard, whom the narrator serves as secretary in *Combat avec l'Ange*. This ill and dying minister (presumed to owe something to Briand) gives the last ounces of his energy in the cause of world peace.

Through these portraits based on living people it is possible to see in what contempt Giraudoux held hypocrisy and vindictiveness, and what esteem he felt for moderation and generous internationalism — his "Briandisme" as Mr. Kohler calls it.[38] Dubardeau, along with his five gifted brothers, is endowed with that Apollonian perfection which seems the birthright of a hero of a Giraudoux work, and which, for that reason, we may take as the author's ideal in politics as in everything else. Dubardeau and Hector, of *La Guerre de Troie n'aura pas lieu,* represent enlightened and noble statesmen, who bring to international problems the sincerity and wisdom lacking in patriots like Rebendart and Demokos, the drum-beating poet of *La Guerre de Troie.*

In a more whimsical vein, we have the portrait of Zelten, who staunchly opposes, in the name of poetry and a legendary past, Siegfried's views on the reconstruction of Germany:

> L'Allemagne de ton Siegfried! Je la vois d'ici. Un modèle de l'ordre social, la suppression de ces trente petits royaumes, de ces duchés, de ces villes libres, qui donnaient une résonnance trente fois différente au sol de la culture et de la liberté, un pays distribué en départements égaux dont les seules aventures seront les budgets, les assurances, les pensions, bref une nation comme lui théorique, sans mémoire et sans passé.[39]

Zelten has a most engaging way of settling border disputes:

> Il arriva un matin avec un puzzle qui était une carte d'Alsace collée sur carton et découpée par district.
>
> — Il faut vider cette histoire du Reichsland, avail-il ajouté, du moins entre nous deux. J'ai la même carte découpée. Quand je t'en jugerai digne, toi ou ton pays, quand je serai pris d'un accès d'amitié, pour toi ou pour ton pays, je te céderai un district. Fais comme moi. Quel bel exemple nous donnerions à l'Europe si dans six mois tu avais toute ma carte et moi toute la tienne![40]

This German Romantic Ariel is vanquished by the Caliban of trusts and cartels, also the foe of Chaillot's madwoman:

> Messieurs, dit Zelten, dans une heure j'aurai quitté le palais . . . Ce qui m'en expulse, ce sont deux télégrammes pour Berlin que voilà interceptés: le premier vient d'Amérique et est adressé à Wirth. Je vous le lis: "Si Zelten se maintient Munich, annulons contrat pétrole." Le deuxième vient de Londres et est adressé à Stinnes: "Si Zelten se maintient Munich annulons contrat Volga et provoquons hausse mark."[41]

But Zelten's defeat is redeemed by Aurélie's victory over the "mecs," and there is no reason to doubt that the chimerical political idealism depicted in *Siegfried et le Limousin* and *La Folle de Chaillot* — works that span Giraudoux's career — represents at least one fundamental aspect of his thinking.

Such an assertion, we know, is always subject to caution when it is a question of a literary theme. As such, attitudes indicated by characters or situations are not necessarily the writer's own and, even if they do describe his feelings at a given time, may not be taken as his full and final word on the subject. The novelist or the dramatist uses his thematic material to meet his artistic needs or to suggest an interesting perspective or a tentative truth. To complete a picture of Giraudoux's politics, to the naïveté of Zelten and Aurélie we must add the sophisticated astuteness of Ulysses of *La Guerre de Troie* and the philosophy of compromise and expediency of Aegisthus of *Electre.* The writer who showed in *Judith* how the slogans that rally nations can be fabricated out of lies was not a dupe. The fact remains, however, as we have remarked in Part One in connection with *Siegfried et le Limousin,* that Giraudoux's political thinking is on the whole extremely idealistic and literary in character.

In calling Giraudoux's political thinking literary, we are not considering only that Zelten's puzzle and Aurélie's trap door are questionable solutions to the ills of the world. We have already agreed that a creative writer — and we see Giraudoux as essentially that — does not work on the level of practical solutions. Even though Giraudoux is inspired in some of his political portraits by living models, through fable and poetry he lifts persons and views to a level of ambiguity and high generality. As persons turn into symbols, debates become duets, problems are motifs, and nations take on traits of character or spiritual natures. Just consider his concept of nations: "Le mot France et le mot Allemagne ne sont à peu près plus et n'ont jamais été pour le monde des expressions géographiques, ce sont des termes moraux."[42] The United States is "ce pays, la patrie des jeunes filles";[43] Germany, "une conjuration poétique et démoniaque";[44] France, "pays des agneaux sans suint, du langage sans hoquet, des Arméniens sans odeur, [qui a] fait de la religion un levain de liberté, de poésie, d'esprit critique."[45] The validity of such definitions, whimsical, humorous, and farfetched as they are, lies in their possible ability to illuminate in a flash an aspect of the moral nature of nations, thereby serving as orientation or as a basis for specific and practical action. But this Giraudoux would leave to others. We know of no treatment of politics in literature maintained more consistently on a purely literary level. And this, incidentally, is why we cannot subscribe to any interpretation of his writing as disguised pamphlets, ideology, or party endorsement.

For Giraudoux seems to think instinctively and spontaneously on the literary level — a matter of poetic temperament, one would say — and it is for this reason in particular that we call his political thinking literary. Even in his essays he envisages a problem in terms of rhetoric. Symbol, parallel, antithesis, etc., remain the patterns of his thought in *Pleins Pouvoirs* as in *Siegfried et le Limousin.* To problems however concrete he offers only the literary solution, reiterating that what the world is seeking is language or style, and presenting La Fontaine in a lecture series devoted to topical subjects.

And lastly let us explain that when we describe Giraudoux's political thinking as extremely idealistic as well as literary, we are not implying that he is necessarily as naïve or uncompromising as Zelten or Aurélie, for his works offer ample evidence to the contrary. But through them all shines the Apollonian ideal that Dubardeau incarnates; and in fiction, drama, and essay as well, the political theme is linked with the noble vision of life.

War.

In *Adorable Clio* and *Lectures pour une Ombre,* Giraudoux was chiefly content to record his reactions to the personal experience of war. After the Armistice, however, when he was back at the Quai d'Orsay, working with the problems of international understanding and observing firsthand the activities of diplomats and politicians, war became for him a subject of philosophical meditation. This is reflected in much of his writing all through the 1920's and into the mid 30's, where the war theme is often linked with the political. *La Guerre de Troie n'aura pas lieu* (1935) constitutes a sort of *summa* of his thoughts on war — there we can learn how wars start, where the guilt lies, what they accomplish, and why they will always occur. But already the works that precede this play — notably *Suzanne et le Pacifique, Siegfried, Bella, Amphitryon 38, Judith, Combat avec l'Ange* — give indications of Giraudoux's mature attitude and his considered views on the subject.

Suzanne on her island witnesses a battle at sea, filled with the anguish and apprehension that are the lot of all women, who can only watch or wait. The realization that nations are at war brings her unhappy visions of parents saying: "My son is dead"; of horses and mules dying of misery and cruelty; of duchesses caring for the wounded in railway stations. Not knowing yet who the antagonists are, Suzanne tries to reassure herself that her own country is not involved. Yet, in spite of her efforts, a poison invades her feelings towards the countries that are possible adversaries of France, and instinctively she rises to the defense of possible war crimes France may have committed: "Si mon pays avait attaqué l'Allemagne, surpris sa frontière, violé la Belgique, ce tout petit nerf de mon âme, infime, qui admet qu'on viole la Belgique, je lui permettais soudain de croître . . ."[46] Suzanne's chauvinistic instincts are, unfortunately, natural enough, and Giraudoux shows here that he really had no illusions that territorial disputes could be arranged by games such as the one Forestier and Zelten play in *Siegfried et le Limousin.*

Although he never lost sight of his Apollonian ideal, Giraudoux scorned self-delusion and admired courageous lucidity. Of his model statesman, Dubardeau, he says, "délié de l'ignorance et de la crédulité universelles, il ne se croyait pas tenu au mensonge."[47] The remark is made apropos of the "constructive lying" of official communiqués.[48] Lack of illusions does not, however, prevent a Dubardeau and a Brossard (the statesman in *Combat avec l'Ange*) from dedicating their lives to peace. Even at the point of death, Brossard, in his efforts to prevent war, has called together the great munition manufacturers. His fainting spells cut short the conversations; and Brossard, left alone, is attended by his secretary and the young woman Maléna. Gazing upon Maléna's lovely features, the dying statesman imagines he beholds the face of peace. — "La paix," as Giraudoux has Sosie say in a cynical moment of *Amphitryon 38,* that "intervalle entre deux guerres."[49]

On the subject of Li-pou-pou (the facetious euphemism coined for war in *Combat avec l'Ange*), Giraudoux reveals himself in a variety of moods: gaiety as he remembers his escapades while in the service; anger and indignation at the thought of the Rebendarts, who encourage hatred and the spirit of vengeance by pompous phrases about the sacrificed dead; admiration for the Dubardeaus and the Brossards; horror and loathing as the spectacle of the battlefield rises before his eyes.[50] But his general attitude, whether expressed in personal reminiscences, in the pithy remarks he lends to his characters, or in the superb description of what people do and think when general mobilization is called, is a philosophical resignation colored by tenderness and irony.

Giraudoux knew full well that towards war a man thinks in two directions. Of course he loves peace and deplores war, but when the bugle blows, the weight of individual responsibility is suddenly lifted from his shoulders, the yoke of routine is taken off. He stands free and strong, eager for adventure, heroism, and glory. Already in the war diaries Giraudoux had depicted these ambivalent feelings towards war. They are brought out again in *Amphitryon 38* in the dialogue between Sosie and the Warrior. But it is in *La Guerre de Troie* that they obtain their most dramatic expression. Andromache asks Hector, "Aimes-tu la guerre?" and her husband must admit that in the past upon going into battle he has felt like a god. War had promised him "la bonté, la générosité, le mépris des bassesses." . . .[51] Hector is now without illusion, but Priam, seconded by Demokos, is there to incite the Trojans to battle by all the conventional appeals to masculine honor and vanity. Only the women are not thrilled by ringing phrases like "dying for one's country" and "war makes heroes of men."

As preparations advance for the war "that will not take place," Giraudoux's irony catches the stock actors of this dreadful comedy in characteristic attitudes. Demokos is already busy with his superpatriotic pen. Priam, true to the Rebendart type of statesman, is shocked that Hector should speak of peace at a moment of national crisis; he exhorts him to pronounce the usual discourse to the war dead. Busiris, expert on matters of form and legality in international disputes, arrives on the scene to demonstrate that force makes the most persuasive diplomacy and that legal condonement can always be had if the incentive is strong enough. The Greeks arrive. First Ajax, who begins by insulting Hector, then turns to praising him when the Trojan chief slaps Demokos. Ajax's instinctive admiration suggests that complicity, that sentiment of caste, which is often stronger than patriotism. Ulysses, too, when he appears, reacts to Hector not as to a stranger or as to an enemy but as to a colleague. Nothing more natural than, after their most cordial conversation, that they should separate, "en se serrant les mains, en se sentant des frères . . .[52] Next day, to be sure, war is declared.

The talk between the Greek and Trojan chiefs has turned to the causes of war. Ulysses executes brilliant pieces of rhetorical bravura on such themes as foreordained destiny, the impossibility of war between natural enemies (contrary to the common notion), the "imperceptibles impolitesses" that nations die of. He speaks like a precious poet, but through all the metaphors and the paradoxes we detect a wisdom that is nonetheless real for being expressed poetically, susceptible as it is of being translated into precise economic and political terms.

Society and the family.

One hesitates to speak of society or social classes as a theme with Giraudoux, for still less than in the matter of politics is there anything like a realistic presentation or an objective study of milieu. Yves Gandon reported after an interview with him that "les études de mœurs, régionales ou autres, ne l'amusent pas."[53] Moïse the banker, Fontranges the aristocrat, the numerous government officials whether modest civil servants or great statesmen, do not come to us as special species in the Balzacian sense, but as symbols of their position about whom Giraudoux can compose fugues on a social theme. The word theme is proper, then, only if taken in a musical sense, the sense we ought to understand — as a matter of fact — whenever we speak of Giraudoux's themes.

Is there any social message, any point of view on social questions in Giraudoux's novels? As a French citizen, he did not hesitate to take the stand for women's rights, for urbanism, and for other social issues which form the subject of his essays. But as a creative artist, he stays out of the forum. In *Combat avec l'Ange,* Maléna — the only one of his characters who worries about her social privileges — is chastised for her concern. All others in Giraudoux's well-off fictional world ignore, along with their author, the lower classes, the unfit, and the underprivileged. Notwithstanding, although it would be improper to call the series of novels from *Bella* to *Choix des Elues* studies of manners, they do involve the institutions of family, marriage, and the couple and do offer reflections of milieu, hence do have sociological implications. The problems and conflicts of Giraudoux's characters, if not altogether peculiar to their group, at least are representative of it.

The Dubardeau and the Rebendart families represent a high stratum of French society. In the first pages of *Bella,* the Dubardeau family is presented: "Mon père avait cinq frères, tous de l'Institut, deux sœurs, mariées à des conseillers d'Etat anciens Ministres, et j'étais fier de ma famille quand je la trouvais rassemblée les jours de fête ou de vacances dans la propriété de mon oncle Jacques, en Berry."[54] We are told that these men, engaged in furthering the world's progress in science, philosophy, and politics, enjoy working together, surrounded by a band of young men and women whom they join in sports and diversions; but we have really nothing of an actual description of these exemplary lives. The Rebendart family is as vigorous as the Dubardeau family. "Elle avait fourni à la France depuis deux siècles un nombre respectable de hauts fonctionnaires, de présidents du Conseil et de grands bâtonniers."[55] The plot of *Bella* is constructed on the sustained parallels established between these two families, different in every respect except in clannishness and in political prominence. It is a sort of Romeo and Juliet situation, with the narrator from the Dubardeau clan and Bella, through marriage, from the Rebendarts. The families are used to symbolize two opposing temperaments and political philosophies, and are accordingly too much abstracted to give much of a social picture. Moreover, there is no question here of intimate family relationships, of spouse, parent, or child.

Such matters are merely touched upon in connection with Fontranges, Bella's father, through whom, incidentally, we catch glimpses of another social group — the landed gentry. Fontranges lives on his estates, busying himself with his thoroughbred horses and hunting dogs. His great passion is his son Jacques, left motherless at the birth of his sisters, the twins Bella and Bellita. In Fontranges, Giraudoux gives us a highly lyrical picture of paternity. Every fatherly care and attention is bestowed upon Jacques as a child. He is a perfect specimen when sent off to Paris for his schooling, but after six months he returns home with a venereal disease. To share his son's misfortune, the immaculate Fontranges goes to Paris for the purpose of soiling himself. This is in 1914 and Jacques goes to the Front. He is killed and his father returns home with uncontaminated blood. His mourning for Jacques, and soon afterwards for his daughter Bella, is a theme on which Giraudoux executes several variations in subsequent works.

There are few other pictures of paternity. Jérôme Bardini has an infant son, but we see them together for just a moment. The relationship of Pierre, of *Choix des Elues,* with his two children, Claudie and Jacques, is barely mentioned. In the later novel the maternal theme is rather important, however.

Between mother and daughter there is a complicity of kindred spirits; Claudie fosters and condones in advance Edmée's abandonment of her husband and son:

> Si la vie d'Edmée avait été heureuse, si jamais elle ne s'était repentie de l'avoir ainsi dirigée, si elle avait passé sur le désespoir de Pierre, sur l'absence de Jacques, si le monde avait été pour elle un asile, un honneur, une facilité, c'est parce qu'elle avait eu l'accord de Claudie.[56]

But Claudie eventually withdraws from her mother and returns to her father. Then it is Jacques' turn to seek out Edmée, and we observe the episode Jacques-Edmée, the son in the presence of the runaway mother. As the book opened, she had been a conventional housewife caring for her comfortable little family. Giraudoux delineates, as nowhere else in his works, the daily life of a middle-class family, with its meals and its bedtime, the hurry in the morning to get off to school or office. Just a bit of this we had seen in *Jérôme Bardini* — the arrival of the mail during lunch, conversation about invitations, guests, and shopping. But Jérôme, like Edmée, makes haste to leave all this behind.

How important is the family theme in *Electre*? There is filial love (Electra for the memory of Agamemnon) and hatred (Electra for Clytemnestra), a closer brother and sister relationship than anywhere else in Giraudoux. But the story was not invented by him; and the family situation that came with it, although presenting the highly dramatic picture of a mother defending herself against her children who are her judges, serves a metaphysical theme.

French literature of the between-wars period took the family as a social unit severely to task. Gide, Mauriac, Cocteau denounced it openly or demonstrated its harmful influence upon the individual. Giraudoux is neither moralist nor sociologist, but the implications of his works endorse the conduct of Gide's prodigal sons. Jérôme and Edmée are never censured for their lack of responsibility to family, and the child who wins our deepest sympathy, the Kid, is a vagabond. Giraudoux's attitude seems to be more one of indifference, however, than of bitter hostility — an assumption which the scarcity of references to the family would seem to bear out. On the other hand, Giraudoux is keenly concerned with the problem of the wedded couple.

The couple.

In Giraudoux's early fiction the subject of the couple is present only incidentally here and there. It is introduced as a theme first in connection with Jérôme Bardini, who leaves his wife and his comfortable life to seek adventures in the world. He has nothing to reproach Renée for. Her beauty, loyalty, attentions are all that any man could ask of a wife. Yet he suffocates in so much well-being. Despite his love for her, the idea of her possible death is not altogether unpleasant. Ah, to be like David Copperfield, he thinks, "qui perdit sa femme enfant avant d'avoir sa femme femme, ah! qui pourra dire son bonheur!"[57] We see Bardini and Renée together only the morning of the day he will depart — a routine morning in appearance with its humdrum occupations and topical conversation at lunch. Yet each in his own mind is carrying on a soliloquy charged with poetry and drama. The first picture of the couple that Giraudoux paints is one already in dissolution.

In *Eglantine* we encounter a strange couple — Moïse, the Jewish financier, and his wife Sarah. Sarah, who is dead now, had been an ugly, sickly woman whose many virtues served for nothing until the moment of approaching death: "Ses qualités étaient l'héroïsme, la patience, l'audace, le dévouement sans limites."[58] If Moïse's life had been marked by failure and misfortune instead of triumph and success, Sarah would have been a good and useful wife. The pathos of her death scene filters through the screen of Giraudoux's unsentimental rhetoric:

> J'arrive à peine à te voir enfin, disait Moïse . . . — Moi, je te vois tout le temps, répondait-elle. Ils disaient tous deux les phrases inverses de leurs sentiments, Moïse se passant au besoin de voir Sarah, mais la portant toujours dans sa pensée, Sarah désirant ardemment sa présence, mais grâce à cette tendre diagonale entre leurs cœurs et leurs bouches, deux amours loyaux et purs étaient exprimés.[59]

This early glimpse of conjugal tenderness is very brief. The Sarahs of the world are not Giraudoux's forte. Nor is pity his frequent mood. When we see happiness in marriage again, it will be associated with persons more to Giraudoux's taste — and to the gods'.

"J'aime votre couple," Jupiter says to Amphitryon, "j'aime, au début des ères humaines, ces deux grands et beaux corps sculptés à l'avant de l'humanité comme des proues."[60] Young and perfect specimens ("elle est blonde et rose; le mari brun, tout brun"),[61] Amphitryon and Alcmene constitute indeed the perfect couple so invulnerable together that heaven itself can do nothing against them. Jupiter is no match for Alcmene in her eloquent defense of conjugal love:

> Si tu n'es pas celui près de qui je m'éveille le matin et que je laisse dormir dix minutes encore, d'un sommeil pris sur la frange de ma journée, et dont mes regards purifient le visage avant le soleil et l'eau pure; si tu n'es pas celui dont je reconnais à la longueur et au son de ses pas s'il se rase ou s'habille, s'il pense ou s'il a la tête vide, celui avec lequel je déjeune, je dîne et je soupe, celui dont le souffle, quoi que je fasse, précède toujours mon souffle d'un millième de seconde; si tu n'es pas celui que je laisse chaque soir s'endormir dix minutes avant moi, d'un sommeil volé au plus vif de ma vie, afin qu'au moment même où il pénètre dans les rêves je sente son corps bien chaud et vivant, qui que tu sois, je ne t'ouvrirai point.[62]

The bourgeois marriage from which Bardini flees is Alcmene's greatest joy. Amphitryon, too, basks in contentment. Their happiness, a little smug and ridiculous for being so middle-class, takes on a nobler countenance in the lyrical duets that constitute their *adieux* to one another before Jupiter arrives. Their mutual love prevails, and as the curtain goes down, in spite of the official legend, Alcmene and Amphitryon are just a happy pair awaiting the birth of a son. Their story of wedded bliss is unique in Giraudoux's theater, where the problem of the couple, one of its principal themes, will hereafter be treated with increasing disillusionment.

In the spoofing *Supplément au Voyage de Cook* the poet of the ideal couple turns cynical and a trifle wistful. Mr. and Mrs. Banks are a caricature of connubial complacency. For years they have lived in their stodgy English virtue and fidelity. But what adulterous sins they have committed in spirit! In spite of the Gallic hilarity of the piece there are touching indications of lifelong frustrations borne in silence. Listen to Mrs. Banks: "A mon âge, j'ai pris des habitudes, mon cher Vaïturou, ou des manies: je n'aime plus que les hommes invisibles. Mes uniques joies viennent d'eux. A la présence de Mr. Banks, tout superbe qu'il est, je préfère même l'absence de Mr. Banks."[63] His life is brightened by the memory of a red-haired Sally Thompson; hers, of a tennis player who also had red hair. Who would say, watching this respectable couple sleeping in proper beds set up for them on the tropical beach, that "Mr. Banks passe sa nuit avec cent femmes expertes et Mrs. Banks avec cent géants!"[64]

To return to a more serious work, let us look at *Choix des Elues,* Giraudoux's last novel, which takes up the theme of escape from marriage that was already treated in *Aventures de Jérôme Bardini.* Edmée, an older and more tragic sister of Suzanne and Juliette, who had their fling and returned to marry the home-town boy, must leave her devoted husband and her family to realize her individual destiny outside of marriage. Pierre is too heavy, too earthy, to follow this star-struck creature into the invisible apartment, into the "maison des airs," as Claudie imagines it. The prosy Giraudoux hero, Bardini excepted, needs a good bourgeoise wife like Alcmene, or one like Suzanne, Juliette, or Isabelle, who after briefly romancing on desert islands, in the "pays des hommes," or in the forest with a specter, is ready to concern herself with housekeeping. Woe to him if he mates with an avenging arm of the Lord, like Judith, or a water nymph who cannot learn to deceive, like Ondine, or a creature like Edmée, over whom even the law of gravity is powerless.

Although stubbornly clinging to his great ideal for humanity, Giraudoux grew less and less convinced of man's ability to realize the happy couple. The gods who looked with pleasure on Amphitryon and Alcmene see in subsequent works only wrecked or abandoned marriages. In *Sodome et Gomorrhe,* they are ready to destroy the world if a happy couple cannot be found. For it is in marriage that man's pride, selfishness, and fanaticism are checked, that he must learn generosity and tolerance. A society in harmony and nations at peace with one another are only chimeras so long as men and women cannot achieve with each other a satisfactory, enduring union. The angel tells Lia:

> De là-haut nous voyons surtout le désert, qui tient les trois quarts du monde, et il reste le désert si c'est un homme seul ou une femme seule qui s'y risque. Mais le couple qui y chemine le change en oasis et en campagne. Et le couple peut être égaré à vingt lieues du douar, chaque grain de sable par sa présence devient peuplé, chaque rocher moussu, chaque mirage réel.[65]

Neither Lia nor Jean, Ruth nor Jacques, can make the desert of their incompatibility bloom. Marriage has brought no happiness to any one of them, and the illusions of love have flown away like so many birds. Not even the idea of the death of their spouses could move them. To save the world, Jacques would be willing to counterfeit an exemplary couple, but Lia balks before hypocrisy. She, burning with a thirst for the absolute, sets about trying to seduce the angel. The couples engage in interminable duets of mutual recrimination punctuated by spasms of rage. There is no hope for them. When Lia, in her frenzy, goes as far as blasphemy, the fiery wrath of the Lord envelops the evil city.

Sodome et Gomorrhe constitutes the term of the evolution we have seen the couple theme take in Giraudoux's works. The despair of this play remains Giraudoux's final stand on the subject. The posthumous publications do not treat the theme directly, and any inference we make from them does not mitigate the conclusion of *Sodome et Gomorrhe.*

Pour Lucrèce starts from the couple theme, but concerns the individual's problem of honor and virtue more than the mutual relations of a couple. Lucile is a proud, self-righteous person, entirely lacking the humility of the other good wives, Alcmene and Ondine. She must be punished for her lack of generosity. But since one can imagine this tragedy of character centered around concepts other than those of a wife's honor, it cannot be thought of as primarily another play about the couple. The husband, one remembers, is scarcely put on stage. Lucile's punishment does, however, touch on familiar ground, for the most painful consequence of her folly is the realization that her husband is unworthy of her and that between them there is really no common ground for understanding. She has been the victim of a bad joke — her idealism has brought about only misfortune and disillusionment. Lucile cannot live in a world that is impure. She dies, leaving it to couples like Paola and Armand who are willing to suffer compromise, voluntary blindness, and hypocrisy. There is nothing in the ambiguous irony of this dénouement to indicate that Giraudoux before his death ever regained the faith in the couple that had inspired *Amphitryon 38.*

The disenchantment which colors Giraudoux's final picture of the wedded couple may be interpreted as frustration at the impossibility of ever fixing for long the dream of love. A large part of his writing is given over to sentimental pursuits and pleasures; but, because of their idealism no doubt, they are condemned to be only transitory.

The shy Simon of the early period, who recoils before sensuality, gradually evolves into the posed and worldly Jacques of *Combat avec l'Ange.* Yet his amorous adventures, that would easily provide material for an erotic novel, are presented almost without sensuality. Jacques has mistresses, regularly visits a dubious hotel with Maléna. But even lying together naked on the bed, they appear like disembodied spirits, so little carnal are the thoughts and fancies that Giraudoux ascribes to them. In the mature novels and plays, the numerous highly erotic situations are decently clad in the author's sentimental and cerebral monologue. Even in the early *Juliette,* a scene of murder and rape is almost hidden by rhetorical play. The lust in the Judith story becomes lost in tragedy, and in the story of Helen of Troy it turns into humor.

One would say that Simon's idealism persists throughout adulthood, permitting him to find fit subjects for his reverie in the most mundane intrigues. If, among the female characters, Indiana is the only real prostitute, the others are no less lacking in conventional moral prejudices. Geneviève the artist and Bellita the society woman both take a succession of lovers. Stéphy engages in a mock marriage that lasts no longer than the honeymoon. Nellie (of the unfinished *Menteuse*) divides her time between two men. Love is their preoccupation, their *raison d'être,* but, as Giraudoux analyzes their sentiments and those of their partners, they appear utterly devoid of physical passion. The sexual instinct, it would seem, has been transformed into a spiritual force and a lyrical impulse.

Thus a theme that is usually treated in literature as comical or grotesque — that of the elderly man who keeps a young mistress — acquires a beauty and poignancy that makes its title, *Cantique des Cantiques,* entirely suitable. In *Eglantine,* the two old gentlemen Fontranges and Moïse invite our sympathy, and the heroine, who is apparently the mistress of both, does not seem unlovely. Actually Eglantine seems purity itself, for poetry and fancy keep the reader from translating her adventures into any sordid prose.

Some critics who attempt to analyze Jean Giraudoux's libido hint that behind the innocence of his stories there is a certain morbidity, that the obvious fascination young women held for him is an unhealthy symptom. Although we are not qualified to refute with professional authority such a suspicion, we believe it entirely without foundation. The young woman in Giraudoux's work is more of a poetic symbol than a sexual object, and there is not any lasciviousness whatever in her depiction. In view of the licence he permits his characters and the amoral situations he does not hesitate to depict, it seems obvious that this *pudeur* is not the result of any inhibition but of a natural delicacy of sentiment — love as the seventeenth-century *précieux* would have it. The only fault that can be imputed to love such as this is the one Giraudoux himself denounces — the element of pride. Simon, Jérôme, Maléna are proud: they adore the impossible and cannot realize the modest happiness of those who do not look at the moon. Hence their restlessness and dissatisfaction, their incapacity to obtain an enduring love. We cannot here pursue an exhaustive investigation of Giraudoux's theme of love. But anyone who might undertake to do so would do well, we believe, to use spirituality rather than morbid complexes as his touchstone.

If Giraudoux grew in time convinced that his dream of love could never be realized, he was never completely bitter. The little idyll of Irma and the young man in *La Folle de Chaillot* indicates that Giraudoux always took pleasure in watching the happiness of two young people, even though he knew that in time they might become like the couples of *Sodome et Gomorrhe.*

Chapter 5

HIS PHILOSOPHY: HUMANITY AND THE UNIVERSE

Although some of the major motifs of Giraudoux's work fall under the headings of psychology or sociology, we have insisted that Giraudoux's treatment of them is purely poetic. In the early books, Giraudoux is poetic chiefly in the lyrical sense, describing his feelings and his sensorial reactions to the world about him. As his work matures, Giraudoux's poetic sensibility acquires greater depth: he contemplates man in his essential nature, muses on his destiny, and rejoices over or laments the order of things. Consider the theme of the couple, just discussed. As Giraudoux treats it, it is not really a social or psychological theme, but a metaphysical one presented in terms of poetry. When man and woman cannot form a satisfactory couple, "la création de Dieu . . . est compromise," the Archangel says.[1] The time has now come to try to reconstruct Giraudoux's notion of the metaphysical universe and determine man's place in it.

The Gods

For Giraudoux, upon the visible world hinges an invisible world.[2] The "certains bibliophiles de Lyon" reported to have been surprised that Suzanne on her island never once mentions God were just quibbling:[3] all Giraudoux's novels and plays attest the existence of unseen forces that determine the movement of history and the course of individual lives here below. They may not always appear directly, or may assume various guises, depending upon the whim of the author or the

Notes to Chapter 5 begin on page 227.

needs of the situation, but their presence can always be felt, and, through the revelations of each successive work, their ultimate nature can be perceived.

Never, however, even though they be referred to as God, can these forces be thought of as the God of mercy and of love worshipped by the Christian faithful. The Biblical plays — significantly drawn from the Old Testament — depict only a fearful avenger and destroyer. But he is not the just and righteous God of the Old Testament either, rewarding the virtuous and punishing the wicked. Hypocrite, deceiver, callously indifferent to human sensibilities and concepts of justice, he is denounced with hysterical vehemence by his elected vessel Judith, forced against her will to be a symbol of murder and hatred. Attitude alone is what this God demands of human beings, intentions do not count: "Dieu exige que notre œuvre ait la robe du sacrifice, mais il nous laisse libres, sous cet ample vêtement, de servir nos propres penchants, et les plus bas."[4] How could he be interested in moral behavior, when, by human understanding, he does not act with rectitude himself? Judith's sensuality is turned into saintliness: "Pourquoi," his outraged victim cries, "de cette nuit de parjure et de stupre faire tout à coup une nuit sainte?" The angel replies, "Ne t'inquiète pas de cela. Dieu se réserve, à mille ans de distance, de projeter la sainteté sur le sacrilège et la pureté sur la luxure. C'est une question d'éclairage."[5] *Judith* is one long blasphemy against the God of the Jews. As she is being led off to the synagogue, there to spend the rest of her days, Judith says, "C'est facile. Ma saleté et ma gloire ne me laissent plus d'autre fréquentation que Dieu."[6]

Is the God of *Sodome et Gomorrhe* any more orthodox? It is clear that he acts with less baseness towards his creatures. They have, ostensibly at least, a freedom of choice which Judith was denied, but, given their unalterable natures, they can scarcely profit from this freedom. What he demands of them is beyond their power to achieve — a happy couple — and this condition of salvation, as well as his rejection of sacrifice freely offered, is preposterous in any Judaeo-Christian frame of reference. Lia's voice joins Judith's in blasphemy: "Dieu est comme vous. Lui aussi se dérobe. Que les êtres qu'il a créés soient de pièces et d'arondes que rien n'ajuste, peu lui importe . . ."[7]

Although the rabbi Joachim in *Judith* declares that Jehovah is not like the Greek gods, in Giraudoux's universe all the gods are actually much the same. But just as the Jehovah of *Judith* is not the orthodox God of the Jews and the Christians, the "grandes distractions" and "grands indifférents" of *La Guerre de Troie* and *Electre* are not the gods of Aeschylus or Euripides. Giraudoux's gods have little to do with any established cult or historical religion, but constitute merely a very personal solution to the riddle of the world invented by Giraudoux's poetic imagination:

> Je les imagine [Aegisthus says] non point occupés sans relâche de cette moisissure suprême et mobile de la terre qu'est l'humanité, mais parvenus, à un tel grade de sérénité et d'ubiquité, qu'il ne peut plus être que la béatitude c'est-à-dire l'inconscience. Ils sont inconscients au sommet de l'échelle de toutes créatures comme l'atome est inconscient à leur degré le plus bas. La différence est que c'est une inconscience fulgurante, omnisciente, taillée à mille faces, et à leur état normal de diamants, atones et sourds, ils ne répondent qu'aux lumières, qu'aux signes, et sans les comprendre.[8]

Hector, in *La Guerre de Troie,* mocks their silence: "C'est curieux comme les dieux s'abstiennent de parler eux-mêmes dans les cas difficiles."[9] But what can one expect of gods who are unconscious? Incoherence, stupid awkwardness, and injustice. Their justice is the same "question d'éclairage" that the angel explained to Judith:

> Il est incontestable qu'éclatent parfois dans la vie des humains des interventions dont l'opportunité ou l'amplitude peut laisser croire à un intérêt ou à une justice extra-humaine. Elles ont ceci d'extra-humain, de divin, qu'elles sont un travail en gros, nullement ajusté. La peste éclate bien lorsqu'une ville a péché par impiété ou par folie, mais elle ravage la ville voisine, particulièrement sainte. La guerre se déchaîne quand un peuple dégénère et s'avilit, mais elle dévore les derniers justes, les derniers courageux, et sauve les plus lâches. Ou bien, quelle que soit la faute, où qu'elle soit commise, c'est le même pays ou la même famille qui paye, innocente ou coupable. Je connais une mère de sept enfants qui avait l'habitude de fesser toujours le même, c'était une mère divine. Cela correspond bien à ce que nous pensons des dieux, que ce sont des boxeurs aveugles, des fesseurs aveugles, tout satisfaits de retrouver les mêmes joues à gifler et les mêmes fesses.[10]

Unconscious or blind though they may be, these forces appear to act with malevolence. "Les dieux infestent notre pauvre univers, Judith," says Holofernes.[11] They plot wars to destroy what they have allowed to fructify — "le déchaînement de cette brutalité et de cette folie humaines qui seules rassurent les dieux," as Ulysses calls war.[12] It is the same story, whether they take the form of a Jewish God, Greek deities, or the familiar spirits of Germanic lore: Oh, to be alone a bit in the universe! cries Hans — "Ce que je demande, c'est vivre sans sentir grouiller autour de nous, comme elles s'y acharnent, ces vies extra-humaines . . . N'y a-t-il donc pas eu une époque, un siècle qu'ils n'aient empesté?"[13] What Hans longs for is the little oasis free from the gods that Holofernes offers Judith:

> Il n'y a pas de Dieu ici . . . dans ces trente pieds carrés. C'est un des rares coins humains vraiment libres. Les dieux infestent notre pauvre univers, Judith. De la Grèce aux Indes, du Nord au Sud, pas de pays où ils ne pullulent, chacun avec ses vices, avec ses odeurs . . . L'atmosphère du monde, pour qui aime respirer, est celui d'une chambrée de dieux . . . Mais il est encore quelques endroits qui leur sont interdits; seul je sais les voir. Ils subsistent, sur la plaine ou la montagne, comme des taches de paradis terrestre. Les insectes qui les habitent n'ont pas le péché originel des insectes: je plante ma tente sur eux . . . Par chance, juste en face de la ville du Dieu juif, j'ai reconnu celui-ci, à une inflexion des palmes, à un appel des eaux. Je t'offre pour une nuit cette villa sur un océan éventé et pur.[14]

Are we right in accepting such verbal exercises as an expression of Giraudoux's serious attitude? Within limits, yes, for underneath the whimsical rhetoric there appears to be a fundamental position regarding the forces that man cannot directly perceive but that affect his life. Man must reckon with them; he must never adore them. Nothing in Giraudoux suggests atheism, but nothing suggests religious fervor either. Discreetly silent on the question of a Christian God ("Je n'assurerais jamais qu'à Dieu que Dieu existe."),[15] hostile towards the God of the Jews, and impatient with all matters of cult, he would have us turn our eyes away from the gods to dedicate ourselves to this world, to fellow men, to the here and now. Giraudoux's dream is of an earthly paradise where human beings live fully and freely according to their natures. Holofernes exhorts Judith to imagine a world of innocence, without preoccupation with God:

> Songe à la douceur qu'aurait ta journée, dégagée des terreurs et des prières. Songe au petit déjeuner du matin servi sans promesse

> d'enfer, au thé de cinq heures sans péché mortel, avec le beau citron et la pince à sucre innocente et étincelante. Songe aux jeunes gens et aux jeunes filles s'étreignant simplement dans les draps frais, et se jetant les oreillers à la tête, quelques talons roses en l'air, sans anges et sans démons voyageurs . . . ! Songe à l'homme innocent . . .[16]

Humanity

Through a large part of his work, Giraudoux pursues a pretty dream of a world before the Fall. He describes himself in the "Prière sur l'Acropole" as the sorcerer of the Garden of Eden:

> C'est que je vis encore . . . dans cet intervalle qui sépara la création et le péché originel. J'ai été excepté de la malédiction en bloc. Aucune de mes pensées n'est chargée de culpabilité, de responsabilité, de liberté . . . Je vois les meubles anciens du monde comme Adam les vit, les arbres, les étangs sans tache originelle, et les meubles modernes, téléphone, cinéma, auto, dans leur divinité. Je suis un petit Messie pour les objets et les bêtes minuscules . . . Les quelques modifications que l'on me doit ici-bas sont celles que j'aurais apportées au jardin d'Eve . . . je suis le sourcier de l'Eden![17]

The early novels depict a world as pure and gratuitous as a child's dream, accented only by a touch of Watteau-like melancholy. Superb young men and women dally at life and love *à la* Mlle. de Scudéry. The experience of the war is chiefly a spree. The hero returns from the war, the heroine returns from her island — yet, in assuming the role of adulthood, they continue to be discreet and elegant. Maléna, Fontranges, Bardini, Edmée have a purity and a perfection that is Edenic. Giraudoux, the sorcerer, has cast a spell over the world. It is the "enchantment" of the village in *Intermezzo:*

> Le droguiste. — Elle est bien plutôt dans cet état où tous les vœux s'exaucent, où toutes les divagations se trouvent être justes. Chez un individu, cela s'appelle l'état poétique. Notre ville est en délire poétique.[18]

To "poetize" life thus is for Giraudoux the supreme adjustment, the essence of civilization. He loves the gods no more than the postwar "Promethean" writers do.[19] But he is more urbane than they, and prefers to remain on polite terms with the universe — "une politesse envers la création."[20] Already in *Siegfried et le Limousin* he defines the attitude of the civilized man towards nature:

> C'est un état de modestie qui pousse l'homme civilisé à vivre parallèlement à la nature (ce qui lui évite d'ailleurs de rencontrer cette personne impitoyable), à attribuer par une juste évaluation du pouvoir humain . . . le moins de prix possible à la vie, à en garder vis-à-vis de son contraire la mort une certaine déférence et à la saluer; — et, d'autre part, en raison de ce doux mépris pour elle, à ne pas la compliquer sur terre par d'autres exigences que les humaines; à exercer, mais sans nuire aux autres et par gymnastique, les qualités qui seraient nécessaires si la vie était juste, agréable et éternelle, telle que le courage, l'activité, quelque parcimonie et la bonté.[21]

Siegfried and the Sisyphus of Albert Camus are not in disagreement:

> Je laisse Sisyphe au bas de la montagne! On retrouve toujours son fardeau. Mais Sisyphe enseigne la fidélité supérieure qui nie les dieux et soulève les rochers. Lui aussi juge que tout est bien. Cet univers désormais sans maître ne lui paraît ni stérile ni futile. Chacun des grains de cette pierre, chaque éclat minéral de cette montagne pleine de nuit, à lui seul, forme un monde. La lutte elle-même vers les sommets suffit à remplir un cœur d'homme. Il faut imaginer Sisyphe heureux.[22]

Life must be lived joyously within its boundaries.

Indeed, man living according to his nature and exploiting the area assigned to him in the universe need not lament his lot. Did not Ondine leave her watery palace to learn how to make pastry for a human husband, do not gods and ghosts seek the company of mortals? Giraudoux's chief spokesmen — Holofernes, Alcmene, the *contrôleur* of *Intermezzo,* Aurélie — reiterate in winsome, albeit ironic, speeches the satisfactions of the human condition and defend with enthusiasm its unique dignity. Alcmene, perfectly comfortable in her housewifely way, cannot be tempted by promises of immortality and divinity. Human she is, and human she will remain. If for nothing else, out of loyalty to her kind: "Devenir immortel, c'est trahir, pour un humain. Je me solidarise avec mon astre."[23] Jupiter must acquiesce with admiration: "C'est que tu es le premier être vraiment humain que je rencontre."[24] Alcmene is indeed the human being *par excellence.* She declares, "Il n'est pas une peripétie de la vie humaine que je n'admette, de la naissance à la mort, j'y comprends même les repas de famille."[25]

Just as Alcmene stands firm against the blandishments of Jupiter, so the *contrôleur* prevails against the specter. He successfully woos Isabelle with a lyrical description of a life spent in civil service. Giraudoux's irony plays lightly over all these defenses of life made by Alcmene, Holofernes, the *contrôleur,* and poor Aurélie (with all her pathetic woes), but their attitude has his wholehearted endorsement.

If these exemplary characters know that the humdrum pleasures of life are not to be despised, they know also that its precariousness, its transitoriness, should not be deplored. Alcmene has no hankering after permanence of any sort: "Mais la beauté de la terre se crée elle-même, à chaque minute. Ce qu'il y a de prodigieux en elle, c'est qu'elle est éphémère."[26] The *contrôleur,* too, marvels that life is at once so rich and so brief. These conscientious human beings, after exploiting life's fullness, meet death as merely a part of the natural course of events. Alcmene remarks, "Je ne crains pas la mort. C'est l'enjeu de la vie."[27] The Dubardeau family in *Bella* confronts death with the same equanimity: "J'étais surpris de voir combien ces savants prenaient, en ce qui les concernait, peu de précaution [contre la mort] . . . Ils s'étaient donnés sans réserve au sort commun . . . Tous d'ailleurs savaient où ils allaient, c'est-à-dire au néant."[28] "To philosophize is to learn to die," said Montaigne. Giraudoux, another amiable stoic, might paraphrase, "To live fully is to learn to die."

The subject of death looms among Giraudoux's major preoccupations. Its fascination for him is evident in his earliest works. In *Provinciales,* the young boy overhears that relatives and townsfolk have died and, mystified, observes the strange manner in which adults speak of death. In *L'Ecole des Indifférents,* the adolescent muses continually over death, and in his dreams holds sweetly melancholy conversations with the departed. The shades of Edith and of André Bovy are tender friends, who exhort him to enjoy his life, "à apprécier tout ce qui court et joue sans raison sur la surface de la terre, les chats, les enfants, les cyclistes ridicules qui pressent des trompes d'automobile."[29] The deaths that Giraudoux depicts are all noble deaths without terror or struggle — those of Geneviève, Bella, the *Président,* Sarah. The ideal death is the simple death: "Le jour vint où Sarah dit. — Je meurs, et, seule mais parfaite traduction qu'elle fit de ce mot, elle fut soudain roide, tendue et pâle."[30] This is Giraudoux's conception of the ultimate "politesse envers la création." Unsupported by assurance of future life, but confident that he has done his duty by this one, man waits for death modestly and courteously. Death is, in the words of the *contrôleur,* just a "repos définitif. Se torturer à propos d'un repos définitif, c'est plutôt une inconséquence."[31]

It is therefore by being most simply man that man achieves happiness and virtue. Everyone and everything in place is for Giraudoux the perfect world. On these grounds, Jean-Paul Sartre calls Giraudoux's world Aristotelian and rationalistic: "N'est-ce pas chez [Aristote] qu'on trouve ce monde propre, fini, hiérarchisé, rationnel jusqu'à l'os?"[32] This is indeed the world that Giraudoux's poetic fancy chooses to create — a world of archetypes, in fact, in which all phenomena — pickles or human beings — strive to attain their own ideal, approximate their "substantial form." Action, event, progression are, as typified most clearly in *Choix des Elues,* the adventure of the character in search of his own essential nature, matter trying to realize its form.

With movement limited to sudden flowering or gradual unfolding of essential natures, this perfect and ideal world of Giraudoux's strikes Sartre as being a static one.[33] It seems, on the contrary, that this process of self-realization makes for great movement as each seeks his own orbit in a universe itself already in harmonious motion. But for Sartre the opposite of immobility may mean only chaotic movement — fortuity and movement towards nothing — for that is the way he himself sees the universe. And Giraudoux's world is orderly, hierarchized, and delicately equilibrated. Hence the moral law, which Sartre quite correctly formulates for Giraudoux's humanity:

> L'homme doit réaliser librement son essence finie et, par là même, s'accorder librement au reste du monde. Tout homme est responsable de l'harmonie universelle, il doit se soumettre de son plein gré à la nécessité des archétypes. Et dans le moment même où cette harmonie paraît, où paraît cet équilibre entre nos tendances profondes, entre la nature et l'esprit, dans le moment où l'homme est au centre d'un monde en ordre, "le plus nettement" homme qu'il se puisse au centre du monde "le plus nettement" monde, la créature de M. Giraudoux reçoit sa récompense: c'est le bonheur.[34]

An ethic, were it not for the element of *"bonheur,"* not unlike the postwar ethic of "authenticity."

In Giraudoux's Edenic world of archetypes, as happiness is harmony, so virtue too is harmony. Not Christian resistance to one's nature but pagan fulfillment, submission to it. Note Giraudoux's definition of innocence:

> L'innocent n'est pas celui qui n'est pas condamné, c'est celui qui ne porte pas condamnation. L'innocence d'un être est l'adaptation absolue à l'univers dans lequel il vit. Elle n'a rien à voir avec la cruauté ou la douceur — le loup mangeant la colombe n'est pas moins innocent, que la colombe expirante.[35]

The "lay miracle" of *Le Cerf* reveals to Fontranges that he must take up the hunt again. Maléna is in error to commiserate with the poor. Her role is to be rich and beautiful and carefree. The stiff-necked couples of *Sodome et Gomorrhe* sin in refusing to be man and woman living contentedly together. The crime of the "mecs" in the *Folle de Chaillot,* with their syndicates, corporations, and combinations, is having left their proper state of modest human beings to participate in a monstrous plan of exploitation. Their cupidity has scorched the earth in its wake and threatens to destroy the world's balance: "Quand nous aurons vidé notre planète de ses équilibres et de ses dosages internes, elle risque de prendre un jour le parcours non aimanté dans les chemins du ciel."[36] It would be interesting to know what Giraudoux's reaction to the development of atomic warfare would have been. His advice to nations was the same as to humanity: nations must remain true to their historical selves.

The wisdom of France, he declares, is that she has done so:

> La réalité, la finesse, la perfection du jugement humain des Français viennent justement de ce qu'ils n'ont jamais voulu couper leur histoire et le développement naturel de leur esprit par un de ces verres réfringents ou colorés que pose l'imagination sur d'autres races.[37]

No mythological creatures hover over French history; her heroes remain perfectly human, even bourgeois: Jeanne d'Arc, Napoléon. "Tous ces héros qui ont émigré de France pour être les personnages mythiques d'autres pays, Guillaume le Conquérant, La Fayette, vivent encore chez nous une existence bourgeoise et précise."[38] Gilbertain muses over the form Catholicism has taken in France:

> Ce pays maintenu raisonnable et fidèle par la façon dont les fonctionnaires l'avaient administré depuis mille ans, non pas en l'as-

> servissant par la force ou le prodige, mais en graduant sagement ce qu'il pouvait porter par siècle en impôts, en croyance et en adoration . . .[39]

> Il était reconnaissant à la France d'avoir épuré la religion . . . Là seulement elle n'était que civilisation, que perfection.[40]

The younger Giraudoux, enflamed with patriotic fervor, like the Giraudoux minister of propaganda, views his country as if it were Holofernes' "trente pieds carrés," and endows it with all the virtues he admires most.

Modern Germany, on the other hand, appears to Giraudoux to have strayed from her historical self: "L'Allemagne," he asserts, "n'a pas à être forte. Elle a à être l'Allemagne."[41] The German people, "au lieu de suivre les leçons et les instincts que donne le sol qui leur fournit les oranges et les pommes de terre, se forgent un modèle . . ."[42] The results of such deviations can only be catastrophic, whether for nations or individuals.

In Giraudoux's plays, the dramatic crisis is characteristically brought about by a person who would surpass the boundaries of his finite nature. The characters of the early works flirt with infinity but retreat in time to the everyday world. Suzanne, Juliette, and even Jérôme Bardini have had a fling, that is all. Before settling down in life, they have slipped away to satisfy a natural human hankering after golden fruits that do not grow in Bellac. Giraudoux, who advocates a moderate indulgence in *Streben* and *Schwärmerei* to keep the French soul supple, gives them his blessing. When they return, they are all the more enriched for their holiday away from the land of measure, practicality, and common sense. The proud Judith, the just Electra, the virtuous Lucile, however, cross the line, and in so doing wreak havoc on earth. We may consider them as moral figures tragic for being excessive, and their dramas as moralities teaching moderation.

Yet we might justifiably ask, can Giraudoux's tragic heroines be blamed for the stiffening, the abstracting of their personalities? It is not clear how they could have prevented being metamorphosed into symbols. They may have struggled to remain simple mortals. "Je vous répète que ce n'est pas pour moi la voix de Dieu," cries Judith.[43] Something in her nature forces this girl, in spite of herself, to step outside the ranks of her fellow mortals. As Electra, too, when she "declares herself," turns overnight into "la justice intégrale."[44] They seem to be obeying the same laws of self-realization as other phenomena in Giraudoux's universe, and if guilty, are guilty because the universe wants them so. To understand them, we must return to the gods.

The somnolent forces that vex the world would go on dozing and mankind would be left in peace, were it not for those excessive persons who cry out to them, clamoring for vengeance or justice. It takes a sign or a signal from a human being to bring about what is to come. The Electras, "femmes à histoires," are among us for that purpose — "rares créatures que le destin met en circulation sur la terre pour son usage personnel."[45] Thus one cannot say they act willfully or maliciously. Their freedom is no more than that of all Giraudoux's creatures — the obligation to try to attain one's archetype. Like Mauriac's creatures bereft of grace, Giraudoux's tragic heroines merely have the ungrateful role. Suppose they did not cry out? Such a supposition is idle, for they must cry out. It is as if there existed some sort of master plan governing events in the universe down to the individual destiny of each mortal. Giraudoux no more than anyone else knows what it is. He calls it destiny or fate and illustrates it by metaphors (a sleeping tiger) or by conundrums (an accelerated form of time). But whatever man's will or ruse, the course of events is unalterable: Alcmene will give birth to a semidivine child, Judith will avenge her people, the Trojan War will take place. The wisdom of the Hectors and the Aegisthes cannot prevent the cataclysms unleashed by the helpless Helens and Electras.

Such, in the main lines, is the notion of the world that can be deduced from Giraudoux's writings.[46] We can construct, by picking out pieces here and there, a philosophic system complete with metaphysics and ethics. It is delightful and clever, winsome in its simplicity, often brilliantly sagacious and inspiring. But let us not misunderstand. Some critics have pondered distinctions Giraudoux may make between destiny and God, have tried to reconcile what appears to be evidence of free will here with the apparent determinism expressed in another passage. It is as if Giraudoux's work were a vast puzzle behind which the author had concealed a precise corpus of ideas about life. Giraudoux is a writer, they seem to forget, not a philosopher; and his work, dictated by intuition and inspiration rather than logic or system, is unorganized and ambiguous. He can, at a given moment, feel one way or another about life, death, and the universe. He may contradict himself, point this way or that way, or no way at all. We may read in meanings that he in no wise intends and hit upon verities, nonetheless real for us, that are not necessarily his.

Morover, Giraudoux is a particularly facile and fanciful writer, whose thought may be led by a nimble pen. The certitudes he affirms, the lines he draws, are at times surely no more than word play. Could we really think that this world of mortals like flowers blooming or waiting to bloom, of denouncers, and of drowsy deities is, for Giraudoux, a literal description of the universe? He would not presume, except in so far as the truth may burst forth from a poet's inspiration, to have penetrated the mysteries of life. To reflect upon whether Giraudoux is more Aristotelian or Platonic is to do violence to his particular genius as well as to that of creative writers in general. They interpret the world to suit their fanciful vision of things. They can project their dream of a better life, imagine gods and angels, jumble the physical and the moral, allegorize, symbolize, create new paths between cause and effect. And, among them, Giraudoux is a most agile prestidigitator. The tricks that he plays often appear to belong, however, less to a philosophy manual than to a book of rhetoric.

Only with these reservations can we speak of Giraudoux's philosophical ideas. When he seems to close his eyes willfully to the ugliness of the world or depict it as if it were lovely, we may regard him as an elegant stoic and call his vision of things Apollonian. When he seems to ascribe a place for everything in the world and dramatize the individual quest for perfection, we can think of Spinoza. In observing the Edenic dream he projects, it may please us to associate him with the gnostic writers who believed in a paradise before the Fall. When he rebels against the confines of reason and looks to nature to reveal her truths by signs, we recall his study of German Romantic authors. We can point to what seem to be echoes of reading in all sorts of philosophy, ancient and modern, including the mystical, prophetic, and illuministic. And, mindful not to equate his work too closely with any one school of thought or to reduce his art to an exposition of a philosophic system, we thereby demonstrate its breadth and manifold nature and suggest possible sources of its nourishment.

But poetic inspiration remains the real key to Giraudoux's universe, the vision of things experienced in moments of rare exaltation.

Sartre remarks that we all have our moments of Aristotelianism — we are walking along the streets of Paris, and suddenly objects turn their faces towards us. That evening is the superlative Paris evening. Time has stopped — we live in a moment of pure happiness, a moment of eternity. This "revelation" experienced occasionally by all has, since time immemorial, been cultivated by the poets. In modern literature, it is thought to have first been described by Rousseau in the *Rêveries d'un Promeneur Solitaire.*[47] Baudelaire calls it a sort of lay grace:

> Il est des jours où l'homme s'éveille avec un génie jeune et vigoureux. Ses paupières à peine déchargées du sommeil qui les scellait, le monde extérieur s'offre à lui avec un relief puissant, une netteté de contours, une richesse de couleurs admirables. Le monde moral ouvre ses vastes perspectives, pleines de clartés nouvelles. L'homme gratifié de cette béatitude, malheureusement rare et passagère, se sent à la fois plus artiste et plus juste, plus noble. . . . Mais ce qu'il y a de plus singulier dans cet état exceptionel de l'esprit et des sens, que je puis sans exagération appeler paradisiaque, si je le compare aux lourdes ténèbres de l'existence commune et journalière, c'est qu'il n'a été créé par aucune cause bien visible et facile à définir. Nous sommes obligés de reconnaître que souvent cette merveille, cette espèce de prodige, se produit comme si elle était l'effet d'une puissance supérieure et invisible, extérieure à l'homme . . . C'est pourquoi je préfère considérer cette condition abnormale de l'esprit comme une véritable grâce . . . une espèce d'excitation angélique . . . le souvenir des réalités invisibles.[48]

We recognize already here in Baudelaire the state of mind Giraudoux seems to be in when he takes up his pen. He himself offers abundant testimony to his moments of poetic illumination. They appear to him moments out of time and space in which he feels in complete harmony with the universe and capable of understanding life's meaning. They are accompanied by a strong sense of well-being, infinite liberty, acute sensibility and lucidity. It is as if, in a state of euphoria, the subject slips out of the human condition to dominate his destiny: "C'est justement que j'ai un poids de moins à porter. C'est que je vis encore, comme l'autre, dans cet intervalle qui sépara la création et le péché originel. J'ai été excepté de la malédiction en bloc."[49]

The universe seems to reveal itself in its primitive clarity. Phenomena which surround man in nature assume the character of symbols, finite expressions of infinity. They suggest the archetypes, the essences of the realm of the absolute, which lend the universe its basic unity and organization. Manifesting themselves through scattered fragments of phenomena, the archetypes impose a system entirely foreign to the rational and logical order which man conventionally attributes to nature. The eternal pattern is thus perceived by the poet: "De grandes ressemblances balafrent le monde et marquent ici et là leur lumière . . . Poète? je dois l'être: elles seules me frappent."[50]

If Giraudoux insists repeatedly on style as the first attribute of the writer, he is in no wise minimizing his function. It is by his use of language that the poet communicates his revelations, by his metaphors that he conveys his intuitions of the intimate structure of the world: "C'est à la poésie, à elle seule que seront toujours réservées la navigation et la découverte."[51] Thus there should be no problem in reconciling Giraudoux of the lofty mission — literature, instrument "de première nécessité" — with Giraudoux the advocate of style and language. We may question the validity of the poet's visions, suspect that he may be dupe of his own fancy, recognize the part of pure fortuity in his writing — the fact remains that Giraudoux's universe is essentially a verbal structure, and whether valued for its possible intimations of the eternal or exclusively for its esthetic delight, it is on the basis of his art that Giraudoux solicits our attention.

Chapter 6

HIS ART: TECHNIQUE AND STYLE

The eminently respectable method of defining by a process of elimination has been practiced time and again in the case of Giraudoux. It has been emphatically reiterated that he is not a novelist, not a dramatist, not a critic. This is quite true, in a sense, for in principle Giraudoux never accepted the limitations of category:

> La forme du livre, pièce, nouvelle, essai, importe aussi peu qu'importaient autrefois la forme du pamphlet de Voltaire, vers libres, dialogue ou conte. . . . Lorsqu'un peuple demande à ses écrivains de ne plus se spécialiser, mais d'aborder chaque genre, lorsqu'il ne les distingue même plus en poètes et en prosateurs, en essayistes et en dramaturges, c'est qu'il a affaire non plus avec les genres, mais avec les écrivains mêmes et la vertu de l'écriture.[1]

In practice, whatever the genre — novel, play, or essay — Giraudoux broke with tradition to adapt the vehicle to his own purposes. A leader in the revolt of his generation against Realism, he rejected *en bloc* the literary canons inherited from nineteenth-century masters — objectivity, observation, documentation as techniques; social history or scientific study as aims and claims; craftsmanship as art.

Paul Valéry declared himself incapable of writing a novel because he refused to write, "La marquise sortit à cinq heures." Giraudoux never felt, as a novelist, that he was obliged to write such sentences. In his earliest pieces he writes only about himself, preferring, he flatly

Notes to Chapter 6 begin on page 228.

states, not to invent characters: "J'écris toujours à la première personne parce que je ne veux pas faire l'artifice de créer un autre personnage."[2] Although his work gradually develops beyond personal reminiscences, his characters — incarnations of his ideas and preoccupations — never acquire realistic density or individualization. The dialogues they engage in bear little resemblance to actual conversation, and they are often not even appropriate to the persons involved. As a study of the versions of a given work shows, speeches may be handed around arbitrarily. The manuscripts offer proof, too, that Giraudoux was little concerned with the development of psychology or situation as we usually find it in the novel, for he arbitrarily trimmed and expanded, or switched the order of episodes.[3] They do not ever constitute what we usually think of as plot.

In his dramatic works and in his essays, Giraudoux exhibits the same unorthodoxy. When *Siegfried* was staged, critics — hostile or enthusiastic — agreed that the play was unlike anything they had come to expect in the theater. Lack of structure, of individualized psychology, or of realism in any measure flouted the time-honored rules. After the première of each new play, critics registered their astonishment. Charming, brilliant, profound, they conceded, but was what they had seen really a play? Of *Sodome et Gomorrhe,* Jacques Houlet says, "L'analyse a beau s'exprimer par la bouche de personnages de chair, ce n'est plus une pièce que nous avons, mais une dissertation."[4] In this play unsustained by plot or psychological action, the only movement is furnished by the progress of the debate between the couples. In Giraudoux's critical writings, we must also be ready for surprises. No one denies that what he says is brilliant, but his fanciful affirmations cannot be judged by the usual machinery of logic and fact.

Neither novelist nor dramatist nor critic, in the accepted sense; no poet either, according to Gabriel Marcel;[5] yet poet is probably the best definition of our author. Although Giraudoux did not write in verse — "Dieu me préserve de faire des vers, d'écrire ce que je pense en lignes, de passer à leur laminoir ma vie"[6] — and is not a purely lyrical spirit (which is the sense in which M. Marcel probably is using the word), how can one better define a writer whose genius is primarily that of a spontaneous creator of images and phrases? It was as a poet that Giraudoux thought of himself: "Poète? je dois l'être."[7] For him the word meant one who has a certain way of looking at things: "Le poète est celui qui lit sa vie, comme on lit une écriture renversée, dans un miroir, et sait lui donner par cette réflexion qu'est le talent, et la vérité littéraire, un ordre qu'elle n'a pas toujours."[8] One for whom writing is only incidental in his life: "L'écriture est un accident dans la vie du poète."[9] Poet would be the only word that Giraudoux would consider as free from the stigma of professional connotation. He sought to avoid (just as determinedly as Proust sought to acquire) the title of *homme de lettres* and made fun of professional literary men "binocle au nez, qui s'occupent à assembler en un roman, comme un jeu de patience, mille pensées qu'ils n'ont eues que séparément."[10] Giraudoux always insisted, at times with irritating coquetry, upon amateur standing among writers. He refused to consider writing as a daily chore and put pen to paper only when the mood was upon him: "J'ai l'impression d'attendre une espèce de commande. Elle vient je ne sais pourquoi. L'ambiance, l'atmosphère se crée, et c'est là-dessus que je travaille."[11] So, if by poet we can understand fanciful improviser, then let us call Giraudoux poet. That will, at least, orient us properly towards his art.

Giraudoux's Composition

"Je prends une feuille blanche et je commence à écrire."[12] Improvisation is Giraudoux's basic method of composition. His manuscripts reveal a spontaneous poet recording his thought patterns just as they take form, with little preconception of where his pen will lead him. "Ce que j'écris correspond à un thème général, mais avant d'avoir tracé le premier mot, j'ignore ce que ce sera. Chaque phrase, chaque chapitre naît de celui qui précède."[13] Often a piece begins with a phrase, and what ensues is embroidery on the theme it states. Each sentence is consequently born out of the preceding — now short and pithy to express a sudden illumination, now sustained over many lines to follow a meandering fancy. In *Adorable Clio,* a chapter opens with the poet before his desk at daybreak. He is looking out of an open window, pressing his forehead "à défaut de vitre, contre l'aube elle-même."[14] The objects that his eye encounters call up fanciful associations and interrelations. Beyond a roof, he sees the top of the plane tree which serves him as weather vane and also indicates, by its leaves, the season. He notes that the "haleine" of night lingers over the water in a basin, although night itself has disappeared. The lights catch his attention — a human hand seems to put out the gas lamps; the street cleaners chase away the shadows by striking the garbage cans.

Suddenly he thinks of a pastor who had discovered a new virtue and then sought it in himself, of a chemist who had discovered a new metal and then sought it in the property of his family. It occurs to him that he has tried on this new virtue and this new metal as one would a new suit; then, his mind wandering back to the subject of dawn, he fuses all these thoughts of newness in the following image: "Jour nouveau, que j'aime à t'essayer sur moi!" A breeze comes up and the sun appears. A butcher boy is wearing a clean apron — "C'est jour sans viande; c'est jour sans sang." An American hurries from the shade of the Odéon across the sunny street to the shade of the Luxembourg. A street sprinkler leaves behind him a snake skin with dripping scales — "chacun combat la nuit comme il le juge bon." The poet now turns away from his window to write: "C'est ainsi, sans pensée, que je commence à écrire au hasard, que j'écris 'Américain,' que j'écris 'joli boucher' dans ma feuille étincelante."

During four days the empty sheet has remained there. Every morning he has removed the books and letters accumulated around it "d'instinct comme autour de la dalle blanche par où l'on plonge en ma mémoire." Every evening he finds his paperweights, the Buddha head, and the mask of Andromeda. But the past is chilly this morning in comparison with the present sunshine. Before he can write about the past, he begs permission to rub against his heart all the things he has just observed, as a bather, standing in the water up to his knees, hesitates and rubs himself with the nearest wave. He lingers further to justify his delay, referring again to the persons in the street and giving fanciful explanations of their actions. He muses: What is the point of being sad if one cannot linger to caress the nostrils of such a fine day; of being happy if one cannot press the lips of Buddha against those of Andromeda; of being tender if one cannot write phrases which do not express one's real feelings, but which begin with O? Now he thinks of the Greek vocatives beginning with O, practicing some nonsensical examples and ending with an apostrophe to the dawn. The postman brings a letter. . . . These ruminations have covered almost six pages. They are typical of Giraudoux's early prose pieces.

One would look vainly for an architectural example among them, a piece structurally conceived and executed, a unit unto itself. Later works have greater autonomy and often more apparent unity. Novels like *Suzanne et le Pacifique* and *Juliette au Pays des Hommes* possess something of an over-all pattern — that, for example, of quest and return. But, as with *Combat avec l'Ange* or *Eglantine,* the beginning and the end of a volume may be entirely arbitrary. Or the story may spin out into sequels or variants like *Siegfried et le Limousin* or *Jérôme Bardini.* A text may be a crazy quilt of fragmentary essays, humorous quatrains, speeches, poems in prose.

The discipline and organization that the theater demanded of Giraudoux did not alter his method of initial composition. Observing that he made several versions of the same play, some critics have spoken of a change in technique, a careful distillation. On the contrary, we see here evidence of the same spontaneous creative process. Out of the welter of improvisations produced, the playwright — in collaboration with the impresario — could cut something stageable. We know how Giraudoux sat with Jouvet at rehearsals, revising and rewriting to put the play in shape. But it never attained a "definitive" form, for such would be contrary to Giraudoux's notion of the writer's art, and the version presented remained a medley of waltzes, fugues, rhapsodies, and laments. In all, the character of inspiration and fortuity is unmistakable, precisely what Giraudoux praised in the Spanish Golden Age dramatists, who turned out hundreds of plays by writing a new one instead of rewriting the old one and executing with virtuosity many variations on a given theme. It was not their practice to have done with a character or a situation once and for all —

> . . . non pas d'en finir avec un caractère, une intrigue, mais simplement, entre la prière du matin et le binage et l'arrosage, de changer les noms des héros et des héroïnes, de dorer leurs épées, de leur donner une nouvelle ombre sous ces deux soleils, l'honneur et l'amour, de planter un nouveau méandre pour leurs allées et leurs venues dans ces deux jardins, l'honneur et l'amour . . .[15]

The patterns upon which Giraudoux embroiders cannot, in sum, be defined by the covers of a book. "Chaque œuvre en elle-même ne compte pas. Un livre, une pièce ne se trouve nullement séparée de celle qui la précède, de celle qui la suit. Je n'ai pas la préoccupation du livre, mais de la série des livres."[16] One moves from *Bella* to *Eglantine* and on to *Jérôme Bardini* as if they were parts of the same work. Where Giraudoux stops one and begins another appears purely arbitrary. The organic units of his work are the motifs, which resemble musical themes. Giraudoux declares in fact: "Un écrivain doit écrire comme un musicien fait sa musique."[17] "Je n'ai jamais compris l'architecture dramatique que comme la sœur articulée de l'architecture musicale."[18] His first piece, *Le Dernier Rêve d'Edmond About,* has divisions specifically entitled prelude, finale, etc. His major fictional and dramatic works are no less obviously musical in character, with their balanced and antithetical themes that cross or echo each other — the theme of France and Germany in the *Siegfried* cycle; of Rebendart and Dubardeau, Moïse and Fontranges, war and peace in the *Bella* group; in *Amphitryon* and in *La Guerre de Troie,* of war and peace again; of innocence and pity in *Combat avec l'Ange;* of purity and justice in *Judith* or *Electre.* The leitmotifs are linked with countless minor ones such as the famous pickle prelude in *Choix des Elues,* which leads into the major theme of lives without savor.

To suggest the general character of Giraudoux's composition, we have referred to music, as he himself has done. More properly, however, we should speak of rhetoric. "Mille exemples pour illustrer un manuel pratique de rhétorique," Gabriel du Genet remarks in his essay on Giraudoux's theater.[19] This is literally true, and to demonstrate we need only to open a book at random. In presenting a problem or developing a theme such as that of national psychology, of political philosophy, of human nature, Giraudoux automatically establishes a polarity, and proceeds by series of parallels, antitheses, and paradoxes. The parallel, as Moïse says, is, "un exercice de style que j'ai pratiqué dès l'enfance . . . et qui m'a singulièrement aiguisé les idées ou facilité le travail."[20] If we glance through *Siegfried et le Limousin,* we note that the moral portraits of France and Germany alternate with regularity, and that there is a French prayer to match the one ascribed to the German children. In *Intermezzo,* two philosophies are juxtaposed as the specter and the *contrôleur* vie for the love of Isabelle. The duet of Hector and Ulysses is built on the parallel-antithesis device in its most obvious declamatory form:

Hector. —Je pèse la joie de vivre . . .
Ulysse. —Je pèse l'homme adulte . . .
Hector. —Je pèse la chasse, le courage, la fidélité, l'amour.
Ulysse. —Je pèse la circonspection devant les dieux, etc.[21]

The entire play, *La Guerre de Troie n'aura pas lieu,* is of course a paradox; just as *Sodome et Gomorrhe* is a monumental example of antithesis. Rhetorical polarity, of which parallel, antithesis, and paradox constitute the principal aspects, is everywhere in Giraudoux's work and may be considered its fundamental structural factor, since it lends form and symmetry to writing that would otherwise be chaotic.

This polarity is strikingly apparent in characterization, accounting in part for the rigidity, the linear and abstract quality that we note in Giraudoux's personages. They are often introduced in pairs — either of opposites such as Lucile and Paola, Eva and Geneviève, Ondine and Bertha, or of doubles such as the two Amphitryons, the two Judiths, the two Holofernes. Giraudoux ascribes to Moïse his own inclination when he speaks of the "parallèles qu'il aimait tirer entre les êtres . . ."[22] Examples of his various uses of rhetorical polarity in characterization could be multiplied countless times. If it is a single portrait that is being painted, the technique remains the same. It is not Giraudoux's intention to present Sarah and Eglantine as a pair, but in the brief sketch of Moïse's wife, Eglantine is a continual source of reference:

> C'était une petite Bernheim, affreusement maigre, mais dotée de telles dispositions à l'obésité qu'il fallait la peser chaque matin pour déterminer le menu du jour. Eglantine, inaltérable, pesait le même poids avant et après ses repas. Sarah avait un teint parfois terreux . . . Eglantine était lisse . . . Sarah n'avait aucune odeur . . . Eglantine avait cette saveur de la chair . . .[23]

Another example, this time from *Combat avec l'Ange:* Maléna and Gladys meet at the races, and we are given one more detail for the portrait of Maléna as well as a sketch of the incidental character Gladys. Each is described by antithetical reference. First we see Maléna as Gladys sees her, in reference to the thoroughbreds of the track. Her hair color — "Tiens, elle avait les cheveux comme Strip avait les poils! Cent noirs pour un blanc! C'était ravissant aussi sur elle . . ." Her eyes — "Au fond les femmes sont plus jolies que les chevaux . . . Quels cils charmants elles ont, partant de l'intérieur et non de la frange des paupières; quel œil pur avait celle-là à côté de l'œil de Strip . . ." Then it is Maléna's turn to think of Gladys. The picture is constructed entirely in reference to Maléna herself in a series of antithetical observations expressed in paradox:

> — Evidemment, pensait Maléna, Gladys est coquette. Mais sa coquetterie est l'esprit de sa beauté. Moi j'ai la modestie d'une beauté médiocre, d'une âme médiocre, d'une bonté médiocre. C'est-à-dire que je ne rassasie Jacques . . . Il verra que j'ai appris à lire pour ne pas lire, à écrire pour ne pas écrire, à aimer, hélas,

> pour ne pas savoir aimer . . . Si seulement Gladys était bonne, dévouée, calme! Idiote que je suis, voilà que je fais d'elle une seconde Maléna! Je veux dire: si seulement Gladys était bonne dans sa cruauté, dévouée dans son égoïsme, calme dans son déchaînement . . .[24]

In the conventional novel the characters emerge from a mass of realistic detail and psychological analysis; here they do not emerge, but seem to be cut out or defined against a background, as their traits are schematically compared or contrasted with those of others. In the conventional play, the characters come to life through realistic dialogue, and we infer their personalities through their acts. Giraudoux prefers the forthright tirade, and a character like Irma in *La Folle de Chaillot* defines herself in a speech of such obvious rhetorical balancing that it is actually an amusing parody of his technique:

> Je m'appelle Irma Lambert. Je déteste ce qui est laid, j'adore ce qui est beau. Je suis de Fursac, dans la Creuse. Je déteste les méchants, j'adore la bonté. Mon père était maréchal ferrant, au croisement des routes. Je déteste Boussac, j'adore Bourganeuf, etc.[25]

Slight as it is in plot and little concerned with succession of events, a work by Giraudoux depends greatly upon rhetorical balancing and parallels for its movement. A novel like *Bella* or *Eglantine,* a play like *Sodome et Gomorrhe* or *La Guerre de Troie,* moves ahead as portraits alternate and antithesis follows thesis. Within the thematic units, progress is achieved in the same manner. Referring back to Moïse and Sarah, we note that the relations between husband and wife are conveyed by a series of antithetical phrases:

> J'arrive à peine à te voir enfin, disait Moïse quand il se trouvait seul avec elle . . . — Moi, je te vois tout le temps, répondait-elle. Ils disaient tous deux les phrases inverses de leurs sentiments, Moïse se passant au besoin de voir Sarah, mais la portant toujours dans sa pensée, Sarah désirant ardemment sa présence, mais grâce à cette tendre diagonale entre leurs cœurs et leurs bouches, deux amours loyaux et purs étaient exprimés.[26]

The brief satirical story of Gilbertain, the lover who has never loved, is a paradox built up through successive contributing paradoxes. He has no time to fall in love — "il avait juste le temps d'achever sa lutte contre l'Eglise catholique, de régénérer l'Etat français dans ses rapports avec les cultes, et de voir se succéder une demi-douzaine de papes." He has no time to write love letters — "lui qui éprouvait déjà le besoin d'écrire à chaque heure à de simples amis, . . . Toute l'occupation amoureuse d'une vie sans amour était déjà trop absorbante pour qu'il pût envisager la possibilité d'aimer."[27] In narrating Suzanne's life on the island, Giraudoux covers "the six days of Creation" in so many parallel sentences describing how she arranges her bed:

> Le second jour, je l'occupai à me faire, dans une des trois niches de la caverne de corail blanc, un lit avec les plumages dont l'île était jonchée. Le troisième jour, je retirai les plumes trop dures et amassai les duvets de gros oiseaux de mer . . . Le quatrième jour, je triai les plumes d'après leur couleur . . . Le cinquième jour, je dus vider ces trois niches . . . Le sixième jour, je retirai certaines plumes . . . Après ces six jours de création, j'étais juste arrivée à faire mon lit.[28]

Much of the dialogue in the plays proceeds by repetition or crisscrossing. In the scene between Andromache and Cassandra which opens *La Guerre de Troie,* Andromache declares, "La guerre de Troie n'aura pas lieu, Cassandre!" Cassandra replies, "La guerre de Troie aura lieu." Andromache: "Cet envoyé des Grecs a raison. On va bien le recevoir. On va bien lui envelopper sa petite Hélène, et on la lui rendra." In her reply, Cassandra repeats Andromache's phrases, but in the contrary sense: "On va le recevoir grossièrement. On ne lui rendra pas Hélène." Andromache: "Quand [Hector] est parti, voilà trois mois, il m'a juré que cette guerre était la dernière." Again Cassandra repeats but twists Andromache's meaning: "C'était la dernière, la suivante l'attend."[29] The conversation goes on, each speech picking up a word or phrase from the preceding, which it doubles or contradicts. *Sodome et Gomorrhe,* which is one long debate, ends thus:

> *Martha.* J'étouffe, Lia.
>
> *Judith.* Lia, je meurs.
>
> *Lia.* Vous entendez, ici nous étouffons d'air pur. Nous mourons de ciel bleu.
>
> *Jean.* O quelles ténèbres!
>
> *Lia.* Quel soleil!
>
> (Et c'est la fin du monde . . .)
>
> *La voix de Jean.* Pardon, ciel! Quelle nuit!
>
> *La voix de Lia.* Merci, ciel! Quelle aurore![30]

In Giraudoux's essays, the ideas develop along the same rhetorical lines. Consider the paradoxes through which "L'auteur au théâtre" progresses. It begins: "Il n'y a pas d'auteur au théâtre." Next: "C'est là aussi le caractère de l'œuvre dramatique, et le privilège de sa beauté quand l'immortalité se pose sur elle: elle est éphémère." Throughout, the essay is marked by such paradoxical affirmations which begin or close a particular discussion: "L'essentiel du théâtre n'est pas l'auteur." "Il n'y a pas de plagiat en art dramatique . . . parce qu'il n'y a pas de propriété." "L'auteur dramatique . . . joue . . . le rôle de l'acteur qui ne joue pas."[31] In the "Avant-propos" to *Sans Pouvoirs,* Giraudoux establishes a distinction between France and Frenchmen and pursues his argument along the two parallels thereby created:

> Où en sommes-nous avec notre pays, et notre pays avec nous? Il règne un malaise, en ce moment entre la France et les Français . . . Le malheur de la nation dépasse de façon disproportionnée le malheur de l'individu . . . Le sang de notre patrie a coulé plus que le nôtre . . . Mais, alors que dans la paix chaque Français irrésolu ou égaré croyait avoir près de lui la ressource d'une France au comble de sa raison et de sa lumière, chaque Français, hier encore, je parle du plus robuste, du plus confiant, avait la hantise d'une France incertaine et déchue . . .[32]

These utterances, which we have brought together, are spaced in the text to reiterate the theme and mark its development, as are the previous examples from "L'auteur au théâtre." Glancing further in the "Avant-propos," we observe syntactical parallels — at least seven paragraphs begin with *celui;* paradoxes and antitheses abound: "Notre colère de nation était douce, notre égoïsme de nation généreux, notre dureté de nation facile, notre paresse de nation active."[33] The antithesis France-Frenchmen is carried through to a depiction of the Exodus of 1940: "Toute la France, ce mois-là, décida de partir pour la France."[34]

Figurative Language

From the broader aspects of structure or composition to the stylistic detail, the rhetoric manual remains a handy reference in analyzing the mechanics of Giraudoux's art. A critical edition of his works could carry the sort of notes that we find in school editions of the classics, where examples of figurative language or devices of rhetoric are carefully pointed out. Illustrations would not be found wanting for many of the most forbidding terms invented by the Greeks. We shall forgo, however, the pedantic pleasure of classifying Giraudoux's figures thoroughly. It will serve our purpose well enough to demonstrate further his general tendencies, the type of figure in which his thought finds its characteristic expression. Parallels, paradoxes, and antitheses have already been studied as structural elements defining not only the broad patterns themselves, but also the patterns of their internal composition. In the mechanics of Giraudoux's writing, the principle of polarity is a fundamental factor. A second fundamental factor is unquestionably the image. "Je suis certes le poète qui ressemble le plus à un peintre," Giraudoux declares.[35] No writer has indulged himself more unrestrainedly in the delights of imagery or exploited more thoroughly its manifold possibilities.

Whether describing a scene or an action, painting a portrait, expressing a thought or an *état d'âme,* Giraudoux invariably has recourse to the image. Note a characteristic rendering of a sentiment — Jacques' infatuation for Maléna:

> Un vernis, un brillant était soudain tombé de toutes les autres. Elles étaient toujours aussi belles ou aussi fardées, mais je les voyais ternes. Cette ombre gagnait même celles dont la fonction est d'être brillantes, les poétesses, les nageuses. Leur voix manquaient de timbre, leurs yeux d'émail. C'est simplement que j'étais fidèle.[36]

The metaphor runs on, saved only by a humorous touch from developing into a rhapsodical song of songs — no longer does the sunlight play over the hands of the typists in the office, the reflectors do not illuminate the *derrières* of the ballet girls in the theater. But Maléna's face seems rubbed with phosphorus.

By giving free course to his pen, Giraudoux sets in movement a continual flow of imagery. We have already watched him compose in *Adorable Clio.* One image calls up another, disappears or blends with still another, in a process of pure association. Observations and stray thoughts are rounded out by a metaphorical corollary. In *Bella,* the narrator explains that it is so early in the morning that only the milkmen are to be seen. The thought is echoed in a whimsical figure: ". . . il n'y avait à taquiner que les mamelles de la ville endormie." The shutters on buildings are closed — "contenaient des morts." The shops have not yet opened — "le soleil seul se distribuait sur les devantures closes comme la seule denrée, le seul vêtement, la seule antiquité à vendre." He crosses the Concorde Bridge — "personne n'a eu à franchir un pont plus bref entre le dernier de ses rêves et son amie." The woman he is expecting comes out of the *Métro* station. Her fellow passengers at that hour are chiefly masons — "elle portait parfois le plâtre sur sa robe, son seul fard."[37]

As Giraudoux's mind rambles on, "bride au cou," it follows the paths favored by a sophisticated wit. Seldom does it stray into those of emotion or unself-conscious lyricism. If Giraudoux uses figures of style traditionally used by impassioned poets, he does so only with a mocking smile. Thus does he treat the apostrophe, the stately simile, and the hyperbole, his favorite device. His fondness for superlatives indicates, according to Jean-Paul Sartre, his Aristotelianism. That there are philosophical implications here we do not doubt: the superlative is a verbal approach to the essences. But when it is a question of pickles,[38] we see more horseplay than metaphysics. The hyperbolic comparisons most frequent with Giraudoux — preposterous compounds in which the trivial is elevated or the grandiose reduced to insignificance — are entirely facetious. In *L'Ecole des Indifférents,* the Greek façade of an American college building is likened to a bridge with gold teeth — "des pilastres aurifiés alternent avec des carrés de marbre."[39] In *La Guerre de Troie,* after the goddess Iris has disappeared, "on voit une grande écharpe se former dans le ciel." Helen remarks, "C'est bien elle. Elle a oublié sa ceinture à mi-chemin."[40] *Elpénor,* that parody of Homer, is full of humorous figures of expansion. It is typical schoolboy banter, which Giraudoux never outgrew.

Another schoolboy trick noticeable in *Elpénor* and elsewhere is to play with clichés. Giraudoux's eye is quick to catch a second meaning, perceive the original color of an expression faded with time; many of his fresh and amusing images are no more than revamped clichés or resuscitated fossil metaphors. Ulysses' sailors have become "hardened" by adversity: "L'agitation sur les terres les plus rocailleuses les a tassés et durcis comme des sacs de sel."[41] The conceit pivots upon the word *durcis*; the physical sense of the verb *durcir* accounts for the comparison. Mock-heroic paraphrases in *Elpénor* often have a cliché basis. Here is a circumlocution obviously used to brighten the faded expression "honeyed words": ". . . il suffit de suivre jusqu'à leur ruche les innombrables abeilles qui sans répit paissent tes lèvres."[42] The "sting" of words is wittily suggested by a similar bee figure: "Ce n'est pas du miel qu'il y a sur les lèvres du Cyclope! Ou alors, avec ce miel, l'abeille oublia son aiguillon. Il a de la repartie comme un diable!"[43] Juggling with the literal and the figurative, Giraudoux indulges in all sorts of verbal play.

His verbal play often involves straight punning. Only birds inhabit Suzanne's island, "et la vie ne se transmettait dans cette île, entre des êtres toujours maigres, comme une jonglerie, que par des œufs verts ou violets piqués de brun."[44] Examples of paronomasia, oxymoron, syllepsis, and zeugma are to be found in great number: "Je ne renouvelle aucun de mes abonnements à la liberté, à l'amour, à la curiosité, et même à mes revues."[45] "Eva se voyait alors dans la nécessité de changer complètement d'âme, sinon de costume."[46] "Elle sortait du sacrifice couverte de bleus et de honte."[47] But often the transition to the image depends not upon a play on words, precisely, so much as just upon verbal association.

Edmée goes to a doctor to ascertain whether her discomfort might have a physical explanation:

> Cette douleur non utile sur cette ravissante et bien portante jeune femme n'était, pour le docteur Raszky, qu'un spectacle, qu'une séduction. Car il la voyait. Certains voient le feu des omelettes au rhum sans que le lustre soit éteint. Lui, avait reçu en partage de voir les douleurs. En ce moment, il contemplait, autour d'un cœur en forme de cœur, une de ces hautes flammes qui ardent, sans la consumer, la poitrine de certaines religieuses d'Europe. La fenêtre du docteur Raszky était entr'ouverte: la flamme ondulait, s'élançait . . . Qu'eût-ce été, dans la nuit![48]

The point of departure is the word *spectacle*. Strictly speaking, the image illustrates only seeing something which is imperceptible, but it is confused with the image of Edmée, making of her nonexistent disease a flaming omelette. Such an identification, although the nonchalant facetiousness of the passage would not reprove it, is of course not intentional. The chain of images involving burning is the writer's only preoccupation. With Giraudoux the associative process works like a reflex. Hence the presence of banal and trivial images mixed in with the rare. One thinks of his Ecclissé (*Elpénor*) rounding out every sentence with *comme,* whether or not the comparison is a good one. Hard as a nut, thirsty as a sponge, inexhaustible as the sea — such comparisons would be rejected by a more careful writer. But any comparison is better than no comparison. As Ulysses (also *Elpénor*) discovered on the raft, life is a bore when the sun shines just like the sun, and the moon resembles only the moon![49]

One may observe characteristic syntactical patterns that develop the image. The simple simile is to be sure the most frequent. Then there is the balanced sentence, the two parts of which being connected by *ainsi que* or *comme* form a sort of equation. The second term is introduced under the guise of an explanation of the first, usually a concrete object to explain an abstraction. "Le soir portait en lui la nuit, ainsi qu'un lait porte sa crème."[50] Night: evening — cream: milk. Aside from the equational figure, there are numerous other instances of images involving fanciful reasons or explanations. They lack the simile connective, but usually have some concessive introduction. The German school children's notebooks are in a handwriting "raide de parade" — just in case the emperor might want to look at them![51] An improper cause or source can serve as link between the literal and the figurative; sometimes, as in the following, the image is just a fanciful perceptual interpretation introduced by a *comme si:*

> J'avais un peu pressé Julia sur mon cœur, et pendant qu'elle dansait ses pyrrhiques avec la marque imprimée de toutes ses perles autour de sa gorge comme si on l'avait retirée à temps, par ses pieds nus, déjà mordillée, de la mâchoire d'un monstre . . .[52]

After adverbs of intensity such as *si* we note many hyperbolic figures: "Sur une bicyclette si neuve, si étincelante, qu'on cherche dans le ciel un nimbe avec sa marque . . ."[53]

Often the image is carried in the set patterns of aphorism, allusion, definition, and paraphrase: "On ne retrouve pas deux fois son empreinte dans le bonheur."[54] "Un nœud finit toujours par se défaire du simple dégoût d'être un nœud."[55] "Porter tout le jour ce sourire douloureux, c'est ressembler à l'élégant qui met déjà un œillet à la boutonnière de son pyjama."[56] "L'amour est un cheval qui se cabre, une antilope qu'on attelle, un traître fidèle . . ."[57] Paraphrases replace a straightforward statement or word by a picturesque image. The pallor of death: "Un aimant intérieur rappelait tout éclat, toute limpidité vers le centre de son corps."[58] Adjectives, frequently involving hypallage, and epithets are also common vehicles for the image. All these patterns seem spontaneously born out of the associative process.

As Giraudoux writes, his inspiration pushes him into paths of expression he has used time and time again. We have indicated some of the most common ones whereby he arrives at his image.

In images produced through the gratuitous play of the intellect, we may expect a minimum of sensory motivation or appeal. Let us not be misled by Giraudoux's insistence on the imagistic manner of his writing[59] into expecting a lush sort of imagery with rich colors, heavy perfumes, and enchanting music. Such heavy sensorial appeal is rare. What an analysis of this aspect of his imagery reveals is rather a subtle and interesting sensitivity, a preoccupation with certain unusual sensory impressions.

Visual imagery is naturally the most common. Color alone — although occasionally used symbolically — is rather infrequent, tending to combine with form to produce the image. Luminosity, on the other hand, proves very suggestive. So do lines and form, which provide the inspiration for many analogies, some humorous, some grotesque, others dainty and exquisite, while in some the vision even approaches the sublime. Motor images are in abundance: they are responsible for the animation characteristic of Giraudoux's nature description. Aural images tend towards minor, nonmusical sounds, attesting perhaps more to ingenuity and wit than to any particular sensitivity or predilection. Tactile imagery, although not abundant, adds a voluptuous touch here and there, particularly in reference to fabrics. The opposite qualities of hard and soft serve as suggestive antithesis. Thermic sensations seem to preoccupy Giraudoux more than most writers. Weight, too, is given unusual prominence. Olfactory and gustatory allusions are few.

Generally speaking, the borrowed terms in Giraudoux's metaphors are the prosaic elements of contemporary life, homely and unpoetic *per se*. They combine provincial and Parisian everyday trivialities with what used to be called the *merveilleux moderne*. To a far less extent do we find allusions to the arts and sciences, although Giraudoux was not coy about showing off (for comic effect) his book learning.

The Limousin, dear to his heart, is drawn upon time and again. Rivers, for example, are as conspicuous in his books as they are in his native province. Being stock in trade for all writers, their depiction in general terms would not seem remarkable, were it not for one particular feature that Giraudoux returns to repeatedly: that is, water locks and flood gates. Everywhere in the moral as well as in the physical world he is reminded of their functions. In addition to landscape, the rural scene is evoked through allusion to animals. Exotic and even mythological creatures furnish his wit and fancy with material, but more commonly we find the familiar domestic animals and the wildlife native to the woods and meadows of France. Their presence creates an air of unpretentious homeliness; this impression is strengthened by the many pleasant glimpses of village life that his metaphor permits — children at games and in school, the housewife engaged in all her humdrum activities. A contrasting note of self-conscious modernity is struck by the occasional reference in metaphor to automobiles, airplanes, typewriters, and radios. These up-to-date touches are noticeable in the earlier prose works.

The arts and sciences inspire a number of images amusing for their novelty and surprising aptness. Painting, sculpture, music, the theater, and the cinema are drawn upon, and to a lesser degree literature. The allusions bespeak the familiarity at least of the *honnête homme,* and some technical knowledge as well. Scientific allusions show that Giraudoux never forgot the days of the classroom and the laboratory. The biological sciences, mathematics, astronomy, geology, archaeology, chemistry, and physics are all represented. But perhaps medicine contributes the greatest number of picturesque images.

Early critics of Giraudoux exclaimed that he would some day have to be read with a glossary. A book like *Siegfried et le Limousin,* for example, bristles with allusions that may escape the average reader. The difficulty is chiefly with direct topical or obscure reference rather than with allusion in metaphorical combination, however. With few exceptions, the allusions employed as basis for metaphor are readily comprehensible, whether they be drawn from city or country life, the world of mechanical objects, or academic knowledge.

The world we enter through Giraudoux's metaphor is a *Märchen* universe where conventional categories do not pertain and where nothing is separate or distinct. Fish swim in the air, leaves flutter in the sea, time and space have nothing to do with clocks or maps, and just as persons respond to laws that govern metals or plants, objects and abstractions take on human characteristics. In fact, all nature seems one, living and beating with a human heart. Animism and personification are basic procedures in Giraudoux's art.

To Suzanne, cut off from the rest of the world on her Pacific island, nature appears as a person "paralysée par le bonheur, par l'impuissance à faire venir des continents ses conduites de venin, et dont les réflexes, oiseau qui s'envole, lézard qui fuit, ne fonctionnaient jamais, même en frappant au bon endroit."[60] Personification with Giraudoux is not, however, exclusively of this whimsical or facetious sort. Here is a splendid image of the sun, enhanced by classical implication: "Puis, peu avant la nuit, le soleil lui-même arrive, escorté de nuées, de bruits et de couleurs. Avant d'enfoncer dans l'horizon, il y jette sa robe, apparaît nu et jaune, et allume de grands incendies d'où montent les fumées qui bourrent les nuages."[61] Personification is a natural vehicle for intensified emotion — War-ravaged France is pictured as a crucified body: "Ce grand corps inerte de la France, tendu pour séparer d'aussi loin que possible les plaies, les pieds cloués, les mains clouées, le visage décharné . . ."[62] In *Siegfried,* personification delineates with maximum economy and effectiveness the moral nature of countries, especially France and Germany.

The constant shifting back and forth between the abstract and the concrete often turns personification into allegory. *Allégories,* the title Giraudoux gave to a group of his early pieces, could have been used also for some of the works he called novels and plays. Jacques of *L'Ecole des Indifférents* represents egoism, Anne of *Simon le Pathétique* sensuality, as is clearly stated. At Anne's dinner party we find her friends who personify in her eyes "la noblesse, le courage, l'automne." But she is mistaken: "Le Courage se révélait vulgaire, l'Automne bavard, l'Honnêteté riait stupidement dès qu'on prononçait le mot femme."[63] No less clearly for not being so labeled does Ondine represent ideal love, Electra justice, Lucile uncompromising virtue. In their stories, as in the old morality plays, virtues and vices take on human aspect to act out the tragedies and comedies of men.

Symbolism is another common procedure by which the physical and the abstract blend. Whatever strikes Giraudoux's retina or consciousness is reflected on several levels. A view, a landscape turns immediately into something else — an abstraction and an emotion in the following example taken from the passage in *Elpénor* where the people of Scheria greet Ulysses: "Changer une maison entourée de chênes-lièges contre une maison entourée de sapins, c'est changer le silence contre le vent, la pensée indolore contre l'angoisse."[64] Although presented as comic, these instantaneous translations and transformations please Giraudoux himself, we can be sure, as much as they do the people of Nausicaä's island: "Ah! quel plaisir ambigu de les unir dans le langage humain, céleste pépinière!" Constantly perceiving ulterior meanings and significances at once profound and whimsical, Giraudoux paints a universe full of signs and omens. Thus he calls teeth "signes de franchise," fingernails "signes de fidelité," complexion and eyes "signes de travail."[65] A spot of sunlight on a German forehead offers two symbolic interpretations: "Il pouvait croire que c'était là le second reflet de la sagesse sur une tête allemande, ou plus simplement, comme dans les music-halls une lumière annonce la fin du numéro, qu'il devait passer maintenant la parole à Siegfried . . ."[66] Sun and sunlight are used repeatedly to stand for happiness. Shade and shadow are frequent too, and the antithesis light and shadow. Water symbolism is a chief feature of *Ondine*. There are certain motifs that are identified with certain characters, such as the allusions to horses in connection with Fontranges. Or characteristic obsessions that are symbolic motifs in a sense, such as Helen's "seeing" and Electra's concern with "poussé" or "pas poussé."

As personification develops into allegory, symbolism develops into myth. The situations Giraudoux describes have an implicit value of universality. Often this is purely whimsical, an amusing game, to attribute to every deed and gesture an abstract significance. Thus of Edmée and Claudie: "Elle s'habilla. Ce n'était pas une petite affaire. C'était la toilette de la mère au matin de la nuit où la fille l'a reniée."[67] But whether whimsical or serious Giraudoux's personages all seem stylized figures of human beings, performing symbolic dramas or rituals of existence. The Siegfried or the Rebendart-Dubardeau cycles are among the most serious and important of Giraudoux's myths. Zelten, representing the old Germany, and Siegfried the new, act out the problem of Germany as Giraudoux sees it. Likewise the two French statesmen act out the French postwar problem. *Cantique des Cantiques* is a myth, too, or, in view of its brevity, a parable. Explicitly stated as such or not, all Giraudoux's works lend themselves to mythological interpretation. But the myth is general and ambiguous in nature. By no means should Giraudoux's myths be interpreted too closely. We have already expressed our belief that critics who look behind everything he wrote to find a specific hidden meaning — for example, political satire — are probably on the wrong track. Giraudoux's works have obvious reference to fundamental human situations and problems; for this reason we may speak of allegories and myths. They should not be confused with pamphlets or riddles.[68]

Procedures of Irony and Preciosity

Critics have been reluctant to classify Giraudoux as a novelist or a playwright because of the absence of realistic techniques in his works and because of the lack of composition such as is found in conventional novels or plays. If one must find a word for him, we have preferred to call him a poet. By analyzing his composition and style we are seeking to demonstrate just what sort of poet he is. In technique, we have found him to be a fanciful improvisator, a rhetorician, an imagist, a creator of allegories and myths. In mood, we believe he will be best defined as an ironist and a *précieux*.

Irony.

The gaiety and humor that bubble over in Giraudoux's improvisation are characteristically of the ironical sort. No sooner has he begun a narrative or a description than a farandole of lighthearted mockery is set in motion — mockery of what he is writing, of self, and of the reader as well. As incongruous images pop into his mind, he records them all without reticence, amused by their preposterousness and trusting the reader will be too. The reader of good will soon understands the game — anything goes and nothing is to be taken very seriously. Good-naturedly he watches this author turn the world topsy-turvy by his tricks and utters chuckling remonstrances from time to time by way of applause. But he is all attention, not only to appreciate all the tricks, but to be certain that some of them are not on him.

In the first chapter of *Suzanne et le Pacifique* we have one of Giraudoux's typical beginnings. From his window, then from the terrace, the author describes the village scene. Lines and angles strike his fancy, and he draws his picture as if with a ruler (anticipating, one might say, a Bernard Buffet or a Robbe-Grillet!): "Le vent du Sud tombait sur le vent d'Est, perpendiculaire, et des souffles Nord-Ouest-Sud-Est vous caressaient dans l'angle droit . . . Le facteur allait en zigzag . . . Puis le soleil se couchait, de biais, ne voulant blesser mon vieux pays qu'en séton."[69] With this last sly absurdity, Giraudoux is in full swing. He adds, "On le voyait à demi une minute, abrité par la colline comme un acteur. Il eût suffi de l'applaudir pour qu'il revînt."

It is probably Giraudoux's all-pervading irony that makes Gabriel Marcel hesitate to call him a poet. Irony does seem, in a sense, the very opposite of poetic inspiration, for it is intellectual in nature and characteristically inhibits lyricism or effusions from the heart. We clearly see how it operates with Giraudoux, whose tendency towards the sentimental and the lyrical (particularly noticeable in the earlier works) is systematically arrested by the intervention of irony. The love of Fontranges for his son Jacques is very tender, so tender in fact that it shows how strong Giraudoux's own paternal feeling was. But, characteristically, it is never presented without a gentle raillery. The young father finds even the most obvious a subject for marvel and delight — "il ne savait trop remercier la Providence que les enfants fussent petits."[70] His indulgence towards Jacques is unlimited, a theme which Giraudoux develops with increasing gaiety. Fontranges tells the boy stories of legendary heroes: "Ce fut un mois délicieux . . . Toute une semaine le fils essaya même, inversant la légende, de placer une pomme sur la tête du père et de l'abattre."[71] We observe the same tendency when a poetic reminiscence shifts suddenly to the comic: "C'était parfois la semaine où les acacias embaument . . . et nous les mangions dans des beignets." After that, we are prepared for the next couplet: "Où les alouettes criblaient le ciel, et nous les mangions dans des pâtés."[72] What begins as a rhapsodical tirade ends in a joke, for Giraudoux will not be guilty of bombast nor let the reader suppose that he is for a moment swept off his feet by his feelings.

As a censor, irony functions indubitably as an anti-lyric element, but it is so closely bound up with lyricism, so often dependent upon the lyrical urge to set itself in operation, that it is with some poets an integral part of their creation. Giraudoux, himself, sees nothing antithetical in the two terms irony and poetry: "Cette ironie," he says in his preface to Evelyn Waugh's book, "dont l'autre nom est la poésie."[73] This remark implies that, for him at least, the whimsical and fanciful play of irony belongs as much to poetry as does lyricism. In this notion he has, of course, many antecedents, extending back to the Romantic philosopher-poets of Germany, whom, as a young man, Giraudoux studied assiduously. Irony was for them, too, the means of maintaining control over their artistic creations, the necessary adjunct of inspiration, the mark of a free and agile spirit.

Among the figures of style that we have already cited, many will be remembered as those of irony. Examples of paradox, catachresis, litotes are everywhere in Giraudoux's works. Their basic ingredient is incongruity, used by Giraudoux in many ways to give his writing an offhand, light and airy quality. We have stressed his constant juxtaposition of elements belonging to categories widely separated. Note in this passage introducing Gérard, Juliette's fiancé, how he leaps nimbly back and forth between categories. Gérard is sitting by a stream, daydreaming in the summer sun:

> Il se trouvait sucer une paille, — et, jouissance exactement égal, il avait deux cent mille francs de rente. Il portait une ombre de merle sur le front, une ombre qui ouvrait le bec, — et, pesée équivalente, sur toute l'âme, la silhouette d'une fiancée riche . . .[74]

Without regard for the barriers that convention has placed between the spiritual and the material, Giraudoux gives just as little heed to divisions within each area. In the matter of time and chronology, like Ondine, he seems to forget that "ce qui a eu lieu ne peut plus ne pas avoir eu lieu!"[75] Notable early specimens of temporal — and geographical — incongruity are the Nativity scene depicted against the background of a power plant in New York, the Crucifixion likewise imagined as taking place in New York, the death of Socrates in Chicago![76] These are just jokes, like the songs the sirens sing in *Elpénor:* prophecies of the discovery of America, of the law of gravitation, of gunpowder. But even when Giraudoux is not joking, he does not fear to shock by incongruities of time and place. *Judith* and *Sodome et Gomorrhe* are no more Hebrew than *Electre* and *Amphitryon* are Greek. Anachronism dispels any historical illusion that may threaten to settle over a text.

Systematically, by a variety of means, Giraudoux keeps his work free from all illusion of reality. In his plays, there are the perpetual incongruities of character, situation, and discourse. Judith is a modern girl whom one might associate with "the fast set"; the royal family of ancient Troy is pictured in terms of the contemporary French bourgeoisie, with Cassandra appearing under the traits of a slightly idiotic maiden aunt, and Paris the younger brother who has got into a scrape. The episode of the rape of Helen is turned into farce with Menelaus being unable to pursue his wife's abductor because a crab has hold of his toe! In the same spirit of parody, the tragic heroes and heroines permit themselves flip and impertinent remarks which break the spell and bring the lofty down with a crash. When Helen explains how her prophetic visions are sometimes in vivid colors, other times colorless, Hector sneers, "Album de chromos!"[77] When Paris explains the irresistible remoteness of Helen — "Même au milieu de mes bras, Hélène est loin de moi," Hector snaps, "Très intéressant! Mais tu crois que cela vaut une guerre, de permettre à Pâris de faire l'amour à distance?"[78] Judith replies impudently to Joachim's solemn utterances:

Joachim. En effet, Judith, Dieu est ici.

Judith. Eh bien! j'ai grand'peur qu'il ne se trompe de maison, cher Joachim.

. . .

Joachim. . . . Notre Dieu . . . appelle chaque être par son nom et par ses entrailles, et l'hermine, et le bouc.

Judith. C'est curieux. Je ne l'entends pas encore nommer Judith.[79]

Whole scenes are marked by this vaudeville technique, whereby two characters stand before the footlights, the one blowing up a magnificent balloon of rhetoric which the other, with a wink to the audience, punctures.

The characters often seem to be mocking each other and themselves. Helen's prophecy of the death of Hector is treated as a joke, with Hector, who is apparently fully informed about his tragic end, "mugging" for a delighted audience (likewise in the know) his discomfort at being reminded of what is in store for him:

Hector. Vous la voyez, la bataille?

Hélène. Oui.

Hector. Et la ville s'effondre ou brûle, n'est-ce pas?

Hélène. Oui. C'est rouge vif.

Hector. Et Pâris? Vous voyez le cadavre de Pâris traîné derrière un char?

Hélène. Ah! vous croyez que c'est Pâris? Je vois en effet un morceau d'aurore qui roule dans la poussière. Un diamant à sa main étincelle . . . Mais oui! . . . Je reconnais souvent mal les visages, mais toujours les bijoux. C'est bien sa bague.

Hector. Parfait . . . Je n'ose vous questionner sur Andromaque et sur moi, . . . sur le groupe Andromaque-Hector. . . . Vous le voyez! Ne niez pas. Comment le voyez-vous? Heureux, vieilli, luisant?

Hélène. Je n'essaye pas de le voir.

Hector. Et le groupe Andromaque pleurant sur le corps d'Hector, il luit?

Hélène. Vous savez. Je peux très bien voir luisant . . . et qu'il n'arrive rien. Personne n'est infaillible.

Hector. N'insistez pas. Je comprends . . . Il y a un fils entre la mère qui pleure et le père étendu?[80]

By these bantering allusions to events outside the play, from the mouth of the protagonist himself, the theatrical spell is broken, a strong sense of incongruity is produced, and the tragedy turns into a farce.

Giraudoux depends greatly upon allusion as a comic device. Much in *La Guerre de Troie* would be lost on those of the audience who did not know their Homer, and a familiarity with La Motte Fouqué's *Märchen* adds to one's enjoyment of *Ondine.* In the *Supplément au Voyage de Cook* and the *Duchesse de Langeais,* as we have already observed, Giraudoux probably counted too heavily on his public's culture. Or else he takes delight in being obscure. Sometimes, it is true, we mistake for allusions remarks that are purely fortuitous. *La Guerre de Troie* has numerous passages that one would take as humorous references to Homer, but which prove not to be. In Helen's vision of Hector's death there is mention of a ring. It sounds very much like an allusion, but we recall nothing of the sort in Homer. When an allusion is understood, however, its mixture of aptness and incongruity is bound to entertain, and if it has been a difficult one, the pleasure of self-congratulation makes us relish it all the more.

Giraudoux's ironical devices are all brought into play in the scenes of *Electre* in which the Eumenides appear. They stand, like the chorus in Greek tragedy, somewhat outside the play, in order to comment upon the action that takes place. However, their function is not to heighten the tragic impression, but to destroy it. These preposterous little girls who become adolescent before our eyes prattle out the events that are to come, recite alternate episodes of the play, and in general so entertain the audience by their burlesque antics that there can be no question of a purge through terror and pity.

To portray the dread tormentors of Greek legend as little girls seems in itself a ludicrous incongruity. Giraudoux doubtless remembered that the Greeks sometimes did represent them as such — just as he must have known that Eumenides was a euphemism for the Erinyes. Accordingly he made of them sweet little fiends — omniscient, malevolent, charmingly ingenuous. From their glee, one would think they were talking about a birthday party instead of murders and horrors, in the following scene:

> *L'Etranger.* C'est sa fenêtre, la fenêtre aux jasmins?
>
> *Le Jardinier.* Non, c'est celle de la chambre où Atrée, le premier roi d'Argos, tua les fils de son frère.
>
> *Première Petite Fille.* Le repas où il servit leurs cœurs eut lieu dans la salle voisine. Je voudrais bien savoir quel goût ils avaient.
>
> *Troisième Petite Fille.* Il les a coupés, ou fait cuire entiers?
>
> *Deuxième Petite Fille.* Et Cassandre fut étranglée dans l'échauguette.
>
> *Troisième Petite Fille.* Ils l'avaient prise dans un filet et la poignardaient. Elle criait comme une folle, dans sa voilette . . . J'aurais bien voulu voir.[81]

Note that the phrase "Elle criait comme une folle," although as absurdly out of place as the rest, is not the phrase of a child. Sometimes the Eumenides drop their candor and sound like *mondaines.* Following the last speech, the first little girl quips, "Tout cela dans l'aile qui rit, comme tu le remarques." (One of the wings of the palace is called "l'aile qui rit," the other is "l'aile qui pleure.") They change their character whenever to do so serves the author's jokes.

The passage quoted above illustrates one more very common device of irony in Giraudoux's discourse. When the third little girl asks for precise details about the cooking of the hearts, she seems completely oblivious to the incongruity of her question. Giraudoux's characters are easily distracted, and can wander off the subject into all kinds of meanders which jibe badly with the seriousness of a scene. The babble of the Eumenides could furnish other examples; the best that comes to mind, however, is not from *Electre* but from *Ondine.* At what otherwise might have been a tragic and ugly moment in *Ondine,* when the faithful water nymph is being tried for her life, the judges become involved in a discussion of pastry-making: "J'adore la pâte brisée, en ce qui me concerne. Elle a dû en user, du beurre, avant la réussite?"[82] In a theater like Giraudoux's, where everybody steps out of character to voice the author's whimseys, none are more amusing than the garrulous judges, who drown salamanders and burn undines, but grow tender at the thought of *pâte brisée!*

Such devices of irony keep the mood detached and remind us continually that we are witnessing a play. Sometimes characters step completely out of their roles and address the audience directly to explain their function. Thus, in *Intermezzo,* the druggist announces that his business is to prepare the transitions. As the curtain falls on the first act of *Electre,* the gardener comes forth to deliver a *lamento* frankly announced as not part of the acting. The play stops in its course to permit him to tell us "ce que la pièce ne pourra vous dire."[83] The author himself may take the audience into his confidence and discuss his craft. In the little play, *L'Impromptu de Paris,* he does exclusively that. In the novel, too, the author reminds us that the work is but an invention. In *Juliette au Pays des Hommes,* he presents a sketch of Juliette's uncle with this explanation:

> L'oncle de Juliette, dont il ne sera plus jamais parlé ici, était un de ces personnages à peine épisodiques, qui ne jouent dans les romans aucune espèce de rôle, mais qui, bien plus que les héros, inspirent le désir irrésistible de connaître la date et le jour de leur naissance, tous leurs prénoms, leurs principaux vices, et naturellement, avec plus de détails encore, tous les faits, gestes et signes particuliers de leurs ascendants . . .[84]

All along his writing Giraudoux confesses his tricks and exposes his techniques. In *Visitations,* he tells us more of the gardener in *Electre.* This character was given all the speeches too sentimental for the hero. It was a compromise device — unwilling to renounce the "purple patches" of sentiment and rhetoric, yet self-conscious about them, the author relegated them to an incidental character. By this subterfuge he protected his hero and himself from the taint of bathos:

> Tous les lamentos, les intermèdes passionnés, les couplets du cœur devant lesquels se dérobent mes vrais protagonistes, tout occupés à mener l'action au plus juste et au plus vite, et aussi par pudeur de leur tendresse, c'est lui qui se les réserve.[85]

This explanation itself is of the tongue-in-cheek sort.

Lyrical inspiration or theatrical illusion — both are checked by irony, which works with Giraudoux like a healthy reflex. It lets him destroy what he has created, free himself before becoming too involved, start afresh on a new track. If, in the universe he creates with his pen, he plays fast and loose with the laws and categories of the real world, he holds his own world no more sacred, razing its walls even as he builds them. He will not exchange one prison for another, even one of his own invention.

Preciosity.

We have seen that through the various processes of irony, emotion is kept in hand and the unpleasant in life is rendered innocuous. The elegant stoic, as we have described Jean Giraudoux in our chapter dealing with his philosophy, would not see man without composure or without disdainful indifference towards the boorishness or the cruelty of nature. His irony is not only a means of asserting the liberty of the artist but also a means of asserting the dignity of man. What we call his preciosity is only another manifestation of this "humanism," the affirmation of man's control over himself[86] and, in so far as his attitude is concerned, over nature. But differing from irony, which can only make fun of emotion and mock the real, preciosity turns emotion into pretty sentiments and alters the real to conform to the civilized ideal:

> Etre précieuse, c'est désespérer alors qu'on espère toujours, c'est brûler de plus de feux que l'on n'en alluma, c'est tresser autour des mots révérés une toile avec mille fils et dès qu'un souffle, une pensée l'effleure, c'est le cœur qui s'élance du plus noir de sa cachette, la tue, suce son doux sang. C'est Mlle de Montpensier suçant le doux sang du mot amour, du mot amant. C'est Mlle de Rambouillet couvrant de sa blanche main tous les mots cruels, et nous les rendant ensuite, le mot Courroux, le mot Barbare, inoffensifs, comme les détectives qui changent le revolver du bandit en un revolver porte-cigares.[87]

This is precisely what Giraudoux does. The world that he presents in his novels and plays is as exquisite as any in literature. It contains nothing crude, awkward, or vulgar; its passions are urbane, and anguish masks itself as tender nostalgia. We recognize the scenes and persons of the everyday world, but purified, as if viewed through a special lens.

This special lens is to be sure the lens of style, and we have seen how Giraudoux imposes upon the world the order and symmetry of rhetoric, how through hyperbole he endows persons and things with the perfection of archetypes, how through metaphor he frees life from causality and all natural laws. His technique recalls some of the very procedures of those refined spirits of the seventeenth century who looked at the harsh facts of life only through a delicate glass of verbal transfiguration.

Just as with the habitués of the *Chambre bleue,* Giraudoux's basic technique is the impromptu, which displays all the resources of imagination, wit, and literary skill. Often he introduces a theme by a sally, an arbitrary assertion that captures our attention as it would that of a *salon* audience, and we follow with amused interest the skillful and subtle elaboration that will follow: "La toilette d'un homme le calme," he begins on a page of *Combat avec l'Ange,* "mais la toilette d'une femme l'exalte."[88] Needless to say, such utterances have no literal truth, nor does the author intend that they should. What he really says is that Jacques is at ease when he meets Maléna for dinner but that Maléna is nervous. Giraudoux characteristically sees situations in general terms, and his fancy binds their elements together in wholly arbitrary fashion. The result is a treasury of sententia which are gambits for verbal games.

The games they introduce are often the very games of the seventeenth century. If, in his writings, the madrigal and the sonnet are transformed because he does not use verse, the epistle and particularly the portrait are little altered. The descriptions of Suzanne, of Juliette, and of many others could find a place in *Le Grand Cyrus.* In *Elpénor,* the Cyclops and Ulysses, like drawing room wits, engage in a game of definition. What is love? The Cyclops answers: "Par aimer, j'entends frissonner d'un feu qui glace, étouffer d'une ombre aride . . ."[89] The sailors of Ulysses sing Penelope's definition: "Aimer, c'est chaque nuit couper des fils de laine,/ Les retendre le jour."[90] One thinks of Benserade's poem: "Amour est un brasier . . ./ Amour est une plaie./ Amour est un désir . . ." Love and its definition were subjects which very much interested the fops and the *belles prudes* of the *salons,* who were as delicate and ethereal as Giraudoux's lovers. *Elpénor* burlesques their manner, but these examples are no more extreme than what other books offer. One may remember the definitions for waiting in "Attente devant le Palais-Bourbon." The author is watching the government officials enter and leave the building. The sight of some specialists in oriental languages prompts his imagination: "L'attente est un tapis vivant. L'attente est une gélinotte entre des mains puissantes . . ."[91] Burlesque is, in any event, a common form of *précieux* humor. When we read the account of the torments that the Cyclops suffered at the hands of the Greeks, we think of the famous letter to

Mlle. de Bourbon in which Voiture described being tossed in a blanket. The same verve and extravagance of imagination transform the humiliating or painful into the comic.

The *précieux* cultivates the excessive deliberately and often as not in a spirit of fun. One always feels that Giraudoux is having as good a time as his audience when he spins his fantasies — the definitions, epithets, or paraphrases that Voiture or Benserade might have envied. "Ce doux sel qu'on appelle sucre. Parce que tu es le miel qui assaisonne tout dessert, ce doux vinaigre qu'on appelle miel."[92] Paradox and antithesis are pushed so far as to become sheer comedy. But the comic blends with the pretty and even with the lyrical, as in the following epithets: dawn, "cadran solaire sans soleil";[93] twilight, "aurore des chouettes, de la sagesse";[94] night, "soleil des chouettes."[95] Some of Giraudoux's inventions are meaningless out of context: "mercredi, hublot ouvert sur le passé" we note in a passage of *Bella.*[96] (We must know that Fontranges is thinking of his dead son, and it is Wednesday, Jacques' birthday.) Others do not depend on the text to be charming or amusing: "Les hommes, moisissure suprême de l'univers!"[97] *Sodome et Gomorrhe* is studded with definitions of the sort. Woman: "la statue volubile du silence, le portrait aux yeux loyaux de la perfidie . . .[98] Tout en elles est ignorance, et elles comprennent tout. Tout vanité, et elles sont simples . . . Elles contiennent la cage de silence . . . Elles sont le sextant de l'innocence, la boussole de pureté."[99] Man: "l'homme est la plus fausse conquête de l'homme."[100] "Un pauvre serpent qui collectionnait toutes ses peaux."[101] In similar language are defined the couple, mankind, and the gods.

Voiture and Benserade surely would have envied the deftness of Giraudoux's epigrams — "La seule promesse que la nature ou Dieu ait tenue: les hommes vieillissaient."[102] — and his daring images perilously prolonged but ending triumphantly in a point. "Cette île, comme dans une auto," Suzanne begins, and there follows a long metaphor comparing an island with an automobile. Many lines later, when the comparison seems to have been dropped somewhere along the way, it reappears to close the passage *en beauté:* ". . . et je désespère sur mon île en panne!"[103] With equal success, Giraudoux achieves delicate balances of oxymoron — "Il toucha et regarda le visage doux du cruel Jacques pour la vie"[104] — or of antithesis — "[Dubardeau] croit aimer les forts et il aime les faibles . . . Rebendart croit mépriser les forts et il méprise les faibles."[105] In the characteristic devices employed by the *précieux* writer, Giraudoux proves himself a past master. They may be found in profusion throughout his work.

To illustrate further Giraudoux's close kinship with the seventeenth-century school, let us open *Sodome et Gomorrhe* again. It is one of the great tragedies, and its language is probably more disciplined than anywhere else in Giraudoux, yet it bears the mark of the *précieux* from cover to cover. Each character expresses the subtlety of his thought and the delicacy of his feelings by means of metaphor often so involved as to challenge the *fins esprits.* Ruth's dissatisfaction with her husband is that he never changes. She has tried everything, but his basic immutability is wrecking their marriage: at her instigation he has dyed his hair, cut his finger nails in a new way, learned to dance — "et j'ai veillé aussi à ce qu'il remplaçât dans son iris son regard de satisfaction par un rayon d'incertitude et de malheur."[106] This final stroke, we are sure, would have been greatly relished by "la belle Arténice." And love described in the very terms of the *Carte du Tendre* would certainly have delighted Mlle. de Scudéry: "Les grands caps de la douceur, les îles de l'entente, les promontoires de la tendresse . . ."[107]

In the definitions quoted above, one notes a marked use of substantives. What happens if we replace them by adjectives? Often we have a perfectly banal description. But instead of writing, "Jean est faible," Giraudoux says, "Jean est la faiblesse,"[108] and thereby lifts his qualifier into the abstract and the absolute, makes of it a superlative. Perhaps too much has been said on the philosophical implications in Giraudoux's use of the superlative, and not enough attention has been given it as a purely esthetic device. Several of his stylistic features are varieties of the superlative. In the form in which it appears above, it was used by the *précieux* as a preliminary flourish to capture attention and introduce the verbal legerdemain that follows. In another form, the superlative is a device of isolation, which has been used by sophisticated artists in all civilizations. In the refined art of China and Japan it is a fundamental esthetic principle. We find it taking this form with Giraudoux: a generalization followed by one exception. For example, the earth of Sodom has been swept by the fires of the end of the world: "Tous les animaux déjà sont tombés et se consument, à part un seul, un cheval, qui . . . galope dans la ville."[109]

The one exception heightens the general impression; a background is created to dramatize the single figure. Again, all the flowers of the earth are burnt — save a single rose. There is a Japanese story about the emperor's visit to a peasant's celebrated garden of morning-glories. When he arrived, he found that to do him honor the peasant had destroyed his entire garden with the exception of one exquisite bloom. The emperor was enchanted at the effect. So may we be, watching the gardener with the only flower that has been spared, one not unworthy of the "Guirlande de Julie."

The *précieux* is a verbal magician who, impatient to dazzle the audience with something else, destroys almost immediately the lovely things he creates. The pose of the gardener with the rose is held but a minute. Then he wonders what to do with it and in a long monologue mimics a comic who has been handed a hot potato. By such pirouettes the *précieux* regains his balance, avoids slipping into emotion. "Mais me voilà obligé de la porter toute la journée à la main, de bêcher d'une main, de ratisser d'une main . . ."[110] The thought of carrying a rose makes him think of himself as a rose bush — "une espèce d'arbuste à une fleur, un arbuste ambulant . . ." Once set in motion, the conceit continues to spin through a series of associations. The audience watches as intently as if it were watching a juggler keep tenpins in the air. The gardener declares it is a privilege to bear a rose "alors que les hommes sont tous en cette heure des arbustes à crime et à péché." He is grateful it is not a zinnia. Of what might it be a symbol? He does not know or need to know. With the rose he carries the will of God. He has only to carry. Moreover, it is not very difficult after all. Soon you realize that man's nature is not to kill lambs or break stones, but to carry a rose. You can hold it even in the open hand by sticking a thorn in your finger. The drop of blood is the same color as the rose. That is why the angel gave me a red rose. The whole matter clears up. In this holocaust, in which the blood of man will flow like rivers, my mission is "celui dont il jaillit en une fleur, et en parfum."

At the rhetorical gymnastics which we witness here, each character is just as skillful as the gardener. Lia's complaint about the presence of angels (the infestation theme already present in *Judith* and *Ondine*)[111] is sustained over several pages. It is followed by the account of her griefs against her husband, likewise expressed in prolonged conceits:

Lia. Tous les charmes se sont posés sur celui que vous épousez. Il est un orme surchargé de pinsons qui vous accueillent. Puis, semaine à semaine, chaque pinson s'envole sur un autre homme, et, au terme de l'année, votre vrai mari est disséminé sur tous les autres.[112]

Then it is Ruth's turn to declaim recriminations against Jacques. The husbands, Jean and Jacques, have their turn, the partners change, and the duets continue. Throughout the play, these couplets alternate, mingling — as in the gardener's speech — the tragic and the lyrical with the comic. Delilah's aria "J'ai choisi" tells how she has arranged to keep Samson faithful by speaking always of his enemies in the feminine: "Toute femme est devenue ainsi pour lui le symbole et le sexe de quelque iniquité." She has contrived to use the masculine gender for "le charme, l'éclat et le prestige," she explains. Suddenly she asks, "Vous connaissez un mot masculin pour candeur? A part Dalila?"[113] This abrupt and witty close saves a passage which was becoming very strained and thin. Samson takes up his side of the "J'ai choisi" song with a succession of images that have a lovely Biblical quality: "Moi j'ai choisi l'amour et la loyauté, le sein et l'œil de Dalila. . . . Il est une pierre de lune que l'on glisse dans la nuit pour la faire prendre, pour que tout en devienne gel de beauté et de resplendissement: c'est le sommeil de Dalila . . ."[114] But Delilah cuts him off with, "On sait ce que tu as choisi . . . Partons."

Wit and artifice camouflage the poignant tragedy of the incompatibility of the couple and the horror of impending doom. The end of the world is described only in general terms, a *précieux* way of meeting it unflinchingly. The minor characters announce their death by "J'étouffe" or "Je meurs" while the protagonists, although reduced to an "amas de cendres," still continue to declaim. This supreme and elegant disdain for nature is preceded by countless minor irreverences and blasphemies. Lia's seduction of the angel is a masterpiece of *précieux* accomplishment; sending the angel off to the orange tree and laughing at his grimace as he sucks a green fruit is derision of heaven. In her arrogance as a woman and a member of the human race, she dares jeer at the master of creation and be witty at the expense of his messengers. To combat the disorder, the ugliness, and the horror of life, man has the resources of language. The weapons Giraudoux puts in Lia's hands are the ones bequeathed by the seventeenth century.

The word *précieux* has perhaps been used more than any to describe Giraudoux and his art. Although it has meant different things to different persons, we believe there is no better word to characterize all his verbal inventiveness and the basic fastidiousness of his vision. Early critics employed it in its pejorative sense to voice their discomfort before a new and dazzling art; later ones stressed its philosophical significance — but each, whether attacking or defending the author, has thrown interesting light on his work. Today, with Giraudoux's high place in the literature of the twentieth century established, we need not fear that the popular connotation of affectation and superficiality attached to the word will be prejudicial; indeed the tendency in recent years seems to be to take him overseriously. The writer once thought of as an impertinent prankster is now regarded almost solely as a tragic poet of the human condition. Actually he is both prankster and tragic poet, and to affirm the one view of him and deny the other is to substitute one partial truth for another. We are not inclined to reject *in toto* any of the views that critics have held of Giraudoux. As his genius unfolded, new elements revealed themselves; and though today some of the critical appreciations seem limited and even mutually contradictory, they represent aspects of the truth that must not be rejected, only brought into proper focus.

Chapter 7

GIRAUDOUX'S WORK BEFORE THE CRITICS

The novelty of Giraudoux's style is what struck his first readers. In 1919, to the reviewers of *Provinciales,* it seemed simply artificial and excessive, and they spoke with disdain of "paradoxes soignés" and "plaisirs de myope."[1] Only André Gide — and he with a word of caution — greeted the new writer warmly.[2] Style would continue for many years to be the main subject of critical comment, as critics tried to label and classify it in literary tradition. They noticed the unusual images, the wit and poetry, the bookish allusions, the tendency towards abstractness, and suggested this writer and that one as spiritual ancestors. Jules Renard was most frequently named among at least six French writers of divergent tendencies. However, the most distinguished commentators — Albert Thibaudet, Francis de Miomandre, Marcel Proust — emphasized Giraudoux's originality. Not until 1923 would his affiliation with German Romantic authors be remarked.[3] By this time the notoriety of the prize-winning *Siegfried et le Limousin* had brought Giraudoux to the attention of a wider circle of critics.

During the period following, that of *Juliette au Pays des Hommes, Bella,* and *Eglantine,* the earlier impressions of Giraudoux were reaffirmed with more precision and emphasis. Not all were favorable. He was treated as a difficult modern, by Catholic critics as a decadent, by some others as the worst writer of his generation! But friend and foe noted the same characteristics. In the mid-twenties the word *pré-*

Notes to Chapter 7 begin on page 232.

cieux was heard openly. Pierre Lafue objected, however, to its exclusively pejorative connotation.[4] Charles de Bonnefon believed, too, that *précieux* need not mean "ridicule."[5] Besides *précieux*, "magicien" was another epithet commonly used to describe Giraudoux's verbal sleight of hand and to indicate the transformation of the world that it effects. The general picture was one of a delicate *fantaisiste* and a prestidigitator whose tricks either delight or repel. Some few critics ventured to suggest that his stylistic feats were not striven for but were simply the products of unbridled improvisation. That was the interpretation of both Humbourg and Bourdet,[6] whose monographs constitute the first volume-length studies on Giraudoux. They are *études d'ensemble*, but, as one may suppose, concentrate heavily on style and method of composition. Critics continued to be interested mainly in explaining, situating, justifying or condemning Giraudoux's fancy writing. Discussion of his universe was limited to brief accounts of his themes; and other than occasional references to his optimism and his delicacy, nothing was said of his philosophy. "L'œuvre de Giraudoux n'a pas de haute portée, mais elle n'y prétend pas."[7] "Aucun souci métaphysique ou éthique, ne le hante."[8]

With *Siegfried*, the novelist of the happy few became the playwright with a smashing popular success. Critical interest increased accordingly. "*Siegfried* classe Giraudoux, un romancier discutable, parmi les meilleurs dramaturges."[9] The unforeseen triumph of this play was explained on the grounds that, after a monotonous fare of triangle plays, slice-of-life dramas, and bedroom farces, the public appetite was ready for "literature" in the theater. Those very qualities that had relegated Giraudoux to the rank of minor — although exquisite — novelist were hailed as the new hope for the French stage. There was surprisingly little discussion of the subject of the play or of Giraudoux's political intention. In the theater as in the novel, he was still thought of first and foremost as a stylist. With *Amphitryon 38*, the word *précieux* was heard again. Although the majority of critics relished the humor and poetry of the play, few seemed to think the content of its pretty speeches worth meditation. Indeed one critic asked, "A quel intérêt humain, moral, ou spirituel peut bien servir *Amphitryon*?"[10] It was more difficult to dismiss the philosophic content of *Judith*, a fact which seems to have annoyed the reviewers, who complained that the play was obscure. The general attitude towards *Judith* was that this time Giraudoux's virtuosity had carried him too far and that the work was an overwhelming display of verbal pyrotechnics. *Intermezzo,* more favorably received, was recognized as a metaphysical comedy. To describe it to their readers, critics spoke of Maeterlinck, Shakespeare, and the German Romantics. But they had not abandoned the epithet *précieux. Intermezzo* was so characterized, just as *Amphitryon* had been, and the novel *Aventures de Jérôme Bardini.*

The important studies that appeared during the early thirties deal mainly with style. Articles by Jean Prévost[11] and Marcel Thiébaut[12] are among the best. Much of the discusion continued to center around preciosity. Robert Brasillach, in analyzing the language of Giraudoux's plays, warned against confusing their opulent "preciosity" with the "dry" art of the seventeenth century.[13] Thierry Maulnier, in another article,[14] developed the paradox that verbal games are often the contrary of preciosity, for, instead of deforming sentiments, they render them more direct and pure. This sounds like Giraudoux's own thought regarding verbal excesses, that they "correspondent du moins à de vrais défauts ou qualités humains."[15] Gonzague Truc, in defending Giraudoux's preciosity, suggested that behind his stylistic games there was depth.[16] But Emile Bouvier distrusted an art that, he said, turned its back on the real world to create one that is purely gratuitous and esthetic.[17] The "world" of the *précieux* was the subject of an essay by Christian Sénéchal, who discussed Giraudoux under the heading "Evasion,"[18] and another by André Rousseaux, who painted the *précieux* world in terms of the Garden of Eden and of eternal springtime.[19]

La Guerre de Troie n'aura pas lieu (1935) represents a landmark in Giraudoux criticism. For the first time reviewers seem generally to have taken quite seriously the thought of a play. *La Guerre de Troie,* called a great poem of despair, was admired at least as much for its handling of the theme of war as for its language. Many heard for the first time the deep philosophical resonances in Giraudoux and recognized the intellectual and human significance of his work. Prompted perhaps by some of the recent *études d'ensemble* such as those we have mentioned above, reviewers of the play began to notice the author's characteristic attitudes. His preoccupation with death caught their attention, and they scrutinized Helen's speeches and Hector's for revelations of Giraudoux's point of view on vital subjects. *Electre,* eventually to be considered by some as Giraudoux's finest work, met at the time of its first performance (1937) less general approbation than the *Guerre de Troie.* But it is clear from reviews of the play that Giraudoux's thought had now begun to evoke almost as much interest as his style. Not without a certain self-consciousness, however, for one does not like to be a dupe, and Giraudoux's mischievousness made many critics wary. Gonzague Truc, who had previously alluded to the depth behind the author's verbal games, ventured an article with a title intended to be taken half-humorously: "La Théologie de Giraudoux."[20] In it he discussed, notwithstanding, the metaphysical implications of *Judith* and *Electre.*

The gradual shift in critical interest was to an extent only a reflection of Giraudoux's own evolution as a writer. It is scarcely surprising that the novel style of his early pieces captured attention and that only gradually would Giraudoux's thought make its presence felt. Giraudoux himself moved only gradually in the direction of the great problems. Yet from *Provinciales* to *La Guerre de Troie* he had traveled a long way, and the critics were far from keeping pace. If the theme of *La Guerre de Troie* had impressed itself upon a public that remembered the last war and feared the next, the themes of *Cantique des Cantiques* and *Ondine* — less topical but nonetheless serious — received scant attention. *Cantique des Cantiques* was taken very lightly, and comments upon *Ondine* were full of the familiar epithets — fantasy, enchantment, poetry. Moreover, in the important articles of the late thirties, style is still the chief consideration. *Le Démon du Style,* by Yves Gandon, referring back to *Juliette au Pays des Hommes,* treats Giraudoux as a "jongleur, rhéteur, sophiste."[21] Another article, by René de Messières, analyzes Giraudoux's use of irony and draws attention to its similarity to *Romantische Ironie.*[22]

Although critics like Messières did not ignore the philosophical implications in Giraudoux's style, the first person really to exploit the subject was Jean-Paul Sartre, in his resounding essay on the Aristotelianism of Giraudoux.[23] From the stylistic singularities which previous critics had, in general, been content to note in passing, Sartre drew precise philosophical conclusions. His picture of Giraudoux's "universe" would stimulate much further discussion in the years to come and serve postwar critics as touchstone and basic reference.

During the war years, however, French writing on Giraudoux was limited chiefly to sketchy comments on the various works he produced at that time — *Littérature,* the scenarios, *Sodome et Gomorrhe.* Political bias dictated some of the comments, and the former minister of propaganda was praised or criticized on extra-literary grounds. The most objective and comprehensive studies of these years were written outside of France. In the United States, a doctoral dissertation was presented on the subject of Giraudoux's imagery;[24] in Norway, an over-all study of Giraudoux and his works appeared;[25] Professor Fernand Baldensperger, teaching in California at the time, wrote a significant article on the "esthétique fondamentale" of Giraudoux, which reaffirmed the affinity with the Germans suggested previously by a number of critics.[26] Upon Giraudoux's death early in 1944, there were a great many homage articles — *Arche, Sur,* the *Cahiers Comœdia-Charpentier, Confluences,* etc. dedicated special issues to his memory. But aside from reminiscences and anecdotes, they offered only brief comments on stock in trade topics.

In 1945 newspapers and reviews continued to print the sort of articles that habitually follow the death of an author — generalizations about his works, summary judgments, and predictions as to his fate before posterity. In them, Giraudoux as a Frenchman was discussed as much as Giraudoux as a writer. During the war, the pro-Germans had attacked him; after the war, it was the patriots' turn. Was Giraudoux himself a patriot or a collaborationist? Stories of his clandestine activity and the rumor that he had been poisoned by the Germans[27] were not enough to quiet all suspicion that Giraudoux had not taken the stand he should have. There developed a *cas Giraudoux.* For some, if Giraudoux was not actually a bad Frenchman, at least he showed himself a thoroughly inadequate minister of the government that could not defend the country. Grave and righteous patriots associated Giraudoux and his writing with what they deemed the criminal frivolity of the between-wars period. They felt little sympathy for a pretty poet who fiddled while Rome was burning. Giraudoux's defenders reiterated that preciosity did not necessarily mean affectation, taste for happiness did not imply scorn for unhappiness, lightness did not mean absence of depth. Some concocted, to suit the taste of the times, a Giraudoux realistic and commonsensical.[28]

Towards the end of 1945, the staging of *La Folle de Chaillot* did far more to restore Giraudoux to favor than the efforts of rehabilitators. True, the delirious praise was in great part for the production itself, a state-sponsored manifestation, but all due allowance made for the part of patriotic zeal, the play brought forth real nostalgic tenderness for France's greatest modern playwright. Several writers thought the time propitious to bring out volume-length studies on the controversial author: Gabriel du Genet, *Jean Giraudoux ou un essai sur les rapports entre l'écrivain et son langage;* Jacques Houlet, *Le Théâtre de Jean Giraudoux;* Claude-Edmonde Magny, *Le précieux Jean Giraudoux.* Despite Genet's title, none of these critics was really concerned with Giraudoux's style. It was his attitude towards language rather than his language itself that interested them — that is to say, a philosophy that conceived of the universe in terms of rhetoric. We may note, incidentally, that, mindful of current prejudices, they felt more or less obliged to murmur against this philosophy. Genet begins his essay with a clear rebuke, which however seems to be forgotten as the essay proceeds. But for or against, it is Giraudoux's thought that primarily concerns them. The same interest in Giraudoux as a moral force is evident in books like Albérès, *Portrait de Notre Héros* (Le Portulan, 1945) and Benda, *La France Byzantine* (Gallimard, 1945), which discuss Giraudoux among other writers of the period. This year demonstrates, due to the temper of the times as much as to the intrinsic importance of Giraudoux's message, a remarkable acceleration in the shift of critical emphasis from form to content. Gérard Bauër echoed a general feeling among admirers of Giraudoux when he wrote: "Ce n'est pas dans son style gracieux que réside le plus grand talent de Giraudoux, mais plutôt dans la conscience qu'il a de la destinée humaine . . ."[29] *Précieux* Giraudoux would continue to be said. But, as is evident in Magny's essay and the subsequent recapitulation of the subject by René Bray[30] (which would appear in 1948), the epithet now had a philosophical meaning rarely implied by earlier critics, who had used it to designate merely a clever and affected stylist.

During the postwar years, great strides were made in Giraudoux scholarship, which, less influenced than general criticism by pressures exerted by the times,[31] concerned itself as much with Giraudoux's expression as with his attitude towards life. Bengt Hasselrot's "Technique et Style de Jean Giraudoux, auteur dramatique" in the *Studia Neophilologica* (1946) was balanced by Wilhelm Kellermann's "Ding, Seele, und Ideal bei Jean Giraudoux" in the *Romistische Jahrbuch* (1947-48). Werner Fink, in his thesis *Jean Giraudoux, Glück und Tragik* (Basel: Helbing & Lichtenhahn, 1947), analyzed systematically and objectively the early optimism and the growth of pessimism that a chronological study of Giraudoux's work reveals. Anne Chaplin Hansen dealt with both philosophy and expression in "Les deux univers de Jean Giraudoux," *Orbis Litterarum* (1948), as she analyzed style to show how Giraudoux typically moves back and forth between the abstract and the concrete. An article by Ruth Elizabeth McDonald ("Le Langage de Giraudoux," *PMLA*, Sept., 1948) pushed on in the field of style; likewise a Sorbonne thesis (Morton Celler, *Une Etude du style métaphorique dans les romans de Jean Giraudoux*, 1952, unpublished) and a University of Oregon monograph (L. LeSage, *Metaphor in the Non-Dramatic Works of Jean Giraudoux*, 1952), the previously mentioned 1940 thesis now recast and printed.

In the late 1940's and early 1950's, scholars and students patiently probed in many areas. The question of Giraudoux's debt to German writers, heretofore suggested or treated briefly, was explored at length in several articles culminating in a monograph (L. LeSage, *Jean Giraudoux, Surrealism, and the German Romantic Ideal*, University of Illinois Press, 1952). Giraudoux and Germany were likewise the subject of a 1950 Sorbonne *mémoire* for the *D.E.S.* (M. L. Knittel, *Giraudoux et l'Allemagne*, unpublished). An American Ph.D. thesis dealt with Giraudoux and humanism (Charles Wahl, *Jean Giraudoux, Twentieth Century Humanist*, Yale University, 1950, unpublished). Giraudoux's heroines were the subject of a thesis by Guido Meister (*Gestalt und Bedeutung der Frau im Werk Jean Giraudoux'*, Basel: Helbing & Lichtenhahn, 1951); his heroes, of one by Will McLendon (*Le Héros selon Jean Giraudoux*, Sorbonne, 1952, unpublished). Giraudoux as a novelist was studied by N. Kirby (*The Evolution of Jean Giraudoux as a Novelist*, Cambridge, 1952, unpublished) and as a playwright by P. B. Bhatt (*Jean Giraudoux dramaturge*, Sorbonne, 1950, unpublished) and Hans Sørensen (*Le Théâtre de Jean Giraudoux*, Copenhagen: University of Aarhus Publications, 1950). Giraudoux as a critic was the subject of an article by Georges May ("Jean Giraudoux: Academician and Idiosyncrasies," *Yale French Studies*, Spring-Summer, 1949).

Although these academic investigations are devoted in the main to exploring aspects of the author rather than to challenging opinions about him, the material thereby produced often authenticates or disproves existing assumptions regarding his art and attitudes and provides the basis for new interpretations. Studies of Giraudoux's metaphor, for example, show clearly that the early charges of artificiality and a labored style were unfounded, that on the contrary those who saw in Giraudoux's writing spontaneity and improvisation were correct.[32] Testimony on the question of Giraudoux's debt to the Germans clarifies considerably his esthetic point of view and the nature of his art.[33] The systematic analyses of his characters provide positive statements of his concept of personality and — along with studies such as Mr. Wahl's on Giraudoux's "humanism" — articulate his views on the human condition.

Leaving the "researchers" and returning to the critics, we note in the latter 1940's Giraudoux was treated as someone quite remote. If critics emphasized his ideas, it was partly because they appeared to constitute a view of life that had been superseded. Giraudoux was a convenient symbol for a period that had ended with the war. This was how Albérès saw him in 1949 (*La Révolte des Ecrivains d'Aujourd'hui*). Giraudoux was the Apollonian writer whose optimism and conciliatory attitude towards the universe seemed the exact opposite of the "Promethean" revolt advocated by the Sartres and the Anouilhs against the unpredictability of a chaotic, indifferent universe. What has been called his preciosity, Albérès declared, is only "un effort poétique et éthique pour reconcilier le règne humain avec les autres règnes."[34] The salvation of man meant for Giraudoux living in accordance with one's foreordained nature, finding one's place in the universal order. For the postwar writers, there existed no foreordained nature, no universal order, no possible salvation.

The picture of a Giraudoux *inactuel* did not, however, survive into the 1950's. Christian Marker, in his introduction to selected texts (1952), insisted that Giraudoux met an urgent need of the times. Unlike the critics of 1945, Marker felt no embarrassment before Giraudoux's cult of the ideal and the beautiful. We do not go to this author, Marker asserted, for an escape from life, but for a true representation of life and for inspiration to live. A taste for living, the frivolous confidence in the instant which is the source of all greatness and all joy — these are his teachings that capture our enthusiastic attention. His initial fame as a magician or an acrobat has been left far behind. Today his glory is that above all he can give us what we earnestly beg for in literature — a face of man that can be contemplated without disgust. In demonstrating the appeal of Giraudoux in 1952, Marker did not basically differ from Albérès as to what constituted his essential characteristics. His point was only that Giraudoux offered a welcome relief from the dreary philosophers of the day. One may note, however, that Marker questioned the famous "serenity" of Giraudoux and suggested that behind it lay real tragedy.

By insisting more and more on the tragic aspect of Giraudoux, critics following Marker have effected a basic transformation of our author. Giraudoux's high seriousness had already, as we have indicated, been established, and nobody in 1954 would have seriously debated the question that heads an article by Albérès: "Jean Giraudoux, écrivain précieux ou poète accordé à l'univers?"[35] But Giraudoux's attitude towards life had seemed so radically different from postwar *angoisse* that critics presented him as a monument of the past and recommended him as a salubrious escape from the present.[36] Since Marker, however, only a few memorialists have continued to sum up Giraudoux by the famous smile. To the critics in general it has seemed only a mask, and they have concentrated their study upon the tragic features it is presumed to hide.

This new orientation towards Giraudoux is illustrated by the lively discussion over *Pour Lucrèce*. As a dramatist, can Giraudoux be called a tragic author? Pierre-Aimé Touchard, we may remember, decided not in an article published in the number of the *Cahiers Jean-Louis Barrault* devoted to Giraudoux.[37] But Barrault found that *Pour Lucrèce* met the specifications for tragedy exactly.[38] Bert M. P. Leefmans, in the *Kenyon Review*,[39] argued that the human victory in Giraudoux's plays prevents their being considered pure tragedy. The question becomes here a technical one. No matter which way it is decided, the fact that the subject under debate is the tragic vision in Giraudoux indicates the trend of the times. The latest major studies of Giraudoux have treated him as a lofty and tragic poet, whose vision of life anticipated our own.

The subtitle of Marianne Mercier-Campiche's book on Giraudoux's theater is significantly *La Condition humaine*.[40] Here Giraudoux appears as the gravest of philosophers, meditating upon the destiny of man. The parts of his work dedicated to war (which once were denounced as shockingly frivolous) strike Mme. Mercier as one of the most profound analyses of the subject ever written. She sees in his treatment of all his major themes — war, love, the "gods" — a man seeking his way out of bitterness and despair. The lesson of his work is that happiness for mankind must be of mankind's own making, for only through his own efforts can he win over "la fatalité stupide, absurde."[41] We see in Mme. Mercier's book a Giraudoux close to Sartre and Camus in philosophical assumptions and preoccupations; man's freedom of action and individual responsibility for his life are obvious implications of such a "lesson."

V. H. Debidour (*Jean Giraudoux,* 1955) attacks the notion of a superficial *bonheur* as characteristic of Giraudoux, pointing out that if happiness is precious to him it is because it is not common. His approach to his themes is, M. Debidour believes, indicative of disappointment and disillusionment. Love, for example, is rarely happy, and the subject of the couple is treated with increasing pessimism. Man cannot escape the curse of solitude any more than he can end wars. If childhood and youth figure often in Giraudoux's works, they are there as a refuge from the grievous problems of adulthood.

The tragedy of the couple is taken up again in an article by André Dumas[42] in *Esprit,* May, 1955; a German critic takes up the subject of death and suicide and traces as far back as the newspaper stories what he considers in Giraudoux to be a morbid obsession.[43] The neurotic presented here bears little resemblance indeed to the sunny and superficial Giraudoux that critics were once pleased to describe. M. L. Bidal *(Giraudoux tel qu'en lui-même,* 1956) rubs out the traditional picture of Giraudoux the humanist to set before our eyes a misanthropist-philosopher who holds the human condition in contempt. Jérôme Bardini, we learn, went off on his adventure out of disgust for his fellow men. Giraudoux and his hero seem in the height of postwar fashion with the sentiments Mme. Bidal ascribes to them — a sort of Sartrean "nausea" before human existence (that "chose ignoble"[44]) and before the absurdity of destiny.

Although this is not the place to discuss at length the extravagance of interpretations such as the above, at least a word of protest may be in order. Giraudoux's allusions to death do not constitute an obsession, nor are existentialist expressions really appropriate to his thought. Bardini's so-called "horror of mankind" is less revolt against the human condition than protest against habit, routine, and all those forces which would stifle the full and harmonious realization of man's basic drives. The fact that Giraudoux's characters are glorified beings is not proof of his disgust for ordinary mortals, but merely of a desire to see them in beauty, their potentialities realized, or of a desire to permit those among them who are his readers to live for a moment beautiful, vicarious existences. To demonstrate Giraudoux's high seriousness and his tragic vision, one need not try to make of him a neurotic or a postwar *révolté*. The critic who first drew the line separating Giraudoux from the authors of today has much more discreetly and effectively erased it himself.

René Marill Albérès, reviewing twentieth-century literature in his *Bilan Littéraire du XXe Siècle* (1956), reverses the position he took in 1949. Instead of a period divided in two by the war, he now sees development and continual evolution during our century. Giraudoux takes a place in line. In the time to which he belongs — also the time of Claudel, Valéry, and Proust — the aspirations of the Symbolists were fulfilled and the way was marked for the writers of today. With the broader perspective the years have brought, Albérès can now see the entire age as a second flowering of Romanticism.

Yet Albérès is careful not to make of Giraudoux a brother to the "Promethean" writers of the postwar revolt. In his thesis *Esthétique et Morale chez Jean Giraudoux,* which examines Giraudoux's thought in great detail at every moment of his career, Albérès stresses the constancy of his idealism. A vision of universal harmony — an orderly cosmos in which man strives to realize his essence — underlies his entire work. Giraudoux's tragic sense is a sort of sensitivity towards discord; it is activated when the universe seems to ring false or when persons or nations — out of ignorance or perversity — seem to go astray, depart from their essential natures, or lose contact with the cosmos. As an artist, he considers it his task to show them where they betray themselves, as it were, and, in general, to communicate the ideal vision which he himself possesses by virtue of intuition and imagination.

If, as we read M. Albérès' voluminous essay, we think at times that he attributes to Giraudoux's thought more coherence and development than is there, we cannot disagree with his fundamental interpretation. We, too, see Giraudoux as Apollonian in his attitudes towards life and, in his concept of art, a partisan of inspiration, prophecy, and ethical intention. But, although we recognize the intellectual interest in Giraudoux, we caution against seeing him first and foremost as a thinker. Early critics treated him too lightly; the tendency today is to place excessive emphasis — however it is interpreted — upon his thought. Not only is there danger of ignoring the gay, elegant, and urbane Giraudoux, who was every bit as real as the tragic poet, but there is even greater danger of neglecting Giraudoux the artist.

Giraudoux himself never lost sight of the fact that he was primarily an artist, not a thinker — as indeed M. Albérès reminds us:

> Giraudoux se considère comme un *artiste,* au même titre que le peintre. Le peintre ne produit pas des idées, mais des tableaux. Il peut même ne point avoir d'opinions conscientes sur le sens de son œuvre, qui n'est pas une métaphysique, mais une peinture. Cette peinture n'est pas destinée à illustrer ou défendre une idée, elle est une création qui ne dépend que d'elle-même.[45]

Giraudoux has left us, through his work, the testimony of a lifetime of impressions, experiences, thoughts, and emotions. But in spite of the intrinsic interest that his vision of the world constitutes, his work must ultimately be judged on the artistic accomplishment of its rendering, which already has placed his writing among the noblest and most exquisite of our times. His place as the great renovator of the French theater remains unchallenged, and the dramatic authors of today acknowledge their debt to him.[46] His significance in non-dramatic prose writing may be just as great. Through the tumultuous acclaim of the plays, one remembers hearing Albert Thibaudet declare that Giraudoux had realized in the novel the long-unfulfilled dream of Symbolism.[47] And an outstanding critic of the present day, Maurice Blanchot, has said that among the novelists of the older generation, Jean Giraudoux was one of the very few to possess "le sens de la création romanesque."[48]

Notes

CHAPTER 1

1. Jean-Paul Sartre, "M. Jean Giraudoux et la philosophie d'Aristote," *Situations,* I (Gallimard, 1947), 98.
2. I have the impression that somewhere Giraudoux himself uses this figure of speech. At any rate, it translates an ideal of discretion typical of the man. See Giraudoux's remarks about Marivaux, p. 97, and about the graduates of Ecole Normale, p. 101.
3. "Bellac et la tragédie," *Littérature (Œuvres Littéraires Diverses,* Grasset, 1958, p. 600).
4. *Provinciales (Œuvre Romanesque,* Grasset, 1955, I, 71).
5. "Bellac et la tragédie," *op. cit.,* p. 599.
6. Jean Loize, *Exposition Rollinat, Giraudoux, Bernard Naudin* (Catalogue of an exposition held at the Galerie Jean Loize, Paris, June, 1954), p. 5.
7. Louis Chaigne, "Jean Giraudoux," *Etudes,* December 20, 1939, p. 622.
8. Preface to Adolphe Jauréguy, *Qui veut jouer avec moi?* (Corrêa, 1939), pp. 8-9.
9. Charles Silvestre, "Le Souvenir de Jean Giraudoux," *Les Nouvelles Littéraires,* April 19, 1945.
10. *Simon le Pathétique (Œuvre Romanesque,* I, 679).
11. *Ibid.,* p. 627.
12. *Ibid.,* p. 628.
13. See Jean-Marc Aucuy, *La Jeunesse de Giraudoux* (Spid, 1953).
14. *Ibid.,* p. 33.
15. *Simon le Pathétique (Œuvre Romanesque,* I, 634).
16. "Discours sur le théâtre," *Littérature (Œuvres Littéraires Diverses,* p. 577).
17. Aucuy, *op. cit.,* p. 27.
18. Loize, *op. cit.,* p. 10.
19. Aucuy, *op. cit.,* p. 31.

20. Paul Morand, *Jean Giraudoux, Souvenirs de notre jeunesse* (Geneva: La Palatine, 1948), p. 25.

21. Quite possibly the prototype of André Bovy in "Jacques l'Egoïste," *L'Ecole des Indifférents.*

22. *Ibid.* (*Œuvre Romanesque,* I, 113).

23. "Nuit à Châteauroux," *Adorable Clio* (*Œuvres Littéraires Diverses,* p. 218).

24. See Aucuy, *op. cit.,* p. 90.

25. *Simon le Pathétique* (*Œuvre Romanesque,* I, 632).

26. Of the six preserved, five can be read in *Hommage à Giraudoux* (Lycée de Châteauroux, June 18, 1949). The one omitted is a poem on the funeral of Alaric, dating from *Quatrième* (March, 1896).

27. See Aucuy, *op. cit.,* p. 113.

28. Christian Marker, *Giraudoux par lui-même* (Editions du Seuil, 1952), p. 64.

29. Giraudoux makes allusion to his early acting in *Visitations* (*Œuvres Littéraires Diverses,* p. 703). Besides *La Rosière de Chamignoux,* there exists also a little magazine in manuscript and illustrated by the author that dates from Giraudoux's childhood. On its cover one reads: *Jean et Jeanne;* directeur: J. Giraudoux; direction: Pellevoisin-sur-Indre. This item of juvenilia, along with a fragmentary *Journal d'un enfant,* is in the possession of M. Jean-Pierre Giraudoux.

30. See p. 12.

31. Loize, *op. cit.,* p. 13.

32. *Simon le Pathétique* (*Œuvre Romanesque,* I, 638).

33. *Ibid.,* pp. 637-638.

34. *Ibid.,* p. 639.

35. Giraudoux played on the football team at Lakanal and received a "mention honorable d'exercices gymniques." If we are to believe his own writing, he also ran races in the Bois de Boulogne, and, according to the following souvenir, indulged in impromptu wrestling before the Carrousel:

> Quand jadis, débarquant du lycée Lakanal à la gare de Médicis le samedi soir pour ma sortie du dimanche, je regagnais l'avenue Henri Martin où habitait ma famille, j'allongeais encore mon chemin des parcours les plus moelleux aux pieds qu'eût Paris, du Carrousel alors sablé, où je luttais une minute en redingote de lycéen contre les champions à poil du Ier arrondissement, et surtout de la descente au Trocadéro qui nous amenait jusqu'à la Seine sous l'œil torse du rhinocéros géant qu'on repeignait de rouge et qu'il fallait prendre soin d'éviter au virage. Tout cela faisait 6 kil. 200, et au printemps nous faisions même un détour de 253 mètres, pour passer sous les acacias en fleurs de l'avenue Mozart.
> *Le Sport* (Hachette, 1928), pp. 54-55.

Incidentally, the reference to his family living on the Avenue Henri Martin is the only indication we have that Giraudoux had relatives living in Paris. It may of course be fictitious.

36. It is unfortunate that the Ecole Normale did not keep in those days the papers of the candidates accepted, for we should enjoy reading the composition which received the very brilliant grade of 7½. The subject was one on which Giraudoux could not but do well: Vigny, who maintained with a young Bavarian prince a literary correspondence now lost, is asked by his royal pupil to explain what French Romantic lyricism is. Romanticism explained by a poet to a German prince is indeed a made-to-order subject for Giraudoux. See Robert Brasillach, "Contes inconnus de Jean Giraudoux," *La Gerbe,* August 10, 1944.
37. Alexandre Guinle, Introduction to Franz Toussaint, *Giraudoux et Giraudoux* (Lyon: Audin, 1948), p. xi.
38. Camille Martin, "Souvenirs de Khâgne à Lakanal en 1902," *Le Figaro Littéraire,* February 11, 1950.
39. *Juliette au Pays des Hommes (Œuvre Romanesque,* I, 551).
40. *Ibid.,* p. 551.
41. "L'Esprit normalien," *Littérature (Œuvres Littéraires Diverses,* p. 538). Giraudoux's *mémoire de licence* on the Pindaric odes of Ronsard would take up the problem of the influence of Luigi Alamanni on Ronsard. See note 47.
42. Robert de Beauplan, "Les Débuts littéraires de Jean Giraudoux," *Aspects,* March 3, 1944.
43. See René Marill Albérès, *Esthétique et Morale chez Jean Giraudoux* (Nizet, 1957), Appendix A.
44. Albérès names Giraudoux's German teacher at Lakanal. *Ibid.,* Appendix B.
45. Louis Chaigne reports that Giraudoux had considered studying for the *agrégation* in Spanish. "Jean Giraudoux," *Etudes,* December 20, 1939, p. 623.
46. See Albérès, *op. cit.,* Appendix C.
47. The outline of Giraudoux's essay can be read in Albérès, *ibid.,* Appendix D.
48. Albérès, *ibid.,* p. 39.
49. See L. LeSage, "Jean Giraudoux, Hoffmann, and 'Le Dernier Rêve d'Edmond About,'" *Revue de Littérature Comparée,* XXIV (January-March, 1950), 103-7. A variation on this piece is woven into "Don Manuel le Paresseux," *L'Ecole des Indifférents.* For later editions in volume or *plaquette,* under the title *Premier Rêve signé,* see L. LeSage, *L'Œuvre de Jean Giraudoux, essai de bibliographie chronologique* (Nizet, 1956).
50. Franz Toussaint, *Sentiments distingués* (Laffont, 1945), p. 280. Maurice Martin du Gard, *Feux tournants* (Camille Bloch, 1925), p. 196. André Billy says that he taught only one afternoon. See *Intimités littéraires* (Flammarion, 1932), p. 121.
51. *Simon le Pathétique (Œuvre Romanesque,* I, 639).
52. *Ibid.,* p. 640.
53. Since 1920, part of Berlin.
54. Memories of Munich are scattered through Giraudoux's early works. *Nuit à Châteauroux* contains some particularly interesting passages.

55. *Siegfried et le Limousin* (*Œuvre Romanesque,* I, 422-423).
56. Paul Morand, *Jean Giraudoux,* pp. 13-14. Compare with Camille Martin's portrait of Giraudoux as he remembered him at Lakanal: "un assez grand garçon élancé et souple, un peu maigre de corps et de visage, souriant avec quelque malice, les mains dans les poches d'un pantalon qui n'arrive pas tout à fait aux chaussures, portant habituellement lorgnon, et coiffé d'un polo bleu et jaune." "Souvenirs de Khâgne à Lakanal en 1902," *Le Figaro Littéraire,* February 11, 1950.
57. Morand, *op. cit.,* p. 15.
58. *Ibid.,* p. 21.
59. "Au cours de l'hiver 1905, il avait surtout vécu à Schwabing, dans les ateliers, parmi les acteurs et les chanteurs d'opéra." See L. LeSage, "Paul Morand's Memories of Giraudoux in Germany," *Modern Language Quarterly,* XIII, 3 (September, 1952), which presents a personal letter from M. Morand.
60. André Beucler, *Les Instants de Giraudoux* (Milieu du Monde, 1948), p. 48.
61. *Siegfried et le Limousin,* Chapters 1, 3.
62. Morand, *Jean Giraudoux,* p. 15.
63. *L'Essentiel du Bridge* (Grasset, 1934). Preface by Giraudoux.
64. Two years, he says here. *Ibid.,* preface, p. 7.
65. "Paul Morand's Memories of Giraudoux in Germany." See note 59.
66. *Visite chez le Prince* (Emile-Paul, 1924).
67. *Simon le Pathétique* (*Œuvre Romanesque,* I, 644).
68. This is of course fictitious, as the dates alone would indicate.
69. See Albérès, *Jean Giraudoux,* p. 39. I believe M. Albérès' dating of the hotel bill may be an error, but I have not verified with the original document.
70. See Albérès, *op. cit.,* p. 39, for documentary evidence of Giraudoux's movements during these months.
71. This letter, as well as the hotel bill referred to above, is conserved by Jean-Pierre Giraudoux.
72. *Siegfried et le Limousin* (*Œuvre Romanesque,* I, 489).
73. *Ibid.,* p. 431.
74. Giraudoux studied carefully the mss. of Platen's Hymns. See Albérès, *op. cit.,* p. 44.
75. See *Siegfried et le Limousin* (*Œuvre Romanesque,* I, 469).
76. See L. LeSage, "Giraudoux's German Studies," *Modern Language Quarterly,* XXI, 3 (September, 1951), 353-359.
77. See L. LeSage, "*Fragments* by Jean Giraudoux," *Modern Language Notes,* April, 1955, pp. 289-292.
78. See note 74.
79. Information offered me in a personal letter by Professor Maurice Boucher of the Sorbonne, based upon a second-hand, unverified anecdote.

80. See Albérès, *Jean Giraudoux,* pp. 44-45 for further discussion of Giraudoux's *diplôme.* Also Appendix E: Procès verbal de la soutenance; Appendix F: Plan du mémoire.

81. Giraudoux apparently took advantage of the fact. In a letter written while he was at Harvard (1917), he tells Paul Morand: "Je fais fortune et bientôt je pourrai envoyer 50 francs à Laveur, qui en profitera pour fermer." Morand, *Jean Giraudoux,* p. 108.

82. See Albérès, *op. cit.,* p. 39.

83. See L. LeSage, "Giraudoux's German Studies," *Modern Language Quarterly,* XII, 3 (September, 1951), 353-359.

84. This information was supplied by Professor Boucher.

85. Professor André Morize, in an unpublished address given June 28, 1949, during the ceremony relative to the commemorative plaque at 89, quai d'Orsay.

86. Harvard records. Giraudoux set down in his notebook the hour of Professor Francke's lectures: three times weekly at 12.

87. *L'Ecole des Indifférents* (Grasset, 1911).

88. *Ibid.* (*Œuvre Romanesque,* I, 135).

89. "Relève de la femme," (1934). See *La Française et La France* (Gallimard, 1951).

90. See Will L. McLendon, "En partant d'un texte oublié de Giraudoux," *French Review,* XXVII, 1 (October, 1953), 30-35.

91. See *Contes d'un Matin* (Gallimard, 1952).

92. For the annotated text of this essay see L. LeSage, "Jean Giraudoux, *La Culture allemande et les universités américaines:* an unpublished manuscript by Jean Giraudoux," *Harvard Library Bulletin,* Winter, 1959.

93. See Albérès, *Jean Giraudoux,* p. 42, note 62.

94. We read in "Quelques souvenirs sur Jean Giraudoux," by José de Bérys (*Rolet,* December 24, 1953), that *La Revue du Temps Présent* was founded by a group of Giraudoux's fellow students in the Latin Quarter at about the time Giraudoux left for Harvard. Knowing that Giraudoux was writing, they asked him for a contribution for their first number. In due time there arrived from the United States "La Pharmacienne." Pierre Chaine and Robert de Beauplan, who were asked to read it — in spite of their admiration for the work — were disturbed about what effect some of Giraudoux's stylistic extravagances would have on their bourgeois and academic public. So, Beauplan crossed out words, phrases, altered paragraphs, and generally fixed up the manuscript. Giraudoux may not have noticed the editing, may not have reread his story; in any event he did not protest, and the version that appeared in the magazine was preserved in the volume edition.

Beauplan himself gives a different account of the episode ("Les Débuts littéraires de Jean Giraudoux," *Aspects,* March 3, 1944). He says that Giraudoux, before leaving for America, asked him to try to place a story he was writing — "La Pharmacienne." When his friend Chaine, with his father's financial backing, founded *La Revue du Temps Présent,* Beauplan succeeded in having Giraudoux's work accepted. According to Beauplan, when Giraudoux returned from America he was furious at the mutilations imposed upon his text and asked that the manuscript be returned. However, when the work appeared in the volume, *Provinciales,* most of the alterations had been retained.

95. Aucuy, *La Jeunesse de Giraudoux,* p. 158.
96. *Les Cinq Tentations de La Fontaine* (*Œuvres Littéraires Diverses,* p. 416).
97. *Simon le Pathétique* (*Œuvre Romanesque,* I, 646).
98. Apparently Giraudoux did not like Jouvenel either. Note Morand, *Jean Giraudoux,* p. 78 and p. 81.
99. See Giraudoux, *Les Contes d'un Matin,* "Remarques liminaires," by L. LeSage.
100. The Bibliothèque Nationale copy of the original edition of *Lectures pour une Ombre* bears this dedication in Giraudoux's handwriting: "A Toulet avec le constant dévouement de son disciple. J. G."
101. See p. 29.
102. See L. LeSage, "A Danish Model for Jean Giraudoux," *Revue de Littérature Comparée,* January-March, 1952, pp. 94-105.
103. *La Nouvelle Revue Française,* June, 1909, p. 463.
104. He would have had the Goncourt prize in 1920, too, if Marcel Proust had had his way. See *Bulletin de la Société des Amis de Marcel Proust,* I, 15.
105. André Beucler, *Les Instants de Giraudoux* (Milieu du Monde, 1948), p. 48.
106. Simonne Ratel, "Jean Giraudoux et le nouveau romantisme," *Dialogues à une seule voix* (Le Tambourin, 1930), p. 12.
107. Jean de Pierrefeu, *Comment j'ai fait fortune* (Editions de France, 1926), p. 160ff.
108. See L. LeSage, "Jean Giraudoux and Big Business," *French Review,* XXXI, 4 (February, 1958), 278-282.
109. Giraudoux's installation in his apartment may be the inspiration for the passage in *Simon le Pathétique* which begins, "Je m'installai enfin . . ." (*Œuvre Romanesque,* I, 664). At Normale, Giraudoux had had a piano in his room.
110. Morand, *Jean Giraudoux,* p. 43.
111. As Morand tells the story, Giraudoux's decision to go into government service was a sudden inspiration. Yet as early as his year of study in the United States there is reason to believe that Giraudoux had it in mind. Lucien Bonzon reports that Giraudoux made inquiries at the consulate in New York about civil service positions abroad. "Jean Giraudoux diplomate," *Jean Giraudoux* (Cahiers Comœdia-Charpentier), pp. 41-42.

CHAPTER 2

1. "Pages de journal," *La Nef*, February, 1949, p. 5. This entry is dated March, 1911. "Bernard, le faible Bernard" had appeared in the February issue of the *Mercure de France*, but I do not find in it the alleged quotation.
2. Paul Claudel, "Adieu à Jean Giraudoux," *Jean Giraudoux* (Cahiers Comœdia-Charpentier), p. 3.
3. Morand, *Jean Giraudoux*, p. 47.
4. See p. 37.
5. Franz Toussaint, *Jean Giraudoux* (Arthème Fayard, 1953), pp. 137-184.
6. *Ibid.*, pp. 180-183.
7. Morand, *op. cit.*, p. 51. Note reference in "Le Retour d'Alsace," *Lectures pour une Ombre (Œuvres Littéraires Diverses*, p. 21).
8. See Albérès, *Jean Giraudoux*, p. 64.
9. Morand, *op. cit.*, p. 76.
10. See Albérès, *op. cit.*, p. 64.
11. Morand, *Jean Giraudoux*, p. 53.
12. The parts of *Lectures pour une Ombre* are not presented in chronological order.
13. Morand, *op. cit.*, pp. 63-64.
14. Still one might think two operations and enteritis contracted at the Dardanelles not really very gay.
15. Morand, *op. cit.*, p. 92.
16. *Lectures pour une Ombre* did not appear until 1917.
17. For an account of the French military mission to the United States, see P. Azan, "Harvard pendant la Grande Guerre," *Harvard et la France, recueil d'études publié pour la célébration du 3ème centenaire à Harvard* (Revue d'Histoire Moderne, 1936), pp. 19-39.
18. *Amica America (Œuvres Littéraires Diverses*, p. 123). Henri Bergson was also crossing on the *Touraine:* "Or, il y avait à bord notre plus grand philosophe . . .", p. 125. The presence of Bergson aboard inspires Giraudoux with wild flights of fancy. See p. 125ff.
19. See Morand, *op. cit.*, p. 104.
20. The Boston *Transcript*, May 9, 1917.
21. Morand, *op. cit.*, p. 109.
22. *Campaigns and Intervals* (Houghton Mifflin, 1918).
23. Morand, *op. cit.*, p. 114.
24. *Ibid.*, p. 118.

25. Beucler, *Les Instants de Giraudoux,* p. 52.
26. Document preserved by Jean-Pierre Giraudoux.
27. *Adorable Clio (Œuvres Littéraires Diverses,* p. 262). The original edition is Emile-Paul, 1920.
28. *Ibid.,* p. 264.
29. See p. 20.
30. *Siegfried et le Limousin (Œuvre Romanesque,* I, 402).
31. *Ibid.,* p. 402.
32. *Ibid.,* p. 428.
33. *Ibid.,* p. 430.
34. *Siegfried,* Act I, sc. 2 *(Théâtre,* Grasset, 1954, I, 8).
35. See, for example, Frédéric Lefèvre, *Une Heure avec . . . ,* lère série (Gallimard, 1924), p. 150. One should not see here, however, a deflection from his basic principle of the primary importance of style.
36. Paul Bourget, "Le Jardin des Lettres," *Le Correspondant,* December 10, 1922.
37. Henri Massis, "Les Lettres: Le Prix Balzac," *La Revue Universelle,* December 15, 1922, pp. 474-482.
38. *Le Correspondant,* December 10, 1922.
39. "Visite chez le Prince," *La Nouvelle Revue Française,* October, 1923, pp. 402-426.
40. This matter is treated at length by Hans Sørensen in his *Théâtre de Jean Giraudoux* (Copenhagen: Publications of the University of Aarhus, 1950) and taken up again by Donald Inskip in his *Jean Giraudoux* (Oxford University Press, 1958).
41. "Siegfried von Kleist," *La Revue Européenne,* February 15, 1927, pp. 81-90.
42. *Théâtre Complet* (Ides et Calendes, 1947), tome XII.
43. Notably, the fourth act of *Siegfried von Kleist* appeared under the title of *Fin de Siegfried* (Grasset, 1934), 64 pp.
44. Pierre Lestringuez, "Notre ami Jean Giraudoux," *Jean Giraudoux* (Cahiers Comœdia-Charpentier), p. 30.
45. Alex Madis, "A la Taverne du Panthéon," *La Revue des Deux Mondes,* April 1, 1956, pp. 510-519.
46. This newspaper clipping is in the possession of M. Jean-Pierre Giraudoux.
47. See G. Champeaux, "Comment travaillez-vous?" Interviews de Paul Valéry, Jean Giraudoux, Marcel Aymé," *Annales Politiques et Littéraires,* September 10, 1935, pp. 252-256.
48. See Frédéric Lefèvre, *Une Heure avec . . . ,* lère série.
49. *Bella (Œuvre Romanesque,* II, 105).
50. See Lefèvre, *op. cit.*
51. Ribadeau-Dumas, "Carrefour de visages: Jean Giraudoux," *La Revue Mondiale,* July, 1927, pp. 63-64.

52. One hopes that there is exaggeration in the stories of the pranks that Giraudoux's friends like Toussaint and Beucler relate with the enthusiasm of old grads. Toussaint's picture of Giraudoux as a young man is that of an insufferable smart aleck, and Beucler portrays the middle-aged Giraudoux as addicted to "gags" that incite street brawls, to jokes at the expense of waiters and doormen, and as exhibiting in general a boorishness that fits badly our notion of Giraudoux's courtesy. Beucler's rhapsodical admiration for the person whom he presumes to paint "en intimité" seems incredible. One not under the spell might consider that a man who never leaves off writing when he has a caller, who habitually insults interviewers, is simply rude; that the sort of person who makes conversation by asking questions to keep another talking, but never offers any confidences himself, is unfriendly and condescending. One should certainly wish to discourage a friend who telephones from time to time with impromptu invitations such as the following:

> Si vous avez cinq minutes, et même plus, venez déjeuner avec moi chez Francis. J'ai déjà mon chapeau sur la tête. Partons ensemble de l'endroit où nous nous trouvons. Le premier arrivé coiffera le heaume de ses ancêtres et portera une pivoine arborescente à la boutonnière pour se faire aisément reconnaître du second." (Beucler, *Les Instants de Giraudoux,* p. 69.)

Beucler is enchanted at such verve and wit. We prefer to hope it is overstated.

53. André Beucler interprets Giraudoux's manner as hiding a fundamental distrust and disappointment. See *op. cit.,* p. 136 and *passim.*

54. *Siegfried et le Limousin (Œuvre Romanesque,* I, 397-398). For more on Dumas, see L. LeSage, "Giraudoux and Big Business," *The French Review,* XXXI, 4 (February, 1958), 278-282.

55. Maurice Bourdet, "La Genèse de Siegfried," *Les Nouvelles Littéraires,* May 19, 1928.

56. Paul Morand, *Jean Giraudoux,* p. 145.

57. Jean Barreyre, "Siegfried," *Candide,* May 24, 1928.

58. See Donald Inskip, *Jean Giraudoux,* p. 44.

59. See Francis Ambrière, "Les grandes premières: *Siegfried* de Jean Giraudoux," *Annales-Conférencia,* January, 1952, p. 49.

60. See Lefèvre, *Une Heure avec . . . ,* I, 149.

61. See G. Champeaux, "Comment travaillez-vous," *Annales Politiques et Littéraires,* September 10, 1935. The painting is reproduced in *Œuvres Littéraires Diverses,* pp. 696-697 (La Troupe Italienne des Andreini).

62. *Intermezzo,* Act I, sc. 6 (*Théâtre,* I, 269-270).

63. *Ibid.,* Act II, sc. 3 (*Théâtre,* I, 287).

64. "Discours sur le théâtre," *Littérature (Œuvres Littéraires Diverses,* p. 574).

65. See interview in *Excelsior,* June 8, 1934.

66. *La Guerre de Troie n'aura pas lieu,* Act I, sc. 3 *(Théâtre,* I, 450).

67. *La Menteuse suivi de Les Gracques* (Grasset, 1958). The date of the manuscript of *Les Gracques* may be open to question. In the postface we read: "Les manuscrits qui ont pu être retrouvés concernent exclusivement un premier acte et sont datés des Etats-Unis (Wisconsin, Lake Louise, Delmonte Lodge) où Jean Giraudoux voyageait en 1936." If the papers are not specifically dated, they may of course belong to another period, for Giraudoux was also traveling in the United States in 1939. Note in the postface: "Le 1er avril 1941, Jean Giraudoux écrivait à son fils: 'Ma pièce sur la guerre civile reparaît à l'horizon.' Des déclarations de Louis Jouvet semblent établir que deux actes de cette pièce lui furent lus, en 1942 à Lyon. S'il existait un manuscrit définitif, aucune trace n'en est restée . . ."
68. Aristide Briand has been suggested as the model. See Inskip, *Jean Giraudoux,* p. 96.
69. This, one may note, is not everybody's opinion of *Cantique des Cantiques.* Mr. Inskip, for example, calls Giraudoux's character an "ageing sentimentalist," and considers the play the least successful of Giraudoux's writing for the theater. What we find particularly praiseworthy in it is its handling of a very difficult theme: love between persons of widely different ages. In the novels of the *Bella* series the theme is already present. Here it attains unusual poignancy as the Sappho situation — the defeat in love of a superior person by mere youth.
70. See L. LeSage, "Fouqué's Undine, an unpublished manuscript by Jean Giraudoux," *Romanic Review,* April, 1951, pp. 122-134.
71. Edouard Bourdet, "Le Théâtre de Jean Giraudoux," *Cahiers de la Compagnie Barrault,* II (Julliard, 1953), p. 20.
72. Pierre-Aimé Touchard, "A la Recherche de l'éternel Giraudoux," *Ibid.,* pp. 45-53.
73. Georges-Albert Astre, "Note sur Jean Giraudoux Poète tragique," *La Grande Revue,* April, 1940, p. 175.
74. Jean-Louis Barrault, "A la Recherche de Pour Lucrèce," *Cahiers Barrault,* II, 80.
75. *Le Film de la Duchesse de Langeais* (Grasset, 1946), p. 164.

CHAPTER 3

1. See p. 76.
2. "Tombeau de Emile Clermont," *Littérature (Œuvres Littéraires Diverses,* p. 515).
3. "Racine," *ibid.,* p. 467.
4. "De Siècle à Siècle," *ibid.,* pp. 560-561.
5. *Ibid.,* p. 569.

6. "Discours sur le théâtre," *ibid.*, p. 576. The sixteenth century was, to Giraudoux's thinking, one of those "époques amples et angoissées." See G. Champeaux, "Comment travaillez-vous?" *Annales Politiques et Littéraires*, September 10, 1935, and Giraudoux's preface to *Portraits de la Renaissance* (Haumont, 1943).
7. See p. 83.
8. "Discours sur le théâtre," *op. cit.*, p. 577. See note 5, above.
9. Note the speech of the Princesse Blamont-Chauvry in *La Duchesse de Langeais,* in which exposure of the century is attributed to writers like Laclos.
10. "Choderlos de Laclos," *Littérature (Œuvres Littéraires Diverses,* p. 489).
11. "Caricature et Satire," *Littérature* (Grasset, 1941), p. 159. The text is somewhat altered in the edition of *Littérature* in *Œuvres Littéraires Diverses,* see p. 550.
12. *Suzanne et le Pacifique (Œuvre Romanesque,* I, 333-335).
13. See note 8, above.
14. See p. 39. For a full discussion of Giraudoux and Claudel, see Albérès, *Jean Giraudoux,* pp. 126-128.
15. See p. 75.
16. Republished in *Portugal* (Grasset, 1958).
17. *Visitations (Œuvres Littéraires Diverses,* p. 695).
18. See p. 93.
19. Marivaux, *Théâtre Complet* (Editions Nationales, 1946), preface by Jean Giraudoux, pp. 6-7. The editor of the recent *Marivaux par lui-même* likewise protests against Marivaux's reputation for artificiality, even denying that the expression "marivaudage" is applicable to him. See *Marivaux par lui-même,* Images et textes présentés par Paul Gazagne (Ed. du Seuil, 1954), p. 37ff.
20. See p. 35. He further expresses his views on the eighteenth century in his lecture "De Siècle à Siècle," *Littérature (Œuvres Littéraires Diverses,* p. 562).
21. Albérès, *op. cit.*, p. 244.
22. See Champeaux, *op. cit.*
23. Alexandre Arnoux, "Notes sur Jean Giraudoux essayiste," *Jean Giraudoux* (Cahiers Comœdia-Charpentier), p. 17.
24. *L'Œuvre de Jean Giraudoux, essai de bibliographie chronologique* (Nizet, 1956).
25. See p. 49.
26. *Siegfried et le Limousin (Œuvre Romanesque,* I, 410).
27. Middlebury, 1954. Unpublished doctoral dissertation.
28. *30 Shots au But* (Paris-Vendôme, 1949).
29. See p. 23.

30. "L'Esprit Normalien," *Littérature (Œuvres Littéraires Diverses,* p. 537).
31. *Portraits de la Renaissance* (Haumont, 1943).
32. Included in *Littérature (Œuvres Littéraires Diverses,* pp. 526-529).
33. Marcel Valotaire, *Laboureur* (Henri Babou, 1929).
34. *L'Œuvre de J. G. Daragnès,* catalogue. Musée des arts décoratifs. Palais du Louvre. Kaldor, 1935. Preface, pp. 17-18.
35. Pierre Lestringuez, "Notre ami Jean Giraudoux," *Jean Giraudoux* (Cahiers Comœdia-Charpentier), pp. 33-34.
36. *Combat avec l'Image (Œuvres Littéraires Diverses,* p. 655).
37. *Les Sept Péchés Capitaux* (Kra, 1927), p. 17.
38. *Simon le Pathétique (Œuvre Romanesque,* I, 735).
39. Published in *Le Figaro,* June 26, 1937, and reprinted in *Œuvres Littéraires Diverses,* pp. 643-650.
40. "La Bête et l'Ecrivain," *Littérature (Œuvres Littéraires Diverses,* p. 556).
41. "Il croit d'ailleurs que la façon de dire compte davantage que ce qu'on dit et ce qui importe avant tout c'est le style." Charensol, "Comment écrivez-vous, Jean Giraudoux?" *Les Nouvelles Littéraires,* December 19, 1931.
42. The importance of style, of form as compared to content, has been affirmed by Buffon, Taine, Flaubert, Gide — to name just a few French writers.
43. See in this connection Agnes Raymond, *La Pensée politique de Jean Giraudoux;* E. Kohler, "Jean Giraudoux et l'Allemagne," *Bulletin de la Faculté des Lettres de Strasbourg,* April, 1954, pp. 310-320; Yves Lévy, "Giraudoux et les problèmes sociaux," *Paru,* June, 1946, pp. 7-14.
44. Lefèvre, *Une Heure avec . . . ,* I, 150.
45. *Les Cinq Tentations de La Fontaine (Œuvres Littéraires Diverses,* pp. 382-383).
46. Lefèvre, *op. cit.,* p. 149.
47. See p. 30.
48. *La Revue Hebdomadaire,* September, 1920, pp. 330-333.
49. Raoul Dautry, in the preface to *Pour une Politique Urbaine* (Arts et Métiers graphiques, 1947), tells us that his first conversation with Giraudoux, in January, 1918, turned to the subject of urbanism. Towards 1930, Giraudoux proposed founding a *Ligue Urbaine.*
50. Henri Milan, "Le vrai théâtre est dans les bibliothèques," *Le Jour,* October 26, 1932.
51. *Marianne,* February 7, 1934.
52. *Ibid.,* April 11, 1934.
53. *Le Figaro,* July 16, 1934.
54. *Ibid.,* September 17, 1934.
55. *Marianne,* February 8, 1933.
56. See p. 48.
57. *La Française et La France* (Gallimard, 1951).

58. *Ibid.*, pp. 39-41.
59. *Les Cinq Tentations de La Fontaine* (*Œuvres Littéraires Diverses*, p. 320).
60. *Littérature*, préface.
61. *Pleins Pouvoirs* (Gallimard, 1939).
62. Claudel, "Adieu à Jean Giraudoux," *Jean Giraudoux* (Cahiers Comœdia-Charpentier), p. 4.
63. Gunnar Høst, *L'Œuvre de Jean Giraudoux* (Oslo: Aschehoug, 1942), pp. 97-98. It may be important to record here the reserve made by Alfred Fabre-Luce in his praise of *Pleins Pouvoirs*. He says: In denouncing the political morass into which France has drifted, why does not Giraudoux put the blame where it belongs? Namely on Alexis Léger, responsible for "la plus grande faillite de la République: celle de sa diplomatie." Of course he cannot — "Giraudoux ne peut pas parler, justement parce qu'il en sait trop long: Giraudoux est fonctionnaire." *Journal de la France*, I (Imprimerie J. E. P., 1941), p. 38.
64. Albérès, *Jean Giraudoux*, p. 463.
65. E. Kohler, *op. cit.*, p. 320.
66. Michel Gorel, "Jean Giraudoux," *Paris-Midi*, August 30, 1939.
67. See James de Coquet, "Siegfried," *Le Figaro*, November 4, 1928.
68. Louis Jouvet, "Dans les yeux de Giraudoux," *Lettres Françaises*, April 14, 1945.
69. Claude Leroux, "A la Recherche de Giraudoux," *Mondes*, June 27, 1945. Another glimpse of Giraudoux in his apartment on the quai d'Orsay is given by G. Champeaux, "Comment travaillez-vous?" *Annales Politiques et Littéraires*, September 10, 1935.
70. Edmond Jaloux, "Jean Giraudoux," *Journal de Genève*, January 27-28, 1945.
71. *Ibid.*
72. Hélène Froment, "Souvenir de Jean Giraudoux," *La France libre*, VII (February 15, 1944), 456.
73. How, asks Alfred Fabre-Luce, could Giraudoux have accepted to be the official poet of war, he who had so systematically debunked its glories? Perhaps the docility of a functionary is the explanation, perhaps the flattery of so important an appointment, but chiefly — concludes M. Fabre-Luce — the *Normalien's* love of paradox, the *tour de force*, which made Giraudoux seize an occasion to play a role "qu'il a raillé toute sa vie." *Journal de la France*, I, 39. The actual facts make Giraudoux far less diabolically clever and criminally irresponsible. Surely he took on his duties in good faith. As for the matter of self-repudiation, Fabre-Luce exaggerates. Giraudoux's lucidity on the subject of war does not preclude an active part in the defense of his country.
74. Roger Peyrefitte, *La Fin des Ambassades* (Flammarion, 1953), p. 43.
75. Fromont, *op. cit.*, p. 456.
76. *Le Futur Armistice* (Grasset, 1940), p. 11.

77. Peyrefitte, *op. cit.*, p. 46.
78. Albérès, *Jean Giraudoux,* p. 500.
79. See Jean Giraudoux, *Portugal* (Grasset, 1958). Note liminaire par Jean-Pierre Giraudoux, p. 13.
80. Giraudoux's disagreement with the guilt and penance psychology will be expressed again in *Visitations (Œuvres Littéraires Diverses,* pp. 701-702), and in the "Avant-Propos" to *Sans Pouvoirs.*
81. *Armistice à Bordeaux* (Monaco: Editions du Rocher, 1945), p. 24.
82. This essay is to be read with the one written the following December, "La France et son héros" (See p. 95 of our study), in which, soothed by the calm of Cusset and the perspective that six months have brought, Giraudoux reformulates his concept of France and composes another message of hope and promise for Frenchmen.
83. *Portugal (Œuvres Littéraires Diverses,* p. 814). Compare this reference to the human attitude with another in *Combat avec l'Image* (See p. 102). The phrase is very revealing of Giraudoux's philosophy: the concern for finding a proper attitude in life, for finding an object to symbolize one's attitude in life, indicates to what degree Giraudoux would carry the stylizing and the abstracting of personality. It suggests also the curious mathematical or mechanical qualities that he would attribute to the universe.
84. *Ibid.*, p. 814. Note Anse's monologue in Faulkner, *As I Lay Dying:* ". . . He aimed for them to stay put like a tree or a stand of corn. Because if He'd a aimed for man to be always a-moving and going somewheres else, wouldn't He a put him longways on his belly, like a snake? It stands to reason He would."
85. See F. W. Müller, "Die dramatische Theorie Jean Giraudoux," *Die Neueren Sprachen* (1957), II, 57-73.
86. *Portugal,* note liminaire, pp. 14-15.
87. *Ibid.*, p. 15.
88. See p. 73.
89. André Beucler, "Dernières idées de Jean Giraudoux," *Gazette de Lausanne,* September 22, 1945.
90. In connection with Giraudoux's clandestine activities, see Beucler, *ibid.*, Jean Blanzat, "Giraudoux et la Résistance," *Le Figaro,* September 23, 1944, and Thierry-Maulnier, "Réponse à Jean Blanzat," *ibid.*, October 7, 1944.
91. *Sans Pouvoirs* (Monaco: Editions du Rocher, 1946), p. 128.
92. *Pour une Politique Urbaine.* Preface by Raoul Dautry, p. 8. I do not find in the text these words of Giraudoux as cited by Dautry, but they summarize exactly his last addresses on the subject of urbanism.
93. See F. Roche, "Le dernier hommage du public à Giraudoux," *Actu,* February 13, 1944.
94. Note, in this connection, an article which ultimately appeared in the French press: "Jean Giraudoux a été empoisonné par la Gestapo nous révèle Louis Aragon," *Ce Soir,* September 20, 1944.

CHAPTER 4

1. *Provinciales (Œuvre Romanesque,* I, 29-30).
2. "Mirage de Bessines," *La France Sentimentale (Œuvre Romanesque,* II, 423-424).
3. *Siegfried,* Act IV, sc. 5 *(Théâtre,* I, 66-67).
4. "Visite chez le Prince," *La France Sentimentale (Œuvre Romanesque,* II, 373-374).
5. *Siegfried et le Limousin (Œuvre Romanesque,* I, 535).
6. *Simon le Pathétique (Œuvre Romanesque,* I, 631-632).
7. *Ibid.,* p. 634.
8. *L'Ecole des Indifférents (Œuvre Romanesque,* I, 108).
9. René Lalou has already collected a few. See *Textes Choisis* (Grasset, 1932).
10. *L'Ecole des Indifférents (Œuvre Romanesque,* I, 106).
11. *Ibid.,* p. 118.
12. *Ibid.,* p. 122.
13. *Ibid.,* p. 122.
14. *Ibid.,* p. 124.
15. *Ibid.,* p. 125.
16. *Ibid.,* p. 172.
17. *Simon le Pathétique (Œuvre Romanesque,* I, 713).
18. *Siegfried et le Limousin (Œuvre Romanesque,* I, 436-437).
19. *L'Ecole des Indifférents (Œuvre Romanesque,* I, 144).
20. *Les Contes d'un Matin* (Gallimard, 1952), p. 148.
21. Marcel Azaïs, *Le Chemin des Gardies* (Nouvelle Librarie Nationale, 1926), p. 232.
22. Jean Schlumberger, "Adorable Clio," *La Nouvelle Revue Française,* November 1, 1920, p. 785.
23. *Lectures pour une Ombre (Œuvres Littéraires Diverses,* p. 61).
24. *Ibid.,* p. 69
25. *Ibid.,* p. 70.
26. *Ibid.,* p. 89.
27. *Adorable Clio (Œuvres Littéraires Diverses,* pp. 239-240).
28. *Ibid.,* pp. 229-230.
29. *Suzanne et le Pacifique (Œuvre Romanesque,* I, 333).
30. *Lectures pour une Ombre (Œuvres Littéraires Diverses,* p. 101).

31. *Ibid.*, p. 27.
32. *Ibid.*, p. 45.
33. *Ibid.*, pp. 32-33.
34. *Adorable Clio* (*Œuvres Littéraires Diverses*, p. 244).
35. *Amica America* (*Œuvres Littéraires Diverses*, p. 181).
36. *Simon le Pathétique* (*Œuvre Romanesque*, I, 647).
37. *Bella* (*Œuvre Romanesque*, II, 7).
38. See pp. 110-111.
39. *Siegfried*, Act I, sc. 2 (*Théâtre*, I, 7-8).
40. *Siegfried et le Limousin* (*Œuvre Romanesque*, I, 404).
41. *Ibid.*, pp. 522-523.
42. *Ibid.*, p. 461.
43. *L'Ecole des Indifférents* (*Œuvre Romanesque*, I, 146).
44. *Siegfried*, Act I, sc. 2 (*Théâtre*, I, 8).
45. "Je présente Bellita," *La France Sentimentale* (*Œuvre Romanesque*, II, 348).
46. *Suzanne et le Pacifique* (*Œuvre Romanesque*, I, 351).
47. *Bella* (*Œuvre Romanesque*, II, 8).
48. In connection with Giraudoux's later function as propaganda minister, it is interesting to reread the pages of *Bella* (p. 8ff.) that describe the ideal statesman in wartime.
49. *Amphitryon 38*, Act. I, sc. 2 (*Théâtre*, I, 103).
50. Note *Judith*, Act I, sc. 6 (*Théâtre*, I, 195): "Il se peut aussi qu'un monstre surgisse de la terre en ricanant — on rit beaucoup . . . dans cette sorte de pays — et charge vers toi sur trois pattes. Ce n'est qu'un cheval blessé. Frappe-le d'un bâton, surtout sur la jambe brisée, et il s'enfuira . . ."
51. *La Guerre de Troie n'aura pas lieu*, Act I, sc. 3 (*Théâtre*, I, 451).
52. *Ibid.*, Act II, sc. 13 (*Théâtre*, I, 502).
53. Yves Gandon, "L'Influence du terroir," *L'Intransigeant*, August 12, 1935.
54. *Bella* (*Œuvre Romanesque*, II, 10).
55. *Ibid.*, p. 29.
56. *Choix des Elues* (*Œuvre Romanesque*, II, 748).
57. *Aventures de Jérôme Bardini* (*Œuvre Romanesque*, II, 241).
58. *Eglantine* (*Œuvre Romanesque*, II, 164).
59. *Ibid.*, pp. 164-165.
60. *Amphitryon 38*, Act III, sc. 4 (*Théâtre*, I, 162).
61. *Ibid.*, Act I, sc. 1 (*Théâtre*, I, 101).
62. *Ibid.*, Act I, sc. 6 (*Théâtre*, I, 119).
63. *Supplément au Voyage de Cook*, Scene 9 (*Théâtre*, II, 125).
64. *Ibid.*, Scene 11 (*Théâtre*, II, 128).
65. *Sodome et Gomorrhe*, Act II, sc. 7 (*Théâtre*, II, 330).

CHAPTER 5

1. *Sodome et Gomorrhe,* Act I, prelude *(Théâtre,* II, 288).
2. See *Bella (Œuvre Romanesque,* II, 110): "Si le monde réel se cousait ainsi à un monde imaginaire."
3. This is, of course, an invention of Giraudoux, a means of introducing the preface he was asked to write for a special edition of *Suzanne et le Pacifique* subscribed to by the "Bibliophiles de Lyon." This preface, which is entirely devoted to the subject of God, was republished under the title "Dieu et la littérature," in *Littérature (Œuvres Littéraires Diverses,* pp. 532-536).
4. *Judith,* Act II, sc. 6 *(Théâtre,* I, 220-221).
5. *Ibid.,* Act III, sc. 7 *(Théâtre,* I, 244).
6. *Ibid.,* Act III, sc. 8 *(Théâtre,* I, 245).
7. *Sodome et Gomorrhe,* Act I, sc. 2 *(Théâtre,* II, 300).
8. *Electre,* Act I, sc. 3 *(Théâtre,* II, 23-24).
9. *La Guerre de Troie,* Act I, sc. 9 *(Théâtre,* I, 470).
10. *Electre,* Act I, sc. 3 *(Théâtre,* II, 24).
11. *Judith,* Act II, sc. 4 *(Théâtre,* I, 217).
12. *La Guerre de Troie,* Act II, sc. 13 *(Théâtre,* I, 503).
13. *Ondine,* Act III, sc. 3 *(Théâtre,* II, 266-267).
14. *Judith,* Act II, sc. 4 *(Théâtre,* I, 217).
15. "Dieu et la littérature," *Littérature (Œuvres Littéraires Diverses,* p. 533).
16. *Judith,* Act II, sc. 4 *(Théâtre,* I, 217-218).
17. *Juliette au Pays des Hommes (Œuvre Romanesque,* I, 601-602).
18. *Intermezzo,* Act II, sc. 1 *(Théâtre,* I, 278).
19. Note that the Rév. P. Léger feels that Giraudoux did an about-face in *Pour Lucrèce:* "Avec Giraudoux qui jusque là dans son théâtre prend le parti des hommes contre Dieu, va prendre le parti de Dieu contre les hommes." *Pour Lucrèce de Giraudoux* (35 rue de la Glacière, 1954, 15 pp. mimeo.), p. 2.
20. *Juliette au Pays des Hommes (Œuvre Romanesque,* I, 615).
21. *Siegfried et le Limousin (Œuvre Romanesque,* I, 514).
22. Albert Camus, *Le Mythe de Sisyphe* (Gallimard, 1942), p. 168.
23. *Amphitryon 38,* Act II, sc. 2 *(Théâtre,* I, 128-129).
24. *Ibid.,* p. 129.
25. *Ibid.,* p. 129. The analogy between Giraudoux and Camus, suggested above, cannot be pushed too far. On the subject of death they part company.
26. *Ibid.,* p. 126.

27. *Ibid.*, p. 128.
28. *Bella (Œuvre Romanesque,* II, 13-14).
29. *L'Ecole des Indifférents (Œuvre Romanesque,* I, 110).
30. *Eglantine (Œuvre Romanesque,* II, 165).
31. *Intermezzo,* Act III, sc. 4 *(Théâtre,* I, 311).
32. Jean-Paul Sartre, *Situations,* I (Gallimard, 1947), p. 96.
33. Claude-Edmonde Magny echoes Sartre's notion of the immobility of the Giralducian universe. See *Précieux Giraudoux* (Editions du Seuil, 1945), p. 58.
34. Sartre, *op cit.*, pp. 95-96. See p. 117.
35. "Charles-Louis Philippe," *Littérature (Œuvres Littéraires Diverses,* p. 510).
36. *La Folle de Chaillot,* Act I *(Théâtre,* II, 354).
37. "Racine," *Littérature (Œuvres Littéraires Diverses,* p. 474).
38. *Ibid.*, p. 475.
39. "Je présente Bellita," *La France Sentimentale (Œuvre Romanesque,* II, 349-350).
40. *Ibid.*, p. 348.
41. *Siegfried,* Act I, sc. 2 *(Théâtre,* I, 8).
42. *Siegfried et le Limousin (Œuvre Romanesque,* I, 513).
43. *Judith,* Act I, sc. 4 *(Théâtre,* I, 184).
44. *Electre,* Act I, sc. 2 *(Théâtre,* II, 21).
45. *La Guerre de Troie n'aura pas lieu,* Act II, sc. 13 *(Théâtre,* I, 505).
46. The most complete and most nuanced treatment of Giraudoux's metaphysical ideas is of course Albérès, *Morale et Esthétique chez Giraudoux.*
47. Cinquième Promenade.
48. Charles Baudelaire, *Œuvres Complètes* (Conard, 1925), X, 3-5.
49. *Juliette au Pays des Hommes (Œuvre Romanesque,* I, 601).
50. *L'Ecole des Indifférents (Œuvre Romanesque,* I, 125).
51. "Choderlos de Laclos," *Littérature (Œuvres Littéraires Diverses,* p. 489).

CHAPTER 6

1. "De Siècle à Siècle," *Littérature (Œuvres Littéraires Diverses,* p. 569).
2. Lefèvre, *Une Heure avec . . . ,* I, 149. Donald Inskip disagrees with Giraudoux himself and the majority of his critics in attributing to him the power of creating characters: "In the stories of *Provinciales,* in those of *L'Ecole des Indifférents,* in various passages from *Lectures pour une Ombre,* it is

quite obvious that the author possessed from the beginning in marked degree the power to conceive motive and depict psychological development." *Jean Giraudoux, The Making of a Dramatist* (London: Oxford University Press, 1958), pp. 173-174.

3. For textual illustrations, see Albérès, *Jean Giraudoux,* chapter 4.
4. Houlet, *Jean Giraudoux,* p. 184.
5. Gabriel Marcel, "Les différentes tendances du théâtre d'aujourd'hui," *Annales du Centre Universitaire Méditerranéen,* 1950-1951, pp. 118-120.
6. *L'Ecole des Indifférents (Œuvre Romanesque,* I, 124).
7. *Ibid.,* p. 125.
8. "Gérard de Nerval," *Littérature (Œuvres Littéraires Diverses,* p. 501).
9. Lefèvre, *op. cit.,* IV, 122.
10. *L'Ecole des Indifférents (Œuvre Romanesque,* I, 141).
11. Charensol, "Comment écrivez-vous, Jean Giraudoux?" *Les Nouvelles Littéraires,* December 19, 1931. In the several interviews he granted, Giraudoux talked freely about his method of writing. He declared to G. Champeaux that he wrote only two months out of a year, but then worked diligently every morning. "Comment travaillez-vous . . . ?" *Annales Politiques et Littéraires,* September 10, 1935.
12. Lefèvre, *Une Heure avec . . . ,* I, 149.
13. Charensol, "Comment écrivez-vous, Jean Giraudoux?" *Les Nouvelles Littéraires,* December 19, 1931.
14. "Mort de Segaux, Mort de Drigeard."
15. "L'Auteur au théâtre," *Littérature (Œuvres Littéraires Diverses,* p. 581).
16. Charensol, *op. cit.*
17. *Ibid.*
18. Preface to *Fin de Siegfried.*
19. Genet, *Jean Giraudoux,* p. 46.
20. *Bella (Œuvre Romanesque,* II, 26).
21. *La Guerre de Troie n'aura pas lieu,* Act II, sc. 13 *(Théâtre,* I, 501-502).
22. *Eglantine (Œuvre Romanesque,* II, 161).
23. *Ibid.,* p. 161.
24. *Combat avec l'Ange (Œuvre Romanesque,* II, 572-574).
25. *La Folle de Chaillot,* Act I *(Théâtre,* II, 378).
26. *Eglantine (Œuvre Romanesque,* II, 164-165).
27. "Je présente Bellita," *La France Sentimentale (Œuvre Romanesque,* II, 362).
28. *Suzanne et le Pacifique (Œuvre Romanesque,* I, 290).
29. *La Guerre de Troie n'aura pas lieu,* Act I, sc. 1 *(Théâtre,* I, 447).
30. *Sodome et Gomorrhe,* Act II, sc. 8 *(Théâtre,* II, 339-340).
31. "L'Auteur au théâtre," *Littérature (Œuvres Littéraires Diverses,* pp. 578-579).
32. *Sans Pouvoirs,* pp. 12-13.

33. *Ibid.*, p. 23.
34. *Ibid.*, p. 25.
35. *Adorable Clio* (*Œuvres Littéraires Diverses,* p. 212).
36. *Combat avec l'Ange* (*Œuvre Romanesque,* II, 494).
37. *Bella* (*Œuvre Romanesque,* II, 18-19).
38. *Choix des Elues* (*Œuvre Romanesque,* II, 644ff.).
39. *L'Ecole des Indifférents* (*Œuvre Romanesque,* I, 122).
40. *La Guerre de Troie n'aura pas lieu,* Act II, sc. 12 (*Théâtre,* I, 501).
41. *Elpénor* (*Œuvre Romanesque,* I, 215).
42. *Ibid.*, p. 206.
43. *Ibid.*, p. 193.
44. *Suzanne et le Pacifique* (*Œuvre Romanesque,* I, 297).
45. *Combat avec l'Ange* (*Œuvre Romanesque,* II, 471).
46. *Siegfried et le Limousin* (*Œuvre Romanesque,* I, 500).
47. *Combat avec l'Ange* (*Œuvre Romanesque,* II, 584-585).
48. *Choix des Elues* (*Œuvre Romanesque,* II, 718).
49. *Elpénor* (*Œuvre Romanesque,* I, 223).
50. *Provinciales* (*Œuvre Romanesque,* I, 71).
51. *Lectures pour une Ombre* (*Œuvres Littéraires Diverses,* p. 23).
52. *Adorable Clio* (*Œuvres Littéraires Diverses,* p. 204).
53. *Lectures pour une Ombre* (*Œuvres Littéraires Diverses,* p. 60).
54. *Juliette au Pays des Hommes* (*Œuvre Romanesque,* I, 542).
55. *Siegfried et le Limousin* (*Œuvre Romanesque,* I, 426).
56. *L'Ecole des Indifférents* (*Œuvre Romanesque,* I, 119).
57. *Amica America* (*Œuvres Littéraires Diverses,* p. 157).
58. "Visite chez le Prince," *La France Sentimentale* (*Œuvre Romanesque,* II, 382).
59. See p. 177.
60. *Suzanne et le Pacifique* (*Œuvre Romanesque,* I, 302).
61. *Provinciales* (*Œuvre Romanesque,* I, 11-12).
62. *Adorable Clio* (*Œuvres Littéraires Diverses,* p. 263).
63. *Simon le Pathétique* (*Œuvre Romanesque,* I, 677).
64. *Elpénor* (*Œuvre Romanesque,* I, 233).
65. *Eglantine* (*Œuvre Romanesque,* II, 219).
66. *Siegfried et le Limousin* (*Œuvre Romanesque,* I, 460).
67. *Choix des Elues* (*Œuvre Romanesque,* II, 751).
68. In view of the many interpretations given to the word myth — as well as to symbolism, allegory, parable, and even metaphor — it may be proper to indicate specifically the sense we have lent these words in our discussion. Metaphor we have used in the broad sense to mean figures involving bor-

rowed images. Our use of the other terms is based chiefly on the movement in the figure from the concrete to the abstract or from the abstract to the concrete. In this restricted and arbitrary sense, we should not care to defend our classification too strongly, or argue whether a given situation should be called a myth or an allegory, for example. And our only qualification for parable is that it is shorter than the other two. The propriety of the terms has not concerned us overmuch, since our purpose was not to classify so much as to illustrate by a variety of examples the manner in which Giraudoux constantly moves between the abstract and the concrete in his writing.

69. *Suzanne et le Pacifique (Œuvre Romanesque,* I, 249-250).
70. *Bella (Œuvre Romanesque,* II, 56).
71. *Ibid.*, p. 57.
72. *Suzanne et le Pacifique (Œuvre Romanesque,* I, 250).
73. *Diablerie* (Grasset, 1938). See pp. 91-92.
74. *Juliette au Pays des Hommes (Œuvre Romanesque,* I, 541).
75. *Ondine,* Act II, sc. 14 *(Théâtre,* II, 259).
76. *Eglantine (Œuvre Romanesque,* II, 206-207).
77. *La Guerre de Troie n'aura pas lieu,* Act I, sc. 9 *(Théâtre,* I, 469).
78. *Ibid.,* Act I, sc. 4 *(Théâtre,* I, 454).
79. *Judith,* Act I, sc. 4 *(Théâtre,* I, 183).
80. *La Guerre de Troie n'aura pas lieu,* Act I, sc. 9 *(Théâtre,* I, 469-470).
81. *Electre,* Act I, sc. 1 *(Théâtre,* II, 14).
82. *Ondine,* Act III, sc. 4 *(Théâtre,* II, 271).
83. *Electre,* Entr'acte *(Théâtre,* II, 51).
84. *Juliette au Pays des Hommes (Œuvre Romanesque,* I, 545ff.).
85. *Visitations (Œuvres Littéraires Diverses,* p. 699).
86. "La préciosité . . . demande la prédominance de l'esprit sur le cœur." René Bray, *La Préciosité et les Précieux* (Albin Michel, 1948), p. 71.
87. *Suzanne et le Pacifique (Œuvre Romanesque,* I, 332-333).
88. *Combat avec l'Ange (Œuvre Romanesque,* II, 506).
89. *Elpénor (Œuvre Romanesque,* I, 194).
90. *Ibid.,* p. 195.
91. *La France Sentimentale (Œuvre Romanesque,* II, 440).
92. *Combat avec l'Ange (Œuvre Romanesque,* II, 594-595).
93. *Lectures pour une Ombre (Œuvres Littéraires Diverses,* p. 101).
94. *Bella (Œuvre Romanesque,* II, 11).
95. *Combat avec l'Ange (Œuvre Romanesque,* II, 602).
96. *Bella (Œuvre Romanesque,* II, 110).
97. *Eglantine (Œuvre Romanesque,* II, 230).
98. *Sodome et Gomorrhe,* Act II, sc. 8 *(Théâtre,* II, 338).
99. *Ibid.,* Act I, sc. 2 *(Théâtre,* II, 302).

100. *Ibid.*, Act II, sc. 8 *(Théâtre,* II, 335).
101. *Ibid.*, Act. I, sc. 3 *(Théâtre,* II, 306).
102. *Eglantine (Œuvre Romanesque,* II, 193).
103. *Suzanne et le Pacifique (Œuvre Romanesque,* I, 366-367).
104. *Bella (Œuvre Romanesque,* II, 58).
105. *Ibid.*, p. 27.
106. *Sodome et Gomorrhe,* Act I, sc. 1 *(Théâtre,* II, 296).
107. *Ibid.*, Act I, sc. 4 *(Théâtre,* II, 311).
108. *Ibid.*, Act I, sc. 4 *(Théâtre,* II, 314).
109. *Ibid.*, Act II, sc. 3 *(Théâtre,* II, 320).
110. *Ibid.*, Act II, sc. 1 *(Théâtre,* 315).
111. See pp. 155-156.
112. *Sodome et Gomorrhe,* Act I, sc. 1 *(Théâtre,* II, 293).
113. *Ibid.*, Act II, sc. 4 *(Théâtre,* II, 321).
114. *Ibid.*, Act II, sc. 4 *(Théâtre,* II, 322-323).

CHAPTER 7

1. Jean Viollis, "Provinciales," *Marges,* May, 1909, pp. 193-194.
2. André Gide, "Provinciales," *La Nouvelle Revue Française,* June, 1909, pp. 463-466.
3. Edmond Jaloux, "Esquisse d'après Jean Giraudoux," *La Revue Européenne,* March, 1923, pp. 37-47.
4. Pierre Lafue, "Bella ou les nouveaux jeux de M. Giraudoux," *La Revue Hebdomadaire,* March, 1926, pp. 118-122.
5. Charles de Bonnefon, *Les Ecrivains Modernes de la France* (Fayard, 1927), pp. 567-568.
6. Pierre Humbourg, *Jean Giraudoux* (Marseilles: Cahiers du Sud, 1926), 83 pp. Maurice Bourdet, *Jean Giraudoux* (Ed. de la Nouvelle Revue Critique, 1928), 61 pp.
7. A. de Luppé, "Jean Giraudoux," *Le Correspondant,* May 25, 1928, pp. 509-522.
8. Humbourg, *op. cit.*, p. 13.
9. René Salomé, "Chronique dramatique," *Etudes,* September 5, 1928, pp. 591-599.
10. Fred Orthys, "Amphitryon 38," *Le Matin,* November 9, 1929.

11. Jean Prévost, "L'Esprit de Jean Giraudoux," *La Nouvelle Revue Française,* July, 1933, pp. 37-52.
12. Marcel Thiébaut, "Jean Giraudoux," *La Revue de Paris,* November, 1934, pp. 397-426.
13. Robert Brasillach, "Le Théâtre de Jean Giraudoux," *La Revue Universelle,* May 1, 1933, pp. 313-335.
14. Thierry Maulnier, "L'Humanisme de Giraudoux," *La Revue Universelle,* December 15, 1932, pp. 745-748.
15. "Gérard de Nerval," *Littérature (Œuvres Littéraires Diverses,* p. 504).
16. Gonzague Truc, "M. Jean Giraudoux et l'artifice dans l'art," *Comœdia,* December 23, 1930.
17. Emile Bouvier, "Deuxième Exemple de vulgarisation esthétique, Jean Giraudoux," *Initiation à la Littérature d'aujourd'hui* (Renaissance du Livre, 1932), pp. 231-256.
18. Christian Sénéchal, *Les Grands Courants de la Littérature Française Contemporaine* (Malfère, 1933), p. 343.
19. André Rousseaux, "Jean Giraudoux ou l'éternel printemps," *Ames et Visages du XXe Siècle,* II (Grasset, 1936), pp. 109-156.
20. Gonzague Truc, "La Théologie de M. Giraudoux," *La Revue Hebdomadaire,* December 25, 1937, pp. 430-439.
21. Yves Gandon, "Jean Giraudoux ou plaisirs et jeux du style," *Le Démon du Style* (Plon, 1938), pp. 135-146.
22. René Escande de Messières, "L'Ironie dans l'œuvre de Jean Giraudoux," *Romanic Review,* December, 1938, pp. 373-383.
23. Jean-Paul Sartre, "M. Giraudoux et la philosophie d'Aristote," *La Nouvelle Revue Française,* March, 1940, pp. 339-354.
24. L. LeSage, *Jean Giraudoux's Use of the Metaphor,* University of Illinois, 1940.
25. Gunnar Høst, *L'Œuvre de Jean Giraudoux* (Oslo, H. Axhehoug, 1942).
26. Fernand Baldensperger, "L'Esthétique fondamentale de Jean Giraudoux," *French Review,* October, 1944, pp. 2-10.
27. Anon., "Jean Giraudoux a été empoisonné par la Gestapo nous révèle Louis Aragon," *Ce Soir,* September 20, 1944.
28. See, for example, Yves Lévy, "Giraudoux et les problèmes sociaux," *Paru,* June, 1946, pp. 7-14.
29. Gérard Bauër, "Le Théâtre," *La Revue de Paris,* February, 1946, pp. 109-110.
30. René Bray, *La Préciosité et les Précieux* (Albin Michel, 1948), pp. 371-386.
31. The fact that most — if not all — of the scholars are foreign is an additional isolating factor.
32. A recent critic, however, argues that Giraudoux labored over his style. See Michael Riffaterre, "Giraudoux: irony and poetry," The *American Society Legion of Honor Magazine,* XXXIX, 1 (1958), 9-19. The evidence presented

amounts to a few minor changes from one edition to another, particularly of *Elpénor.* No one has assumed, I believe, that Giraudoux never altered a text, but those who have examined a great many manuscripts as well as editions find nothing to substantiate M. Riffaterre's thesis. Doubtless Giraudoux took more pains than he chose ever to admit. He did correct and recast his texts. But very little in comparison with most writers. His basic technique was improvisation; and when he was dissatisfied with a draft, he would lay it aside and begin afresh. For further studies of textual changes see Albérès, *Esthétique et Morale chez Giraudoux* and Professor Inskip's publications.

33. The matter is now taken for granted. Note ". . . né à la vie littéraire au contact de ces romantiques allemands chez lesquels il avait, très tôt, puisé toute sa philosophie." Pierre de Boisdeffre, *Une Histoire Vivante de la Littérature d'Aujourd'hui* (Le Livre Contemporain, 1958), p. 194. Of course such a statement is too flat to be exact.
34. Albérès, *La Révolte des Ecrivains d'Aujourd'hui* (Corrêa, 1949), p. 249.
35. *Le Figaro Littéraire,* February 6, 1954.
36. This does not mean that signs pointing towards the concept of Giraudoux as a tragic poet cannot be found earlier. Note, for example, Georges-Albert Astre, "Note sur Jean Giraudoux, poète tragique" (see p. 83). But neither *Judith* nor *Sodome et Gomorrhe* inclined most critics to see Giraudoux's nature as essentially tragic. Gabriel du Genet closes the introduction to his study (1945) with these words: "Il a suivi la pente du langage, et lui, qui aurait pu devenir l'un de nos plus grands penseurs, l'un des écrivains les plus douloureux, les plus bessés par le mal incurable d'être un homme, il s'est abandonné à la grâce, c'est-à-dire à la facilité." *Jean Giraudoux,* p. 12.
37. "A la recherche de l'éternal Giraudoux," pp. 45-53. See p. 83.
38. "A la recherche de *Pour Lucrèce," Cahiers Barrault,* II, 80.
39. Bert M. P. Leefmans, "Giraudoux's Other Muse," *Kenyon Review,* Autumn, 1954.
40. Marianne Mercier-Campiche, *Le Théâtre de Giraudoux* (Domat, 1954).
41. *Ibid.,* p. 296.
42. André Dumas, "Giraudoux ou la tragédie du couple," *Esprit,* May, 1955, pp. 156-157.
43. Franz Walter Müller, "Die 'idées obsédantes' im Werke Jean Giraudoux," *Die Neueren Sprachen* (Frankfort), Neue Folge (1955), Heft 3, pp. 106-117; Heft 4, pp. 165-173.
44. M. L. Bidal, *Giraudoux tel qu'en lui-même* (Corrêa, 1956), p. 40.
45. Albérès, *Esthétique et Morale chez Giraudoux,* p. 7.
46. See the tribute of Jean Anouilh, "A Giraudoux," *Chronique de Paris,* February, 1944, pp. 1-3.
47. Albert Thibaudet, *Réflexions sur le Roman* (Gallimard, 1938), p. 84.
48. Maurice Blanchot, *Faux Pas* (Gallimard, 1943), p. 246.

Index

Note: This index is intended only for general orientation and is limited chiefly to names of persons and to titles of Giraudoux's works discussed or alluded to in the text. Sources of quotations have not been included.

From his childhood spent in the heart of provincial France to his sudden death in Paris during the Occupation, Jean Giraudoux is presented here in every stage of his life and career. We see the model schoolboy such as the writer presents himself in his early books, a swan among the ducks of Châteauroux; the university student who interrupted his nonchalant life in the Latin Quarter only to pursue it abroad in Munich and then at Harvard; the soldier in the trenches, and then the officer with monocle and sky-blue uniform on missions abroad. We see the writer and the diplomat rising in twin careers to attain glory in the one and notoriety in the other. Behind the celebrated dramatist and the minister plenipotentiary, we catch glimpses of the husband, the father, the addict of Saturday night poker parties, and the host at Sunday dinners *entre amis*.

In Part One, which traces Jean Giraudoux's life and career, each of his works is situated and described: the fictional prose pieces, the plays, and the essays. Part Two is devoted to an analysis of his creative writing in general. Themes and motifs, attitudes, composition and style — all aspects of this writer of genius are analyzed and demonstrated. In a final section we are offered a review of his changing and evolving reputation through critical eyes — Giraudoux's growth from the role of prince of precious nonsense to that of tragic poet "in tune with the universe."